Henry Miller: The Inhuman Artist

Henry Miller: The Inhuman Artist

A Philosophical Inquiry

Indrek Männiste

BLOOMSBURY
NEW DELHI • LONDON • OXFORD • NEW YORK • SYDNEY

BLOOMSBURY INDIA
Bloomsbury Publishing India Pvt. Ltd
Second Floor, Building No. 4
DDA Complex LSC, Pocket C – 6 & 7
Vasant Kunj, New Delhi 110070
www.bloomsbury.com

BLOOMSBURY, Bloomsbury Academic India and the Diana
logo are trademarks of Bloomsbury Publishing Plc

First published in India 2019
First published 2013

This edition published with permission from Bloomsbury Publishing Plc,
50 Bedford Square, London, WC1B3DP, UK

British Library Cataloguing-in-Publication Data
A catalogue record for this book is available from the British Library.

Library of Congress Cataloging-in-Publication Data
A catalog record for this book is available from the Library of Congress

ISBN: 978-93-88912-34-1

2 4 6 8 10 9 7 5 3 1

Typeset by Deanta Global Publishing Services, Chennai, India
Printed and bound in India by Replika Press Pvt. Ltd.

I am of the order whose purpose is not to teach
the world a lesson but to explain
that school is over.
– Henry Miller

Contents

Acknowledgments

I would like to express my deepest gratitude to those who helped me to face one of the most demanding academic, and perhaps also personal, challenges of my life. To begin with, I would like to thank Haaris Naqvi and *Bloomsbury* (formerly *Continuum*) for providing me this wonderful opportunity to publish a book on the topic that I have been passionate about for several years. To continue, I thank everybody in the Department of Philosophy at the University of Auckland, where I carried out most of the research that has now evolved into this book. I thank John Bishop and Robert Wicks particularly for believing in my project and for helping making things happen administratively. I am immensely grateful to Matheson Russell, my doctoral supervisor at the time, whose professional input and ever-encouraging attitude helped me to stay on the course of writing through even the most demanding and uninspiring times. I am enormously thankful to Jordan Collins, my main pre-publishing *consigliere*, and also to Andrew Triggs, David Nickless, Bernadette Waller, Paul McLaughlin, and Veiko Palge for helping me with numerous editorial and technical tasks in the different stages of writing this book. I also thank James Decker and Geoffrey Boucher for their helpful comments and suggestions. On a less academic but equally important note, I cannot thank enough my friends Tim Erson, Brendan Callies, Claire Mottershead, Danny Pantoja, and Johan Wielanga who all took me into their homes and hearts while I lived in New Zealand. In the same vein, for their lasting support, inspiring discussions, and comforting company, I would like to thank my long-time friends Andreas Ventsel, Mari-Liis Madisson, Toomas Lott, and Tiina Nuum. Last but not least, I owe debt to my parents Sirje and Matti Männiste whose unconditional support over all these years I couldn't even begin to describe.

Abbreviations

All the works of Henry Miller are cited in this book using the following abbreviations along with relevant page numbers referring to these particular editions that were used.

ACN *Air-Conditioned Nightmare* (New York: New Directions, 1945).

AP "Artist and Public," in *Remember to Remember* (New York: New Directions, 1947).

BIML *The Books In My Life* (New York: New Directions, 1969).

BS *Black Spring* (New York: Grove Press, 1963).

BSOHB *Big Sur and The Oranges of Hieronymus Bosch* (New York: New Directions, 1957).

CAN *Tropic of Cancer* (London, New York, Toronto and Sydney: Harper Perennial, 2005).

CAP *Tropic of Capricorn* (London, New York, Toronto and Sydney: Harper Perennial, 2005).

CD "Creative Death," in *The Wisdom of the Heart* (London: Editions Poetry London, 1947).

CHM *Conversations with Henry Miller*, eds. Frank L. Kersnowski and Alice Hughes (Jackson: University Press of Mississippi, 1994).

COM *The Colossus of Maroussi* (Aylesbury: Penguin Books with William Heinemann LTD, 1974).

DML *A Private Correspondence* (with Lawrence Durrell), ed. George Wickes (London: Faber and Faber Limited, 1963).

HAM *Henry Miller's Hamlet Letters* (Santa Barbara: Capra Press, 1988).

LE *Letters to Emil* (New York: New Directions, 1989).

LP *A Literate Passion: Letters of Anaïs Nin and Henry Miller 1932–1953* (New York: Harcourt Brace Company, 1987).

MM “Murder the Murderer,” in *Selected Prose,* vol.1 (London: MacGibbon & Kee, 1965).

NEX *Nexus: Book Three of “The Rosy Crucifixion” Trilogy* (Manchester: Panther Books, 1969).

OLAS “On Open Letter to All and Sundry,” in *The Plight of the Creative Artist in the United States of America* (Privately published by Ben Porter, 1944).

OLSE “An Open Letter to Surrealists Everywhere,” in *The Cosmological Eye* (New York: New Directions, 1939).

PCA *The Plight of the Creative Artist in the United States of America* (Privately published by Ben Porter, 1944).

PLEX *Plexus: Book Two of “The Rosy Crucifixion” Trilogy* (New York: Grove Press, 1965).

PWP “The Philosopher Who Philosophizes,” in *The Wisdom of the Heart* (London: Editions Poetry London, 1947).

ROW “Reflections on Writing,” in *The Wisdom of the Heart* (London: Editions Poetry London, 1947).

SEX *Sexus: Book One of the “Rosy Crucifixion” Trilogy* (London: Granada Publishing Limited, 1972).

TOA *The Time of The Assassins: A Study of Rimbaud* (New York: New Directions, 1949).

WOL *The World of Lawrence: A Passionate Appreciation* (London: Calder, 1988).

WOS *The World of Sex* (Unknown: The Olympia Press, 2004).

Introduction

The question of Henry Miller's relation to philosophy is positively vexing. While he considered professional philosophy to be "an activity removed from life," he still thought that "philosophy itself" was exciting, "not only as a legitimate part of life but *sine qua non,* a without which no life" (PWP, 75). Although there is little doubt among commentators today about the philosophical influence of Nietzsche, Bergson, and Spengler on Miller, most researchers have found it difficult, if not impossible, to agree what, as a matter of fact, Miller's philosophical *sine qua non* is or whether there is such a thing at all. Skeptics like John Parkin, for example, have tried to make us believe that conducting in-depth philosophical investigations of Miller would be effectively fruitless because of the markedly contradictory nature of his philosophical alignments. "To attempt to pin Miller down to a coherent system of thought is clearly a waste of time: enough has been said about paradox, incongruity and nonsense to indicate that no explicit or systematic philosophical approach could possibly emerge from a work whose very task indeed is to subvert such a possibility,"[1] Parkin observes. Miller himself certainly has only added to such despairing diagnoses regarding the questions of his philosophical constitution by declaring wholeheartedly that he is "somewhat of a juggler" who has no problem balancing "such incongruous ponderables as *The Decline of the West* and the *Tao Tí Ching*" (PLEX, 628). Having been unable to find "one unified attitude" behind Miller's "ideas, judgments and opinions" made Anaïs Nin give up the search and conclude tellingly: "You don't have *a* philosophy. You have feelings" (LP, 194). At the other end of the spectrum, and certainly fewer in numbers, there have been people like Paul Weiss and Count Hermann von Keyserling who, regardless of the supposed ambiguities, have claimed to have seen "a philosophical position" in Miller's work.[2]

The seemingly widespread inability of critics and commentators to set their hands firmly on Miller's philosophy seems to have resulted in exactly the situation Parkin proposed above: they no longer attempt to do it. Taking for granted that the road goes nowhere, philosophical inquiries into Miller's oeuvre seem to have stopped, period. Or rather, they have never really begun. To be sure, most of the higher-quality studies and better biographies do mention the names of philosophers and may even suggest connections between Miller's ideas and certain general philosophical tendencies. However, these otherwise high-caliber studies do not stem from, and are not directed by philosophical interest but, for example, set out to explore Miller's "ambiguous status in the literary tradition,"[3] examine his works "for their commentary on American and Western civilization,"[4] or trace the roots of the "unique form" of his fiction.[5] Miller's philosophy *per se* is not the main research question of any major study.[6] Besides literary and cultural inquiries, which seem to dominate the field, the biggest genre of Miller scholarship seems to be biographies. The beginning of the 1990s alone gave us three more Miller biographies[7] to be added to the already existing six. Nine biographies! How many solely biographical treatments needs one author whose entire oeuvre is supposed to be autobiographical (even if we acknowledge the suggestions that the latter should be, perhaps, taken with a grain of salt)? One can only hope that the fact that we haven't seen new Miller biographies in this century yet can be taken as a sign of a realization that the niche has been positively over-exploited.

This book, then, grows out of a twofold concern. The major part of the concern lies in the fact that not only have the questions regarding Miller and philosophy not been settled in any philosophically significant way, but also it is assumed that there is no need for revisiting existing opinions. Because of the self-imposed apathy, we have listened to those who, by rendering the philosophy-question in Miller undecidable, consider the matter decided. By pointing out that the issue is difficult or unclear, commentators like Parkin and Nin expect to have made it clear to us. Surely, by accepting this unfortunate situation, we would not only underestimate ourselves as scholars but also we would agree that an important part of the Miller-discourse has reached its end: that there is not, in principle, anything to be asked about Miller and philosophy. It seems, however, that even apart from the question of whether Miller indeed has any worthwhile philosophical ideas, the scholarly discussions over any given topic should be kept alive for the reason of avoiding dogmas, premature conclusions, and closing down of our critical sense alone. A healthy scholarly debate is a necessary (although not always sufficient) condition for saving any discipline from degeneration: the mild signs of which *Milleriana* has displayed for years. And precisely this regrettable tendency forms the second part of the twofold concern: we don't have enough intellectually challenging academic studies of Henry Miller. Indeed, while "Nexus: The International Henry Miller Journal" does its best to keep the Miller debates alive, it is hardly enough. The situation with more substantial monographs and books concerning Miller's work, while not voluminous and satisfactory in any sense, shows at least some degree of variety in interpreting Miller's texts. Over the last 10 years, we have seen, for example, books examining Miller's intertextuality, views on emotions and religion, comparisons to Dostoyevsky, his relation to surrealism and the city, and several other interesting phenomena.[8] Still, there is not a single book on philosophy.

These concerns, then, form the ideological basis of this book. I believe that we need to re-awaken the philosophical readings of Miller's works and free ourselves from the old prejudices. In encouraging such philosophical investigations, I also call for moving on from the questions of the philosophical influence of others on Miller and focusing more on what those influences resulted in: that is, something that we could positively call Henry Miller's own philosophy. In this book, I present one such attempt. Against skeptics, I argue that Miller does indeed have a philosophy which underpins most of his texts. Furthermore, I demonstrate that this philosophy forms a system, the understanding of which is necessary to adequately explain even some of the most basic of Miller's ideas.

It needs to be clarified in what sense philosophy—and Miller's relation to it—is understood in this book. If D. H. Lawrence is right "every novelist who amounts to anything has a philosophy."[9] Indeed, philosophy is something that writers *have* rather than something that they *do* as opposed to professional philosophers. Philosophy in this largely hidden and often unexplainable sense is ultimately to do with one's life as lived day to day. It is existential by nature. It guides and permeates one's life and thinking and manifests in the writer's works indistinctly, not explicitly. I call this type of *lebensphilosophie* a metaphysical sense of life. Metaphysics can be experienced and voiced both as a professional doctrine and as an "intuitive relation to reality."[10] It is largely in this latter sense that I have understood and undertaken to investigate Miller's philosophy in this book. Indeed, following D. H. Lawrence, I take his thought that metaphysics must always "subserve the artistic purpose beyond the artist's conscious aim. Otherwise the novel becomes a treatise,"[11] to be an accurate description of the role of philosophy in any writer's works. In the last analysis, Miller's philosophy *is* his idiosyncratic sense of life that metaphysically saturates his being.

Another stipulation is in order. Miller's thinking, in its qualified philosophical sense, results, by and large, from four main strains: European, American, Indian, and Chinese.[12] In this book, the predominant emphasis lies on the impact of the European philosophers and literary and cultural movements, which to me seemed to influence Miller the most. While perhaps often cited, I have always felt that the real philosophical depth of, for example, Nietzsche and Spengler has been still largely unexplored and unwritten in the truly scholarly fashion it deserves. With this book, limited as one always is, I hope to have catered for that particular void in *Milleriana*.

Before introducing the content and structure of this book, a few very general remarks about the methodological situatedness of the book are in order. Since my approach in dealing with Miller's philosophy consists of interpreting a vast number of his texts as crucial parts of the manifestation of some all-encompassing idea(s), it can be said to be sympathetic to the hermeneutical tradition. One important principle of the hermeneutical method, implicitly adopted here, is that we give up pretensions to objective truth and absolute knowledge and, instead, read and interpret texts with the view to "disclosing" aspects of their meaning and significance. While such "disclosures" never purport to be objective, one indicator of their usefulness or value could be said to lie in the range of explanations they offer. If an interpretative disclosure provides a structure for understanding many thus far seemingly incoherent or puzzling concepts based on an extensive number of an author's texts, then it can genuinely be said to be useful as well as proof of its hermeneutic consistency and overall credibility.

The book consists of five chapters. While each chapter could be read reasonably well independently, they do form altogether a more or less harmonious progression. In fact, the chapters are organized to reflect the kind of *germinal* approach I have chosen for disclosing Miller's philosophy. Indeed, between the first and the last chapter I have compressed around 65 years worth of Miller's intellectual torments. The structure of the book is, in an important sense, genealogical or evolutionary: it traces Miller's philosophy throughout his life.

In Chapter 1, "Prelude to a Future Philosophy: Modernist Melancholy, Dadaist Dances, and Surrealist Songs," I deal with the early influences on Miller's thinking. I claim that the intellectual foundation he built by reading Nietzsche, Spengler, Bergson, Hamsun, and others in the early 1910s and 1920s grounded the very basis of his philosophy to come. These sources, I argue, also prepared Miller for becoming a decidedly modernist writer. I also discuss Miller's engagements with Surrealism and Dadaism, which made important contributions to his views on art and the artist's role in society.

In Chapter 2, "Apocalypse Now: The End of History and the Twofold Present," I show that by rejecting a linear sense of history, Miller postulates the first important feature for his thinking. In attacking the *progressive* notion of history, Miller effectively strives against the *metaphysical ground* of the industrial age. I demonstrate that, based on his ahistorical bent, he introduces the distinction between the *traditional* and the *full present,* which to Miller represent the incommensurable realms of modern industrialist man and artist. This crucial divide, I argue, reflects, in the case of the *traditional present,* the essence of Miller's philosophical anguish; while in the instance of the *full present,* it conceals avenues for overcoming it. I uncover how this distinction of two senses of the present enables Miller to deal effectively with the modern notions of crisis and offers a response to the prominent modernist writers who, by insisting upon a *transitional view* of the modern crisis and maintaining an historicist stance toward the present appeared, quite paradoxically, far too traditional for Miller's literary tastes and philosophical appetite.

In Chapter 3, "The Anxiety of *Enframing*: Miller, Modern Technology, and Work," I expand upon the distinction made in the previous chapter and reveal two more features of the *traditional present*: *modern technology* and *work.* I suggest that by constituting, along with a linear notion of history, the *metaphysical ground* of the age, the modern sense of technology and work poses a major problem for Miller by closing off the possibilities for artistic self-determination in the modern society. I defend a view that in fighting against these imposed age-specific axioms, Miller philosophically seeks to overthrow Western metaphysics and pave the way toward his post-metaphysical or transcendental concept of *full present* and art.

In Chapter 4, "Behold, I teach you the *Inhuman*!: *Inhuman Artist, Übermensch* & *China*," I lay bare Miller's idiosyncratic notion of the *inhuman artist* which I show to be at the very centre of Miller's mature philosophy, and hence to provide the key to the overall interpretation of his work. Stemming from the conflict between the *traditional* and *full present,* the *inhuman artist* in Miller's thinking is meant to resolve the quarrel. I argue that, on the one hand, while the *inhuman artist* is supposed to inveigh against all the above-mentioned features of modern society *qua* the *traditional present,* on the other hand, he must also direct people toward the *full present* by practicing art in Miller's specific sense. The call for a personal awakening or metamorphosis via art becomes the most important task of Miller's *inhuman artist.* Despite the similarities, I dismiss the idea of the direct correspondence of Miller's *inhuman* to Nietzsche's *overman* but accede to their affinity through (Miller's) *human* and (Nietzsche's) *last man.* In the second half of the chapter, I lay bare Miller's concept of *China,* which, according to my interpretation, marks the final destination in the *full present* where the *inhuman artist* arrives by means of art but which he then must give up. Indeed, I show that by abandoning the *esthetisized view* of art, Miller ascribes only an intermediary role to art, albeit an ethically significant role. Art should guide one to a more meaningful life, and after this is achieved, art *per se* is no longer needed.

I claim that the *China*-experience denotes the ultimate goal of the *inhuman artist* for Miller and as such finalizes one's philosophical voyage. In such an experience, one has managed finally to overcome the metaphysical limits and false artistic pretensions that reign in the *traditional present*. In the transcendental *China*-occurrence, life itself becomes art.

In Chapter 5, "From *Theoria* to *Praxis*: The Poetry of Life," I sketch the outcome of Miller's *inhuman philosophy* from his early post-Paris days until the last years of his life in Palisades, California. I claim that while Miller, in his writings from the 1930s, was mainly driven by the artistic excitement that his *inhumanism* offered to him, its application as a practical doctrine became dominant in the later periods in his life. Analyzing Miller's texts from 1940s until late 1970s, I conclude that Miller not only remained faithful to his Paris-born *inhuman philosophy* but also that he sought actively the avenues for introducing it to the public and, more importantly, for living by it himself. Since his attempts were not without serious drawbacks and occasional self-doubts, I end the chapter with the discussion of the overall value of Miller's *inhumanism*.

Notes

1 John Parkin, *Henry Miller, the Modern Rabelais* (Lewiston, N.Y: E. Mellen Press, 1990), 183.
2 Jay Martin, *Always Merry and Bright: An Unauthorized Biography* (Santa Barbara: Capra Press, 1978), 414.
3 Raoul R. Ibargüen, "Narrative Detours: Henry Miller and the Rise of New Critical Modernism" (PhD diss. Yale University, 1989), 2.
4 Stephen L. Starck, "Hacking Away with an Ax: Henry Miller and Modernity" (PhD diss. University of Oklahoma, 1999), 9.
5 James M. Decker, *Henry Miller and Narrative Form: Constructing the Self, Rejecting Modernity* (New York: Routledge, 2005).
6 While it is true that Lehman sees himself as dealing with Miller's "aesthetic philosophy," a short article as this, however valuable, hardly qualifies as a major philosophical study. See Eric D. Lehman, "Henry Miller and Jean Francois Lyotard: The Aesthetics of 'The Inhuman' in *Tropic of Cancer*," *Nexus: The International Henry Miller Journal* 5 (2008): 275.
7 Robert Ferguson, *Henry Miller: A Life* (New York: Norton, 1991); Mary V. Dearborn, *The Happiest Man Alive: A Biography of Henry Miller* (New York: Simon & Schuster, 1991); Erica Jong, *The Devil at Large: Erica Jong on Henry Miller* (London: Chatto & Windus, 1993).
8 See Katy Masuga, *Henry Miller and How He Got That Way* (Edinburgh: Edinburgh University Press, 2011); Katy Masuga, *The Secret Violence of Henry Miller* (Camden House, 2011); Amy M. Flaxman, *New Anatomies: Tracing Emotions in Henry Miller's Writings* (MLA-IB. Belfast, ME: Porter, 2000); Thomas Nesbit, *Henry Miller and Religion* (New York: Routledge, 2007); Maria R. Bloshteyn, *The Making of a Counter-Culture Icon: Henry Miller's Dostoevsky* (Toronto: University of Toronto Press, 2007); Paul Jahshan, *Henry Miller and the Surrealist Discourse of Excess: A Post-Structuralist*

Reading (New York: P. Lang, 2001); Caroline Blinder, *A Self-Made Surrealist: Ideology and Aesthetics in the Work of Henry Miller* (Camden House, 2000).

9 D. H. Lawrence, "The Novel," in *Complete Works of D. H. Lawrence* [Kindle Edition] (Delphi Classics, 2011).

10 Julian Young, *Heidegger's Philosophy of Art* (Cambridge: Cambridge University Press, 2001), 123.

11 Cited in Frank Kermode, *Lawrence* (Fontana/Collins, 1973), 26.

12 While authors like Paul R. Jackson (1971) and Arnold Smithline (1966) rightly point out Miller's enthusiasm for American transcendentalists, Emerson and Thoreau, as well as Whitman; important as they are, their impact (with a few exceptions), to these ideas of Miller's on which I am focusing in this book does not stand out to the degree comparable to the sources selected. In any case, there seems to be no need to overstress the issue of Miller's intellectual background as *either* being American, European, Chinese, or Indian for it decidedly was a mixture of all of them. For example, there is very little in a way of explicit evidence for saying that Miller's *individualism* was indeed rooted in American thinkers (Emerson, Thoreau, Whitman) (which seems to be Caroline Blinder's view) and not European ones (Stirner, Nietzsche, Spengler). Indeed, Harold McCarthy, for instance, fully subscribes to the latter view by saying that while Miller ". . . accepted the wisdom of Emerson's and Thoreau's writings, those of Nietzsche and Spengler made a profound impression on his mind." See Harold T. McCarthy, "Henry Miller's Democratic Vistas," *American Quarterly* 23, 2 (1971): 223. Likewise, Miller's visions of himself as a sage or seer can be explained equally by the influences of Nietzsche's Zarathustra and by the teachings of Lao Tzu and Krishnamurti.

1

Prelude to a Future Philosophy: Modernist Melancholy, Dadaist Dances, and Surrealist Songs

I was against life, on principle

—Henry Miller

The aim of this chapter is to lay bare the connection between Miller and some of the early sources of his thought. Revealing this bond will help to define and categorize Miller's ideas in the historically relevant context in which they found their inspiration, maturation and point of departure. To an extent, Miller is being scrutinized here in a manner similar to the way he himself insisted on in his study of D. H. Lawrence. That is, as in this study, we can only understand Miller himself, if we investigate him, in his own words, "against the background of his age, by situating him, as it were, in his particular soil and climate" (WOL, 57).[1] This preliminary historico-intellectual contextualization will then open up a path to Miller's thinking, which we will unpack, layer by layer, throughout the book. Miller's early encounters with the works of different thinkers and artistic movements, scrutinized in this chapter, have been presented as preliminary intellectual exercises that Miller subsequently used to inaugurate his conceptual and spiritual basis for finding a refuge from the modern age and establishing himself as a writer. These "exercises" lasted more than 10 years. However, it is precisely these early sources and influences that attuned Miller to think the way he did and resulted in something that we can call his *inhuman philosophy*.

In what follows, we mainly focus on three artistic-intellectual movements as their impact, in my opinion, appears to be the strongest in influencing the pertinent ideas that need to be highlighted in Miller's works. First, Miller's relation to modernist ideas is to me a crucial but still sadly often overlooked topic. To remedy this, we start this chapter by uncovering Miller's early interactions with pre-modernist and early modernist sources and, indeed, his decidedly modernist stance will be continually emphasized throughout the book. I regard modernism here as an umbrella term under which both Dadaism and Surrealism are to be situated. Miller's relationship with modernism is still regarded as very much open to debate. Unlike Dadaism and Surrealism, several important pre-modernist as well as early modernist writings were accessible to Miller even before the 1920s, although he wasn't able to incorporate these ideas into his first literary attempts. While "established literary quarters" have often refused to identify Miller as a modernist on the grounds that his works fall outside of the "golden era" of modernism in Europe, several commentators, on the contrary, regard him as rightfully belonging to the modernist scene. I seek to substantiate and defend the latter view. Rather than insisting that modernism be defined predominantly as a certain historical period, I suggest we instead focus on *themes* or *concepts* that modernist literature has evoked. If we take this *conceptually* modernist approach, as I have, we will see that Henry Miller's works offer a rich treatment of some of the most prominent themes common to all modernist literature, namely the critique of modern technology, the treatments of crisis and history, and the ongoing question of the role of the modern artist, all of which we will take up in the later chapters of this book.

Dadaism and Surrealism, the other two prominent sources of Miller's thought examined in this chapter, were both important stimuli for his thinking in their own right. Although having experienced Dadaist art already before the 1920s, Miller studied both Dadaism and Surrealism "academically" only in the 1930s. Through their influence he acquired the conceptual apparatus for capturing the spirit of his own life of the 1920s in New York. The influences of Dadaism and Surrealism were realized perhaps most effectively in his *Black Spring* (1936) in which he made ample use of impressionistic images, dream symbols, and stream of consciousness techniques. While Miller very much enjoyed Surrealistic cinema and its other art forms, he soon became disillusioned with the ultraintellectual goals and socio-political agendas of the Surrealists. This resulted in his "An Open Letter to Surrealists Everywhere" (1938), in which he directly objected to Surrealism as a movement and defended his own thoroughly individualistic view of art and artists.

Just as his personal engagement with the ideas of these early sources and movements served for Miller as "prolegomena" to his mature writing, the following introductory section will serve as "prolegomena" for readers entering the hallway of *Milleriana*, who can thereby familiarize themselves with the type of thinker Miller is being cast as in this book.

A modernist who got left out in the cold

Though contemporaneous with James Joyce, Ernest Hemingway, Gertrude Stein, Virginia Woolf, Ezra Pound, T. S. Eliot, and several other celebrated modernist writers, Miller, in literary discussions, is typically not considered to be a modernist writer. In his recent study, James Decker concedes that "most critics of late modernist period completely ignore Miller" and that "Miller's representation in broad surveys of modernist era, literary histories, anthologies, reference works, conference panels, and other indicators of academic interest proves rather scant."[2] He also points out that some of the major anthologies of American literature fail to include any of Miller's work.[3] At first blush, this seems to have occurred for a few superficial but compelling reasons. First of all, there is something we may call the historical reason.

Miller's first "official" book, *Tropic of Cancer*, was published in 1934. To those who believe the heyday of literary modernism ended in 1925,[4] this alone would automatically provide a good reason for his exclusion from the modernist canon. Still, as so much is still unclear about what the best way to define modernism is, it may well be that our understanding of modernism as a temporally restricted phenomenon is simply inadequate, or at least not the only possibility. Do ideas cease to interest and influence people with the turn of a particular year or even a decade? Indeed, even during the period that is thought to include "modernism proper," most of the literature produced was not modernist.[5] Thus, denying Miller access to modernism on historical grounds only seems to be nitpickingly narrow-minded to say the very least.

Few as they are, some recent positive tendencies toward including Miller among the modernists can be found. Sarah Garland, for example, in her recent essay, finds Miller to be an interesting voice in articulating "a late apocalyptic modernism."[6] Nicola Allen, too, in *The Modernism Handbook* (2009) lists the publishing of Miller's *Tropic of Cancer* as an important event in the timeline of modernism, which she defines as lasting from 1890 to 1941.[7] We can see, however, that when it comes to the historical definition of modernism, different views abound and it seems to be much like the question of the end of the world where "any date can be justified on some calculation or other."[8] Owing to these apparent difficulties with historical categorization, my treatment of Miller focuses on what we may call a *thematic* or *conceptual* identification of modernism. To be sure, the *conceptual* reading of modernism is nothing but a difference in perspective on the overall phenomenon of *esthetic* modernism which took up the fight against the bourgeois modernity in the late nineteenth century.[9] However, instead of engaging in an analysis comparing the particular literary and artistic similarities or differences between Miller and other esthetic modernists, my approach concentrates rather on the affinity and discord of their more universal philosophical ideas. It seems to me that Miller's relationship to modernism is best demonstrated and explained precisely in such terms.[10]

The other reasons for Miller's traditional exclusion from the modernist canon, or any literary canon for that matter, seem to be due to the use of "frank Anglo-Saxon vocabulary"[11] and explicit sexual depictions in his *Tropic* books. Ample descriptions of sex and the choice of a publisher of questionable reputation certainly ostracized Miller from wider literary discussions for decades. Miller's *Tropic of Cancer* was published in Paris by Obelisk Press: a publishing house that was, alas, mainly focused on publishing books which ". . . were condemned under obscenity laws in England or America."[12] It was more or less guaranteed, then, based on Obelisk's reputation alone, that Miller's book would be banned in English-speaking countries immediately when published. The banning of both Miller's *Tropics* for nearly 30 years in both the United States and Britain, certainly tempered, although not exclusively, the tone of the reception of Miller's works throughout these decades, during which most of the scholarly commentators were not willing to jeopardize their careers and reputation by dealing with a "banned author" who took liberties with sexual matters. To many, the sexual content in Miller's books seemed so extremely over the top that for years it placed Miller "entirely off the map as an ideologue."[13] The mentality that sees Miller predominantly as a pornographer is sadly still felt today in the English departments of universities throughout the world. It has made it extremely difficult, if not impossible, to "pigeonhole him [Miller] into traditional literary classifications," a noted commentator rightly observes.[14] In addition, as Miller's most important books were banned, the few critics who were bold enough to discuss his works between the 1930s and the early 1960s were necessarily limited to those Miller texts—mainly short stories and essays—which had been officially published by that time. As Frank Kermode, a distinguished scholar of English letters, admitted in his early Miller review, any critic at the time would struggle to make up his mind about Miller's literary merit, not being able to read "the *Tropics* in their entirety."[15] Furthermore, drawing on the example of D. H. Lawrence's *Lady Chatterley's Lover*, which similarly was banned, Kermode thought that Lawrence's legal proceedings "would look like tea at the vicarage compared with a Miller case."[16] Referring to Miller's anti-intellectual stance and his well-known contempt for academics, Kermode put forward a warranted question: would the dons really queue up for Miller's defense? It was not until the 1960s that academic criticism really began to take Miller seriously. Miller himself loathed the analyzes by serious university critics who "sought to put him in what they regarded as his proper place – as if he needed to fill a pigeon hole in literary history."[17] Miller did not want to be reduced to a theoretical framework he had never believed in. Indeed, his distrust of "classical models and conventional literature" is central to his works.[18] In addition to being constantly viewed as a dirty writer, things turned even worse for Miller in the mid 1970s when Kate Millet's infamous *Sexual Politics* (1970) brought along vigorous feminist attacks on his works and Miller fell out of favor even more.[19]

Now let's proceed to examine Miller's path to modernism in the way in which it is understood and emphasized here. Literary modernism, with its prime in the 1920s, was mainly a European phenomenon, although many prominent modernists were American expatriates (e.g. Eliot, Pound, Stein, Fitzgerald, Hemingway, etc). The members of the *Bloomsbury Group* in England and the so-called *Lost Generation* writers in Paris produced, around that time, some of their very best works; works that in effect came to define modernism.[20] Without going too deeply into the subtle layers of the history of literary modernism, the perspective I share here with several commentators sees modernism very much as a reaction or response to modernity or the Enlightenment. Modernity, also called the *Age of Reason*, has been most often associated with the explosive increase of rationalism, rejection of religion, self-determination, the advancement of science and modern technology, and the belief in progress. Peter Childs characterizes modernity as having attempted to place

> . . . humanity and in particular human reason at the centre of everything, from religion and nature, to finance and science. Modernity describes the rise of capitalism, of social study and state regulation, of a belief in progress and productivity leading to mass systems of industry, institutionalisation, administration and surveillance.[21]

In his own discussions of modernity in "The Age of World Picture," Martin Heidegger importantly also adds "art's moving into the purview of aesthetics" and the "fact that human activity is conceived and consummated as culture" as essential features of modernity.[22] In one way or the other, although in an overly simplified sense, literary modernism can be viewed as growing out of the disillusionment with the above-mentioned ideals.

World War I had an enormous impact on modernists who now felt that the heightened ideals of humanism, largely initiated by the Enlightenment, were dead and buried forever. Katherine Mansfield, for example, wrote in 1919, about the effects of the war, that she felt "in the profoundest sense that nothing can ever be the same — that, as artists, we are traitors if we feel otherwise: we have to take it into account and find new expressions, new moulds for our new thoughts and feelings."[23] This represented the overall mood of the modernists. Several of them voiced their growing concerns about science and industrialism. D. H. Lawrence, for example, expressed his skepticism toward the prevalent belief in science so characteristic of the attitudes of the age of his day. He seems to suggest that a scientific world view is unable to capture the complexities of the new life or of "man alive" and that only the (modern) novelist can hope to achieve such things. Lawrence writes:

> . . . To the scientist, I am dead. He puts under the microscope a bit of dead me, and calls it me. . . . My heart, my liver, my stomach have all been scientifically me, according to the scientist; and nowadays I am either a brain, or nerves, or glands, or something more up-to-date in the tissue line.[24]

T. S. Eliot, another pre-eminent modernist, in "The Idea of a Christian Society," observes of the ideas inherited from modernity that "for a long enough time we have believed in nothing but the values arising in a mechanized, commercialized, urbanized way of life . . .."[25] And it is precisely because of these and similar anxieties inherited from modernity that Henry Miller, too, should be viewed as intersecting with literary modernism. As J. Gerald Kennedy aptly observes, Miller, especially in his 1930s' works, expresses both his "personal psychodrama" and the "collective experience of the modern age."[26] By connecting "public and private crises" in his texts, Kennedy notes, Miller's views form "a complex response to the crisis of modernity."[27] As Miller's tie with modernist thinking at the time was in many ways vague and indirect (i.e. not geographical but spiritual), we need to turn to the early sources which influenced Miller's thinking and, in however roundabout a way, prepared him for the thought of the modernists.

Modernists in Europe, Miller in America

In the 1920s, while modernists blossomed in Europe, Henry Miller was trapped in New York, his home town, doing odd jobs that he hated and dealing with an unsuccessful first marriage. He only started to contemplate writing around 1922 when he wrote his first novel *Clipped Wings* (never published).[28] Even so, whatever Miller missed out on in virtue of not exactly being at the epicenter where the "canons roared," he made up for by raw experiences and ample, if erratic, reading: primarily of the same literature that had inspired the modernists in Europe. Indeed, it is as "a reader and an enthusiast" that Miller, however late, comes to modernism.[29] For instance, Robert Ferguson, a biographer of Miller, claims Miller read Emma Goldman's *The Social Significance of Modern Drama* (published in Boston 1914) before 1920, in which he would have come across discussions of the works and thought of Ibsen, Strindberg, Maeterlinck, Shaw, Yeats, Tolstoy, Chekhov, Gorky, and others.[30] It was also Emma Goldman, on Miller's own later (though contested) account, from whom he bought Friedrich Nietzsche's *The Anti-Christ* (1895) and Max Stirner's *The Ego and His Own* (1844) in 1913.[31] The impact of both of these books can hardly be overestimated in providing the stimulus for the type of iconoclastic thinking Miller had so vigorously sought but not yet found. It is my view that Miller's path to modernism was, thus, largely laid out and importantly nurtured by the critique of the core ideas of modernity, which both Stirner and Nietzsche, and later Oswald Spengler, vehemently voiced in their books.

Let us now have a closer look at some of these sources. One can only imagine the magnitude of the intellectual rupture, which, for example, Stirner's *The Ego and His Own* presented to a young Miller. James J. Martin, the editor of a recent English edition, calls Stirner's book "one of the most formidable assaults on authoritarianism ever launched."[32] In Stirner's passionate words Miller found a foremost basis for his decidedly anti-traditionalist view of life, which contrasted with his conservative German immigrant upbringing and his mother's adherence to the protestant work ethic. "My concern," writes Stirner, "is neither the divine nor the human, not the true, good just, free, etc, but solely what is mine, and it is not a general one, but is — unique, as I am unique. Nothing is more to me than myself!"[33]

Importantly then, Stirner abandons both the religious and everyday political worlds and seeks something that is thoroughly "one's own." Stirner opines that "man must first become so completely unconcerned and reckless, so altogether without relations, so altogether indifferent to the world that even its falling in ruins would not move him — before he could feel himself as worldless; that is, as spirit [*Geist*]."[34] "Only after all worldly care has left him" is man, Stirner continues to elaborate, "all in all to himself, is he only himself, is he spirit for the spirit."[35] Stirner's idea that, in order to become spirit, one "must create for itself its spirit world, and is not spirit till it creates it"[36] never left Miller and reveals its full prophetic significance, perhaps, in the light of his later (mainly 1930s) ideas of *full present* and *inhuman*, which we will discuss at length in Chapters 2 and 4.

In the 1920s, although these ideas clearly made an enormous impression on him, Miller found neither the personal nor the literary stamina for living out his newly gained wisdom. In fact, the whole of the 1920s for Miller can be described as the ambivalent struggle between his alienation from the *human* world and his becoming *spirit* in Stirneresque fashion. His *Tropic of Capricorn* (1939) particularly captures early strivings of this kind both on a personal and a literary level since it deals with the period when Miller left his first wife, quit his job at the Western Union, and attempted his first novel. I will revisit these issues later on.

Miller's interactions with Nietzsche's *The Anti-Christ* (1895) paralleled his reading of Stirner. Despite the fact that Miller read it quite early on in his life, or perhaps precisely because of that, we can discern and analyze the impact of Nietzsche's teachings, in a scholarly sense, on Miller only from the early to mid-1930s onward. Yet, *The Anti-Christ* made a tremendous impression on Miller at the time (around 1913). So much so, in fact, that he wrote an essay on it "during slack hours" at his father's tailor shop in 1915.[37] Unfortunately, this essay has not survived. Even so, one familiar with Miller's later writings can, without difficulties, sense the allurement *The Anti-Christ* must have presented to Miller. From the first pages it is clear that Nietzsche's book "belongs to the very few" and thus emphasizes the uniqueness of the reader. "One must be accustomed," Nietzsche writes, "to living on mountains — to seeing the wretched ephemeral chatter of politics and national egoism beneath one."[38] Nietzsche's readers are only those, he writes, who have "reverence for oneself; love for oneself; unconditional freedom with respect to oneself." The rest does not concern Nietzsche. The rest are "merely mankind" to which one must be "superior in force, in loftiness of soul — in contempt . . .."[39] Nietzsche considered the values of the present mankind, especially Christian values, as decadent and aimed for the "revaluation of all values" which "free spirits" will establish.[40] In many ways, *The Anti-Christ* can be read as a continuation of his *Thus Spoke Zarathustra* (1885) where he had introduced the notions of the *Übermensch* and the *last man*. It is precisely "the man of today, the man with whom I [Nietzsche] am fatefully contemporary," the *last man* of Zarathustra, who makes Nietzsche "suffocate of his impure breath" and haunts him "by a feeling blacker than the blackest melancholy" in *The Anti-Christ*.[41] The *Übermensch*, or *overman*, can be seen as being present in Nietzsche's descriptions of the "free spirit" who should intensify the "will to power" in him as this promotes, according to him, both nobility and happiness.[42]

Similarly with Stirner, Nietzsche's revolutionary ideas stayed with Miller and found a vital role in his thinking and later texts. It unfolds that the influence is not only that of *The Anti-Christ* but also that of *Thus Spoke Zarathustra* (1885), *The Birth of Tragedy* (1872), and several other Nietzsche texts which Miller read later in his life. It is a fairly uncontroversial view that Nietzsche "remains essential for an understanding of Modernism" and that his "theorization of modernity as a moment in which traditional social values and institutions had eroded remains a clear and important insight."[43] This makes him also one of the most important direct links to modernism for Miller. We examine the Miller-Nietzsche connection at length in Chapters 2 and 4, particularly in regard to the ideas of history, *inhuman*, and art.

Another book mandatory to mention in this list of early influences is Henri Bergson's *Creative Evolution* (1910). "Bergson belongs to my 'youth' (tailor shop days). How much he influenced me is imponderable," wrote Miller to his friend Lawrence Durrell in 1949 (DML, 261). Throughout *Creative Evolution*, Bergson's crucial point is that life must be equated with creation, as creativity alone can adequately account for both the continuity of life and the discontinuity of the products of evolution.[44] It is precisely this notion of creativity that appealed to Miller the most and which, one way or other, found its way into his ideas later on. In *Tropic of Capricorn*, Miller tells of his very first experiences with the book:

> If I had never understood a thing which was written in this book, if I had preserved only the memory of one word, creative, it is quite sufficient. This word was my talisman. With it I was able to defy the whole world, and especially my friends. (CAP, 199)

Without being able to communicate Bergson's complex ideas to his mainly blue-collar friends Miller felt positively alienated and, as his friends were not likely to become Bergson's disciples, Miller felt no need for their company any longer.

> ... This book became my friend because it taught me that I had no need of friends. It gave me the courage to stand alone, and it enabled me to appreciate loneliness ... with this book in my hands, reading aloud to my friends, questioning them, explaining to them, I was made clearly to understand that I had no friends, that I was alone in the world. (*ibid*)

Bergson helped Miller to understand what was manifestly his "own" at the time and to realize how he was situated in relation to his friends, family, and society. Armed with Bergson, Miller was ready to move on "to new fields of battle, to new triumphs or defeats" (200) while, it seemed to him, the rest of the world, and sadly even his own friends, were quite happy to stay put and settle with the status quo. One can sense Miller's desire for something beyond the existing conditions of man when he says that, with the help of Bergson, he wanted to seek out "new specimens of the human race whom you patiently instruct and equip with the new symbols" (*ibid*). This may well be the earliest point at which Miller's search for the idea of the *inhuman artist* started to take its first embryonic shape. Although Bergson's legacy and its relation to Miller will not be discussed directly in this book, its tacit presence is sensed the most in the treatments of time and history in Chapter 2 and *China* in Chapter 4.

In the early 1920s, Miller also read and became infatuated by an important literary precursor of modernism, Norwegian author Knut Hamsun. "Hardly anyone knows," Miller revealed in an interview "that it was Knut Hamsun who was my — the man I was trying to model myself upon" (CHM, 35). Hamsun's *The Hunger* (1890) Miller particularly singled out, repeatedly, as his biggest influence in becoming a writer. In another interview from the mid-1960s, he confessed to an interviewer:

> Knut Hamsun! He's the one who got me started. I've sat with his books and tried to squeeze the magic out of the pages! Because magic is what it is. (101)

Miller intimated that it was precisely *The Hunger* which "made me realize that what I wanted to do was to tell what I was seeing" (101). Miller said he had even studied Hamsun's style "line by line, to find out where is the secret of this" (36). *The Hunger* is considered to be one of the first examples of psychological literature and the stream of consciousness technique later developed by prominent modernist writers such as James Joyce and Virginia Woolf. Miller, too, made use of the stream of consciousness technique in his *Tropic of Cancer* and even more so in *Black Spring* (1936). The story of *The Hunger* was a constant reminder to Miller of his own misfortune of the 1920s as the protagonist in Hamsun's novel is, likewise, an artistic type looking for food and lodging and trying to succeed as a writer. The bleakness of the city and the indifference of his surrounding bourgeois class, which Hamsun's main character experiences in the book, no doubt added to the picture Stirner and Nietzsche had already started to paint in Miller's head. The following passage from *The Hunger*, for example, could be easily read in somewhat Nietzschean fashion as depicting the increasingly growing divide between the "man of today" or *last man* and that of the artist or "spirit":

> How gaily and lightly these people I met carried their radiant heads, and swung themselves through life as through a ball-room! There was no sorrow in a single look I met, no burden on any shoulder, perhaps not even a clouded thought, not a little hidden pain in any of the happy souls. And I, walking in the very midst of these people, young and newly fledged as I was, had already forgotten the very look of happiness.[45]

The mood of the passage is quite characteristic of many later modernists who felt distinctively isolated as artists in the emerging mass of people. Perhaps the protagonist's uncompromising nature and wish to stick to his writing at all costs and in whatever conditions also helped Miller through the 1920s and relieved somewhat the pain of his rejections at the time as a struggling literary man. The important thing was not to give up, to stay on the course chosen, and not to doubt one's own convictions, much like the narrator in *The Hunger*:

> The consciousness that I was yet pure and honourable rose to my head, filled me with a splendid sense of having principle, character, of being a shining white beacon in a muddy, human sea amidst a floating wreck.[46]

Hamsun, Stirner, and Nietzsche without a doubt amplified Miller's feelings as "other" in respect to his family and friends. Later generalizations on a grander scale were only natural consequences of this.

It is evident that Miller, in the 1920s, did not only build up his way to modernism via the criticism of the pre-modernist thinkers and writers but also had direct encounters with modernist literature. In a letter to his friend Emil Schnellock in 1922, Miller, for example, reveals an important source of his early exposure to modern poetry:

> Say, many thousands of thanks to you for introducing me to Ezra Loomis Pound. I have him and the whole tribe of modern poetasters on my desk. Eight volumes of modern poetry all at once, and one taken surreptitiously from the public library . . . Sounds like stuff I say to myself all day long. (LE, 4)

While early on Miller seemed to sympathize with Pound in accurately describing the horrendous nature of the present inherited from modernity, I will point out, in Chapter 2, their differences in regard to their views on history: an important feature that also sheds light on an idiosyncrasy of Miller's in comparison to several other leading modernists.

Miller had definitely also read Ernest Hemingway in the 1920s and, despite what he had said against him all along, he admitted later that "as much as I put him down, that first book, *The Sun Also Rises,* had a lot to do with my going to France, it inspired me to go. It shows something doesn't it?" (CHM, 222).

Another philosophical rupture from which Miller never recovered came through reading Oswald Spengler's *The Decline of the West* (1918) sometime between 1925 and 1928. In his *Plexus* (1963), which deals with the years in question, Miller described it as "another momentous moment in my life" (PLEX, 618).

> The Decline of the West! I can never forget the thrill which ran up my spine when I first heard this title . . . For many a year I had been aware that I was participating in a general decline . . . What we hadn't understood so clearly, most of us, was that we were part of this very 'West' . . .. (620)

Spengler's ideas were built naturally upon the foundation already bolstered up by Stirner, Nietzsche, and Bergson. Portraying modern civilization as the "arteriosclerosis of culture," abandoning the traditional notion of history as linear and necessarily progressive and being outspoken about the nature of modern technology, Spengler became an ally and mentor for life for Miller.

> On every page, virtually, there is an assault upon the dogmas, conventions, superstitions and modes of thinking which have characterized the last few hundred years of 'modernity.' Theories and systems are battered about like ninepins. The whole conceptual landscape of modern man is devastated. What emerges are not the scholarly ruins of the past but freshly recreated worlds in which one may 'participate' with one's ancestors, live again in the spring, the fall, the summer, even the winter, of man's history. (638)

Spengler's view that the modern western world is about to come to its natural end most likely played a part in Miller's later notion of *creative death:* the idea that only with the apocalypse of the "man of today" and contemporary society can there be a new and better world. The end or death then does not signify *the end* of human existence but a new and *creative* beginning.

> . . . thanks to this historical maestro, we glean that the truth of death need not be sad, particularly when, as it happens, the whole "civilized" world is already part of it. Suddenly we are asked to look into the depths of the tomb with the same zeal and joy with which we first greeted life. (622)

Spengler's notion of the "ahistoric spirit," somebody who renounces "world as history," guided Miller toward his own idea of the *full present* which we will discuss in depth in

Chapter 2. Spengler's and Miller's congruity also reveals itself explicitly in our discussion of Miller's relation to *modern technology* in Chapter 3.

The above thinkers are naturally not the only ones who fascinated Miller in the 1920s. There is evidence of a whole array of other prominent writers and philosophers Miller read at that time. In one of his letters from 1922, for example, he claims to have read Haeckel, Darwin, Spencer, Freud, Huxley, Weininger, Rolland, Dewey, France, Schopenhauer, Tolstoy, Gorki, and Mencken among those already mentioned (LE, 4–5). Their impact, however, at least at the time, did not seem to stand out to the same degree as, for example, Nietzsche and Spengler. The important thing to remember from his life in the 1920s is that through reading Stirner, Bergson, Nietzsche, and Spengler, the crucial seed of Miller's thinking was planted and his path toward modernism was, thus, theoretically prepared. Although being "home schooled" rather than systematically taught, Miller was, as we can now see, familiar with many important sources of modernist thinking. In order to release his full potential as a modern spirit himself, however, he needed guidance from like-minded people and different surroundings, both of which he found when he moved to Paris in 1930.

Raoul Ibargüen, in his *Henry Miller and the Rise of New Critical Modernism* (1989), provides a valuable account of Miller's literary, and also spiritual, transformation toward modernism when he settled in Paris in 1930. "Miller in Paris in the 1930s," Ibargüen writes, "was not the novelist he had tried to become in New York in the 1920s."[47] In Paris, Miller met Michael Fraenkel, Walter Lowenfels, and Alfred Perlès, who called themselves *The New Instincitivists*. They suggested, based on *Clipped Wings* and other early efforts, that Miller's novelistic techniques "were obsolete and outdated by an emerging modernist aesthetics."[48] Under the guidance of his new group of friends, especially Michael Fraenkel, "Miller reread Shakespeare, Goethe, Dostoevsky, Proust, Lawrence, Eliot, Joyce, Nietzsche, Spengler, Faure, and others. For the first time he studied Dada, Surrealism, Freud, Jung, and contemporary British-American literary criticism," says Ibargüen. Allegedly, it was Fraenkel who told Miller to start writing in the first person and about his own experiences:

> Write as you talk, I told him. Write as you live. Write as you feel and think . . . Forget the fancy stories and novels and that sort of thing. Write about yourself, your life. Get all this pent-up emotion out of your system. Evacuate the trenches! A writer's duty now is to himself — to liberate himself, to come clean of his past, his death, to come alive. A personal record. No time for anything else. Anything else is literature — with a bad smell![49]

Supposedly, Miller "took to heart Fraenkel's critique of his aesthetics" and understood that "he had failed as a realist, at best managing a slavish imitation of Dreiser."[50] Miller finally realized, Ibargüen argues, that "realism was not his forte."[51] Miller, however, did not follow Fraenkel blindly and, Ibargüen concludes, his "challenge to the emerging modernist aesthetics began, as had every turn of his literary development, on a personal level, when he set out to surpass Fraenkel and by extension all the writers Fraenkel admired."[52] Ferguson has in his biography seriously questioned the extent of Fraenkel's real impact as "the éminence grise" behind Miller's *Tropic of Cancer* as he liked to present himself in later years. Ferguson also points out that several of Fraenkel's ideas were treated as household jokes between Miller and Alfred Perlès.[53] It would be hard to deny the significance of the Miller-Fraenkel *Hamlet* correspondence, however, in which Miller explains some of his most original ideas.

The publication of *Tropic of Cancer* in September 1934 finally made it possible to evaluate Miller to some extent as a writer and place him in some relation with existing literary trends. Miller sent complimentary copies to some of the most pre-eminent modernists such as Pound, Eliot, and [Aldous] Huxley. The response from these literary giants was largely favorable and encouraging. T. S. Eliot deemed *Cancer* a "remarkable book . . . a rather magnificent piece of work" that was "a great deal better in depth of insight and of course in the actual writing than *Lady Chatterley's Lover.*" Dearborn points out, however, that "Eliot became a bit guarded when Miller wanted to use his complimentary letter in advertising."[54] Ezra Pound considered Miller to have made a bigger impact on literature than Virginia Woolf had and thought that *Tropic of Cancer* even "out-Ulyssed Joyce." Lawrence Durrell, who came to be Miller's close friend later, thought *Tropic of Cancer* was "the copy-book for my generation."[55] As J. D. Brown suggests, however, such high praise was likely to be exaggerated by the censorship issues of the time. Because of the ban, there was virtually no response from America to the book at the time.

In their early reviews of *Tropic of Cancer*, Edmund Wilson (1938) and George Orwell (1940), despite their mostly negative (Wilson) or ambivalently favorable (Orwell) attitudes toward the book, perceived in Miller's writing strong resonances with the attitudes of the 1920s (rather than the 1930s). Wilson regarded *Cancer* as "a product of the decadent expatriate culture"[56] and Orwell observed that "the subject matter of the book and, to a certain extent, its mental atmosphere belong to the twenties rather than to the thirties."[57] Even if these observations were intended to count as reasons to view Miller's work as old hat and unoriginal, they nonetheless represent interpretations of Miller that place him in line with the modernist trend in literature. At least according to these two commentaries there was no significant difference, as far as literary labeling went, between what Miller had just written and what the *Lost Generation* writers such as Hemingway, Fitzgerald, Stein, and others had produced in Paris in the 1920s.

In more recent years, there have been other commentators who have associated, in one way or the other, Miller's works with modernism or late modernism. J. D. Brown himself, for example, in his book, calls Miller "the late-bloomer of modern literature"[58] and draws attention to the importance of Miller's development of the autobiographical form and to the fact that Miller "drew upon the narrative strategies of modern fiction."[59] Brown has a high regard for Miller's input into the twentieth-century autobiographical form, in particular, for "introducing Surrealism, Dadaism, and dark humour to the autobiographical form, with savage results."[60] For Brown, Miller managed to successfully combine "the colloquial voice and surrealistic style."[61]

Jeffrey Bartlett in his essay "The Late Modernist" (1992) observes that the "modern spirit was in the air Miller breathed, even if he was unable to capture it in writing while in New York. He felt the anarchy of Dada and the unconscious forces and images of Surrealism, experienced life in cubistic fragments."[62] Bartlett sees Miller's relationship with modernism as a spiritual bond and his sympathy with some of its ideals as perhaps even largely unconscious on Miller's part. Bartlett notes: "Miller is a modernist in that he understands himself, however ambivalently, as of his times. The Zeitgeist of the modern helped him to break the constraints of writing 'museum stuff' and to discover his personal voice."[63] As we'll learn later in the book, Miller not only understood himself as a bearer of the modern spirit but he also became a severe critic and a reformer of several its canons and practices.

For James Decker, it is Miller's *spiral form* technique of narrative development that links him to modernism "as an attempt to come to grips with the sense of alienation promulgated by World War I and its attendant urbanization, scientific Fordism, and depersonalized mass communication."[64] Decker sees Miller's spiral form technique of time development, which enabled him "to expand freely in any direction at any given moment"[65] as one his most original contributions, making him an "important figure in the transition from romanticism and transcendentalism to modernism and postmodernism."[66]

Dadaist dances

Miller's conscious engagements with both Dada and Surrealism started in the 1930s, but they probably still qualify as *preludes* to Miller's thinking, as much of his "studies" took place in the sense that he could read a treatise in the morning and "apply" its wisdom already in the afternoon. Dadaism and Surrealism influenced Miller deeply in his early Paris days. As the emphasis of this book lies decidedly on modernism and its influences, both Dada and Surrealism are, alas, treated here only in a sketchy manner, mainly with the view to simply illustrating the scope of the sources of Miller's thinking.

Dadaism emerged rather independently in several parts of the world roughly at the same time. While Dada in Zürich found its place in 1916 at the *Cabaret Voltaire* under the leadership of a poet and theorist Hugo Ball and his associates Tristan Tzara, Marcel Janco, Walter Sterner, and others, it was also born in 1915 in New York with the help of two French expatriates Marcel Duchamp and Francis Picabia.[67] Apparently, while having found little success with the Parisian *avant-garde*, Duchamp's painting *Nude Descending a Staircase no2* had traveled to New York and was shown at the Armory Show exhibition already in 1913. In an interview with the *Paris Review* in 1962, we find Miller intimating that he, then 22 years old, had visited the very same show: "I was infatuated, intoxicated. All this was what I was looking for, it seemed so familiar to me" (CHM, 53). It is rather safe to assume, however, that young Miller at the time knew very little, if anything, about European Dada and its principles. Unfortunately, then, Miller's real acquaintance with Dada took place *post mortem* as Dadaism is claimed to have faded out around 1922 giving way to its heir, Surrealism. There is no doubt that, however late, Dadaistic ideas indeed left an impact on Miller's thinking:

> The Dadaist movement was something truly revolutionary. It was a deliberate conscious effort to turn the tables upside down, to show the absolute insanity of our present-day life, the worthlessness of all our values. (53)

Dadaism was not identifiable with any one personality, viewpoint or style, nor did it ever acquire a single coherent program. It has been suggested that "Dada had to remain fugitive and imponderable, that it would die the moment it began to take itself seriously or become fixed in any stance."[68] The focus or emphasis within the movement was continually shifting. As such it was able to appeal to many individually very different artists. It has been said to be Dada's "common spirit of rebellion" more than anything else that touched the artistically minded.[69] World War I no doubt confirmed a growing conviction that the "West's obsession with technological advance and the over-estimation of reason at the expense of feeling led straight to destructive megalomania."[70] Their art, according to Dadaists, was in many ways a reaction to, but also a cure for, the ills of the age. Hans Arp, one of the Zürich Dadaists, commented: "We were seeking an art based on fundamentals to cure the madness of the age and a new order of things that would restore the balance between heaven and hell."[71] As we will see, this attitude toward an artist's role makes itself felt in many of Miller's writings about art's purpose.

Miller welcomed Dadaist thinking in his works just after he moved to Paris. "I was open to everything that was going on when I reached Europe," he confessed to an interviewer (CHM, 53). His second novel, *Black Spring* (1936), is considered by several critics to have been closest to the Dada spirit. "I was most impressionable then," said Miller of the particular era (53). In texts like *The Angel is My Watermark!* in *Black Spring*, Miller embraces the immediacy of a thought without an attempt to rationalize it. Instead, he would endeavor to give himself over completely to the power of a random impression or idea. It was not about what he as a writer could do by tinkering with an idea but vice versa: the important thing was to see what an idea could do with him. Miller recalls it thus:

> It is about ten in the morning when this line shrieks at me. From this moment on — up until four o'clock this morning — I am in the hands of unseen powers. I put the typewriter away and I commence to record what is being dictated to me . . . I am lying on the floor with a pencil, feverishly annotating my work. This continues and continues. (BS, 58)

With the same sense of spontaneity Miller also welcomes a sudden impulse to paint:

> It comes over you like that: you feel like a watercolour and you do one. In the insane asylum they paint their fool heads off. They paint the chairs, the walls, the tables, the bedsteads . . . an amazing productivity. If we rolled up our sleeves

> and went to work the way these idiots do what might we not accomplish in a lifetime. (60)

We can see above that Miller, similarly to the Dadaists (especially Hans Arp), believed that art helps to overcome an unwanted reality; by painting even a madman can restore the "balance between heaven and hell."

In Miller's next novel, *Tropic of Capricorn* (1939), which he wrote simultaneously with *Black Spring*, we find him explicitly expressing his feelings toward the Dadaists. It needs to be kept in mind, however, that he is describing his experiences of 1923–1924; that is, with the present sense of his past self. He exhibits the feelings of remorse over the fact that he wasn't familiar with the Dadaists' ideas earlier. Miller declares that he was

> . . . ignorant of the fact that on July, 14, 1916, at the Saal Waag, in Zürich, the first Dada Manifesto had been proclaimed — 'manifesto by monsieur antipyrine' — that in this strange document it was stated 'Dada is life without slippers or parallel . . . severe necessity without discipline or morality and we spit on humanity.' Ignorant of the fact that the Dada Manifesto of 1918 contained these lines. 'I am writing a manifesto and I want nothing, yet I say certain things, and I am against manifestos as a matter of principle, as I am also against principles . . ." (CAP, 265).

The two documents Miller is referring to are obviously the *Manifesto of Mr. Antipyrine* from 1916, presented in the first public Dada soirée in Zürich, and the *Dada Manifesto* from 1918, both written by Tristan Tzara. These manifestos are aimed at ridiculing bourgeois life, its sense of tradition, its morals, and its notion of art. For instance, the whole sentence from the *Mr. Antipyrine Manifesto* that Miller quotes reads:

> Dada is life with neither bedroom slippers nor parallels; it is against and for unity and definitely against the future; we are wise enough to know that our brains are going to become flabby cushions, that our anti dogmatism is as exclusive as a civil servant, and that we cry liberty but are not free; a severe necessity with entire discipline nor morals and that we spit on humanity.[72]

The bourgeoisie's naive belief in science, its sense of national pride and self-importance as artists is further mocked in the manifesto:

> Then came the great ambassadors of feeling, who yelled historically in chorus: Psychology, Psychology hee hee; Science Science Science; Long live France; We are not naive; We are successive; We are exclusive; We are not simpletons, and we are perfectly capable of an intelligent discussion. But we, DADA, don't agree with them, for art isn't serious, I assure you, and if we reveal the crime so as to show that we are learned denunciators, it's to please you, dear audience, I assure you, and I adore you.[73]

Dada's sense of de-intellectualizing art and embracing its joyful and playful aspects over rational ones is one that Miller took away with him for the rest of his life.

There is little doubt that several other Dada proclamations ended up, consciously or not, in Miller's thinking and writing in some form or the other. For example, if Dada "spits on humanity," then Miller with his *Tropic of Cancer* (1934) does just that:

> This is not a book, in the ordinary sense of the word. No, this is a prolonged insult, a gob of spit in the face of Art, a kick in the pants to God, Man, Destiny, Time, Love, Beauty . . .. (CAN, 10)

When Dada says that in true art "each page must explode . . .," Miller seconds with "Art consists in going the full length. If you begin with the drums, you must end with dynamite or T.N.T" (83). There is also a good chance that the Dadaist insistence on "humans" as "them," that is, as somebody other than Dada, helps Miller later to coin his own counter-term: *inhuman.* This is even more likely in the face of the fact that Miller particularly picks up on the "new beings" theme from the 1918 *Dada Manifesto* after he quotes the excerpts of the manifestos in *Tropic of Capricorn:* "New beings, yes! We have need of new beings still. We can do without the telephone, without the automobile, without the high-class bombers — but we can't do without new beings" (CAP, 267). Clearly, the victory march of technology is called into question here and a desire for an individual with different values is professed. This is a call for a reform of humanity. In the second *Manifesto*, Tzara also says:

> How can anyone hope to order the chaos that constitutes that infinite, formless variation: man? The principle: 'Love thy neighbour' is hypocrisy. 'Know thyself' is utopian, but more acceptable because it includes malice. No pity. After the carnage we are left with the hope of a purified humanity.[74]

This goal of a "purified humanity," as we will see, can be said to tacitly undergird Miller's writing ever since *Tropic of Cancer* and is nowhere better captured than in his notion of the *inhuman.* The rejection of technology, an important principle of Dada, also proved to be crucial in Miller's development of the concept of the *artist/inhuman,* as we will come to see in Chapter 3.

Surrealist songs

By the time of the mid-1920s, the Dadaist project is said to have become precisely "what it wanted to avoid becoming: another movement in art history."[75] It is principally André Breton who distinguished himself from Tristan Tzara's Dada and paved the way toward a new movement: surrealism. Breton and his associates, as they became more familiar with Sigmund Freud's ideas of the unconscious, systematically explored the notion of psychic free play. They used Freud's ideas for their poetic interests which resulted in techniques like "automated writing."[76] Freudianism, however, became the last straw for Breton's ties to Tzara's Dada. While Breton believed that Freud's theories would result in "revolutionary self-awareness," Tzara dismissed it vehemently as "a dangerous illness."[77]

Surrealism was formally born with Breton's "First Surrealist Manifesto" in 1924. In the manifesto, surrealism is described as being "based on the belief in the superior reality of certain previously neglected associations, in the omnipotence of dreams, in the disinterested play of thought." The artist, according to Breton, is no longer simply an esthetic producer but "human explorer" carrying out "investigations."[78] Breton credited Freud with turning our attention from the rationally governed reality to the dream, and he hoped that, eventually, the sharp distinction between the two would disappear:

> When the time comes when we can submit the dream to a methodological examination, when by methods yet to be determined we succeed in realising the dream in its entirety, when the dream's curve is developed with an unequalled breadth and regularity, then we can hope that mysteries which are not really mysteries will give away the great Mystery. I believe in the future resolution of these two states — outwardly so contradictory — which are dream and reality, into a sort of absolute reality, a surreality, so to speak.[79]

Though the term surrealism was originally coined by Guillaume Apollinaire, he, according to Breton, "possessed only the letter of surrealism (which was still imperfect) and showed himself powerless to give it the theoretical insight that engages us." Accordingly, Breton defined Surrealism "once and for all" as "pure psychic automatism by which it is intended to express, either verbally or in writing, the true function of thought. Thought dictated in the absence of all control exerted by reason, and outside all aesthetic or moral preoccupations."[80]

As with Dadaism, Miller's evident connections with Surrealism started with his moving to France in 1930. As early as on his first Sunday in Paris, he went to see Luis Buñuel's and Salvador Dali's *Un Chien Andalou* at the famous Studio 28 cinema. The movie "fascinated him utterly."[81] On the same day, Miller wrote to his friend Emil in New York:

> . . . never in America do I expect to see such a picture — not even when the millennium comes. What is *Un Chien Andalou?* I don't know. I don't know what it was all about, except subconsciously, if I may use that word glibly. (LE, 25)

Miller was also there for the showing of Buñuel's *L'Age d'Or* later in 1930, which left, perhaps, an even bigger impression on him. Miller is said to be the first major American writer to apply the thought of such visionaries as Lautréamont, Baudelaire, and Rimbaud to his own work.[82] As there was no important Surrealist movement in the United States, Miller may well be as close as any American writer came to adopting French Surrealist techniques in his writings.[83] When in 1962 asked by an interviewer what he meant by surrealism, Miller answered thus:

> When I was living in Paris, we had an expression, a very American one, which in a way explains it better than anything else. We used to say, 'Let's take a lead.' That meant going off the deep end, diving into the unconscious, just obeying your instincts, following your impulses, of the heart, or the guts, or whatever you want to call it. But that's my way of putting it, that isn't really surrealist doctrine; that wouldn't hold water, I am afraid, with an André Breton. However, the French standpoint, the doctrinaire standpoint, didn't mean much to me. All I cared about was that I found in it another means of expression, an added one, a heightened one, but one to be used very judiciously. When the well-known surrealists employed this technique, they did it too deliberately, it seemed to me. It became unintelligible, it served no purpose. Once one loses all intelligibility, one is lost, I think. (CHM, 52)

Surrealist cinema, in particular, has been suggested by several commentators as having had a major impact on Miller.[84] After seeing Buñuel's *L'Age d'Or*, Miller apparently wrote to him and he intended, when *Tropic of Cancer* was completed, to preface it with an open letter to Buñuel proclaiming the filmmaker's influence upon the work: "The showing of *L'Age d'Or* was for me a revelation. I date everything of importance in my spiritual life from that moment, not having seen it I could not have written this book."[85]

Caroline Blinder, in her study of surrealist influences on Miller's works, contends that the relationship between the two was in effect twofold. On the one hand, Miller was certainly fascinated with surrealism as an art movement but, on the other hand, it was a movement "which he felt at liberty to both critique as an outsider in a political sense, and use it as an overt inspiration stylistically and thematically in a literary sense."[86] Also, as with modernism, the encounter with surrealism importantly "encapsulates Miller's desire to immerse himself in a distinctly European cultural heritage," writes Blinder.[87]

Of his fictional writings, the *Into the Nightlife* section in *Black Spring* is considered to be Miller's closest attempt at adopting the Surrealist technique. The story is based on his *dream book*, a record of his dreams that he kept collecting at Anaïs Nin's suggestion. Borrowing the title from Freud's slogan "Into the night-life seems to be exiled all that once ruled during the day," Miller deliberately employs the dream technique in the story in order to mediate the images of his past. There is no order or rationale connecting the images. As in a dream, one image, situation, or character fades into something else in the next minute. The story is full of Freudian dream symbols starting from the apartment (the self) where Miller starts his story, the chains that attach Miller to the bed (the conscious ego that needs to be liberated or unrestrained), the cross (suffering, martyrdom, death), the old hag with a revolver from whose "mouth, her eyes, her hair, from her vagina even, the cobras are streaming forth" (BS, 152) (Miller's mother, the gun represents unconscious resentment or hostility), and so on and so forth.[88] It is hard, however, not to agree with a commentator who notes that the story seems, perhaps, "a bit like a textbook example of the Surrealist method."[89] To an interviewer's question: "is Surrealism what you mean by the phrase, 'into the night life,'"? Miller himself gave the following answer:

> Yes, there it was primarily the dream. The surrealists make use of the dream, and of course that's always a marvellous fecund aspect of experience. Consciously or unconsciously, all writers employ the dream, even when they're not surrealists. The waking mind, you see, is the least serviceable in the arts. In the process of writing one is struggling to bring out what is unknown to himself. To put down merely what one is conscious of means nothing really, gets one nowhere . . . . (CHM, 52)

As with Dadaism, Miller was not really concerned with slavishly following the die-hard Surrealists and their agendas. Rather, having always been an avid dreamer and interpreter rather than a disciple, he took pieces of ideas from here and there and mingled them all together into a Milleresque cocktail. Soon, Miller began to question the merits of the psychoanalytic method that the Surrealists were so fond of. In the mid-1930s, it was mainly Anaïs Nin, an ample user of psychoanalytic therapy herself, which was then still rare, who tried to direct Miller toward astrology and psychoanalysis. When, on Nin's persuasion, Miller agreed to meet Freud's former colleague of 20 years, Otto Rank, Miller tried to act cool, probably more because he didn't want be seen as less sophisticated than Rank to Nin, with whom he was having an affair at the time. "And where Rank stands after thirty years of struggle, diligence, research, exploration etc. there I stood, equally firm, firmer I'm telling you, despite all the temperamental diffidences and all the questions and obscurities and contradictions in my soul," wrote Miller to Nin after the meeting, which is described by one biographer as an "ego-battle."[90] According to another commentator, Miller considered Freud more like an artist type, "one of the finest examples of a sage in our time," than a scientist; hence his work possessed for Miller only "a fictive value." Miller loathed the whole "patient mentality" aspect of psychoanalysis and considered the idea of a patient talking about his life while lying on a couch as an ego-trip *par excellence.* Miller insisted on trusting himself, and he thought that it is precisely human weakness, or frailty, or neuroses that makes one's life interesting.[91]

In the mid-1930s, Miller was still very much interested in Surrealism as a technique or *Weltanschauung* but grew more and more weary of its socio-political agendas, which contradicted his own more individualistic notions of the artist. As James Gifford's study has shown, the correspondence between Miller and Herbert Read, a *grand old man* of English Surrealism, sheds light on the crucial differences between the socially driven English Surrealists and an individualistic version of Surrealism à la Miller.[92] Out of these epistolary discussions Miller developed his essay, "An Open Letter to Surrealists Everywhere" (1938), which was meant to be a response to Read's book *Surrealism* as well as to his speech at the 1936 London International Surrealist Exhibition. Miller's larger ambition, however, was to address the (English) Surrealist movement as a whole.

In this long essay, Miller presents his vigorous defense of the individual nature of the life of an artist who doesn't need to belong to a group or have unitary principles to guide him. "The brotherhood of man," Miller writes, "is a permanent delusion common to idealists everywhere in all epochs: it is the reduction of the principle of individuation to the least common denominator of intelligibility" (OLSE, 152). The role of the true artist, according to Miller, is "to revive the primitive, anarchic instincts which have been sacrificed for the illusion of living in comfort" (156). Also, an artist should be ultimately free of the cult of leadership:

> I am not against leaders per se. On the contrary, I know how necessary they are. They will be necessary so long as men are insufficient unto themselves. As for myself, I need no leader and no god. I am my own leader and my own god. I make my own bibles. I believe in myself — that is my whole credo. (158)

Miller's view of the role of Freud and Jung in the Surrealist movement only confirms his leader-free attitude.

> They are trying to eliminate themselves as doctors, scientists, philosophers, theoreticians, trying to reveal to us the miraculous nature of man, the vast possibilities which stretch before him. They do not want disciples and expounders, they do not want to be imitated — they want merely to point the way. (174)

While Miller acknowledged the Surrealists for this by saying that "scarcely anything has been as stimulating to me as the theories and products of the Surrealists" (188), he just could not look past, let alone approve of, its current directions. More particularly, Miller blamed English Surrealists for their "effort to get together" with French Surrealists, which he likened to a "courtship between the serpent and the eagle" (168). That to Miller would serve no purpose whatsoever. Miller absolutely rejected the socialism of Paul Gascoyne, another English Surrealist, who in his 1935 Surrealist Manifesto had declared "complete adherence to the historical materialism of Marx, Engels, and Lenin" as one of the aims of Surrealists.[93] In addition, Miller thought that the works of the Surrealists of the day lacked "guts and significance" (OLSE, 181). Surrealists were in error for "trying to establish an Absolute" (*ibid*). "They are trying," Miller writes,

> . . . to usher in the glory of the Unconscious. They believe in the Devil but not in God. They worship the night but refuse to acknowledge the day. They talk of magic, but they practise voodooism. They await the miracle, but they do nothing to assist it, to bring about an accouchement. They talk of ushering in a general confusion, but they live like the bourgeoisie. (181–2)

The path of an artist for Miller is necessarily a personal one: "It has to do with making poetry, or if you will, with making life a poem. It has to do with the adoption of a creative attitude towards life" (152). The artist should abandon the idea of unity, leadership, and brotherhood and change this "confused outer struggle" with an inner one (186). "Let each one," Miller intimates,

> . . . turn his gaze inward and regard himself with awe and wonder, with mystery and reverence; let each one promulgate his own laws, his own theories; let each

> one work his own influence, his own havoc, his own miracles. Let each one as an individual assume the roles of artist, healer, prophet, priest, king, warrior, saint. No division of labor. Let us re-combine the dispersed elements of our individuality. Let us reintegrate. (175)

Despite Miller's harsh sentiments toward several aspects of the Surrealist movement, he later became quite well acquainted with André Breton himself. Miller met Breton twice in New York in 1941 and they exchanged letters, ideas, and excerpts of each other's works regularly between 1947 and 1950.[94] Breton invited Miller to participate in the 1947 Surrealist Exhibition in Paris (Miller didn't go) and chose Miller's story *Paysages* to appear in the event's catalogue. A passage from one of Miller's letters is also quoted in Breton's book *La lampe dans l'horloge:* a gesture which touched Miller profoundly.[95] All in all, a comment by Caroline Blinder, perhaps, sums up Miller's ambiguous relationship between both Dadaism and Surrealism the best. While he "wanted to be part of intelligentsia committed to the creation of a new form of literature" he, at the same time, it seems, "wanted to be seen as a provocative outsider: a form of literary anarchist."[96]

Where do we go from here?

Having seen Miller's engagement with some of his most beloved authors, and experiments with Dadaism and Surrealism, we should be able to determine the direction toward which his thinking is pointing. Miller's sympathy with premodernist thinkers like Stirner, Nietzsche, Spengler, and others is evident. What is crucial about their relation to Miller is that, one way or another, they all stood out against the modern age. Through these thinkers Miller not only found support but, in effect, also crystallized his attitude toward the climate of his time. It is precisely the "absolute insanity of our present day life, the worthlessness of all our values" (CHM, 53) from which Miller seems to have sought a release. Since the modernist movement in literature, and the Dadaists and Surrealists in *beaux arts* and in cinema raised very similar worries, it is largely through their influence that Miller comes to think that "the ills of the age" can be addressed by means of art. This patent confrontation between the horror of present-day life and the envisioned freedom of the artist's life becomes then an underlying yet conflicting tension for Miller, which he sets out to resolve.

The above characterization of Miller's plight is, thus, also precisely that by which our inquiry "gets guided beforehand."[97] Since the epicenter of Miller's anguish lies, however abstractly, in the conflict between modern society and the artist, exactly this, then, should be the focal point for our further inquiry. As Miller's quest comes forward thematically interwoven with modernist thinking, and since he insisted upon reckoning with one's "soil and climate," Miller himself predetermines, as it were, that we should trace his thinking in conjunction with the intellectual context in which he was immersed. Owing to that fact, we need to throw ourselves literally in the midst of modernist debates in order to find a firmer basis or point of entry to Miller's own philosophy. Naturally, we should choose the debates where Miller's voice sounds fresh and intriguing since only that promises to direct us toward something that is truly intrinsic to Miller. For this reason, we will continue our inquiry with the exploration of the issues of *history* and *modern crisis* since Miller's vocalizations about these topics are heard afar.

Notes

1 Caroline Blinder, likewise, has emphasized the need for more age-contextual studies of Miller because "Rather than insert Miller into a more complex historical, political, and aesthetic framework, the effect has been to neglect the period in which he actually wrote . . .." See Caroline Blinder, *A Self-Made Surrealist: Ideology and Aesthetics in the work of Henry Miller* (Camden House, 2000), 1.

2 James M. Decker, *Henry Miller and Narrative Form: Constructing the Self, Rejecting Modernity* (New York: Routledge, 2005), 148–9.

3 Ibid., 168.

4 This is the date Michael Bell (among numerous others) suggests in Michael Bell, "The Metaphysics of Modernism," in *The Cambridge Companion to Modernism*, ed. Michael H. Levenson (Cambridge: Cambridge University Press, 1999), 9.

5 Peter Childs, *Modernism* (London: Routledge, 2008), 18.

6 Sarah Garland, "'The Dearest of Cemeteries': European Intertexts in Henry Miller's *Tropic of Cancer*," European Journal of American Culture 23, 3 (2010), 197.

7 Nicola Allen, "Timeline 1890–1941," in *The Modernism Handbook*, eds. Philip Tew and Alex Murray (London: Continuum, 2009), 24. In a less qualified sense, Miller has also been thought to be a modernist writer by commentators such as Frank L. Kersnowski and Alice Hughes who, in their introduction to *Conversations with Henry Miller*, write "modernists, such as Henry Miller . . .." See CHM, ix. Michael Whitworth, also, seems to think of Miller as a modernist writer, stating in his foreword to "Regendering Modernism," ". . . two modernist writers, D. H. Lawrence and Henry Miller." See Michael H. Whitworth, *Modernism*, (Malden, MA: Blackwell Pub, 2007), 217.

8 Frank Kermode, *The Sense of an Ending: Studies in the Theory of Fiction* (New York: Oxford University Press, 1967), 98.

9 Matei Calinescu, *Five Faces of Modernity: Modernism, Avant-Garde, Decadence, Kitch, Postmodernism* (Durham: Duke University Press, 1987), 41.

10 I don't intend, by all means, to ignore several decidedly literary modernist features that Miller unquestionably shared with the "golden era" modernists such as *stream of consciousness* writing, addressing the *representational crisis*, and the like. Since my aim here is to lay bare the structure of Miller's philosophy, however, investigating these literary features of his work in depth would have resulted in an altogether different book.

11 Elizabeth Ladenson, "Henry Miller: A Gob of Spit in the Face of Art," in *Dirt for Art's Sake* (Ithaca & London: Cornell University Press, 2007), 172.

12 Mary V. Dearborn, *The Happiest Man Alive: A Biography of Henry Miller* (New York: Simon & Schuster, 1991), 155. Dearborn adds, however, that in the 1930s "when

English-language writers were defying sexual conventions freely," Kahane and Obelisk press built up an "impressive list" of books which included Radcliffe Hall's *The Well of Loneliness*, James Joyce's *Pomes Penyeach*, Frank Harris's *My Life and Loves*, and several other well-known authors.

13 Ladenson, "Henry Miller: A Gob of Spit in the Face of Art," 159.

14 Blinder, *A Self-Made Surrealist*, 1.

15 Frank Kermode, "John Betjeman and Henry Miller," in *Puzzles and Epiphanies: Essays and Reviews, 1958–1961* (New York: Chilmark Press, 1962), 141.

16 Ibid.

17 Jay Martin, *Always Merry and Bright: An Unauthorized Biography* (Santa Barbara: Capra Press, 1978), 488.

18 Ladenson, "Henry Miller: A Gob of Spit in the Face of Art," 162.

19 As the topic has been covered extensively in the Miller literature, there's no need to repeat it here.

20 James Joyce's, *Ulysses*, 1922; T. S Eliot's, *Waste Land*, 1922; Virginia Woolf's, *Mrs. Dalloway*,1925; and Ernest Hemingway's, *The Sun Also Rises*, 1926 are only a few paradigmatic examples.

21 Childs, *Modernism*, 19.

22 Martin Heidegger, "The Age of The World Picture," in *The Question Concerning Technology, and Other Essays*, trans. William Lovitt (New York: Harper & Row, 1977a), 116.

23 Cited in Chris Baldick, *The Modern Movement: Oxford English Literary History* v. 10, 1910–40 (Oxford: Oxford University Press, 2004), 10.

24 D. H. Lawrence, "Why the Novel Matters?," in *Selected Literary Criticism*, ed. Anthony Beal (London: Heinemann, 1955), 2–3.

25 T. S. Eliot, "The Idea of a Christian Society," in *Selected Prose of T. S. Eliot*, ed. Frank Kermode (London: Faber, 1975), 290.

26 J. Gerald Kennedy, "The Secret Paris of Henry Miller," in *Imagining Paris* (New Haven & London: Yale University Press, 1993), 165.

27 Ibid.

28 The book is commonly considered as a literary failure not the least for its mimicking of Theodore Dreiser's *Twelve Men* (1919). Ibargüen suggests that in *Clipped Wings* Miller attempted to write the way realist and naturalist writers had done, writers with whom Miller sympathized at the time. See Raoul R. Ibargüen, "Narrative Detours: Henry Miller and the Rise of New Critical Modernism," (PhD diss. Yale University), 103.

29 Garland, "'The Dearest of Cemeteries': European Intertexts in Henry Miller's *Tropic of Cancer*," 198.

30 Robert Ferguson, *Henry Miller: A Life* (New York: Norton, 1991), 34.

31 Ibid., 24. Ferguson points out, however, that Emma Goldman did not lecture in San Diego that year. Although she was in town she was prevented from speaking because of a riot. As of Miller's own account, he says "maybe he got mixed up, or maybe he was lying" (26). Mary Dearborn suggests in her biography *The Happiest Man Alive* of Miller-Goldman encounter that although "she was not allowed to speak" Miller had "buttonholed her on her way out" (50).

32 Max Stirner, *The Ego and His Own: The Case of the Individual Against Authority*, trans. James J. Martin (New York: Dover Publications, 2005), vii.

33 Ibid., 5.
34 Ibid., 19.
35 Ibid.
36 Ibid., 28.
37 Dearborn, *The Happiest Man Alive*, 55.
38 Friedrich Wilhelm Nietzsche, *Twilight of the Idols; and, The Anti-Christ*, trans. R. J. Hollingdale (Harmondsworth: Penguin, 1986b), 124.
39 Ibid.
40 Ibid., 133.
41 Ibid., 159.
42 Ibid., 125.
43 Emmet Stinson, "Literary and Cultural Contexts: Major Figures, Institutions, Topics, Events," in *The Modernism Handbook*, eds. Philip Tew and Alex Murray (London: Continuum, 2009), 52.
44 Leonard Lawlor and Valentine Moulard, "Henri Bergson," in *Stanford Encyclopedia of Philosophy*, ed. Edward N. Zalta, url: http://plato.stanford.edu/entries/bergson/.
45 Knut Hamsun, *Hunger*, trans. George Egerton (Alfred A. Knopf, 1921), 11–12.
46 Ibid., 26.
47 Ibargüen, "Narrative Detours," 363.
48 Ibid., 106.
49 Michael Fraenkel, *The Genesis of the Tropic of Cancer* (London: Village Press, 1973), 12–13. Ibargüen rightly points out, however, that Fraenkel's account was written considerably after the publishing of *Tropic of Cancer* in 1934.
50 Ibargüen, "Narrative Detours," 363.
51 Ibid., 107.
52 Ibid.
53 Ferguson, *Henry Miller: A Life*, 214.
54 Dearborn, *The Happiest Man Alive*, 173.
55 Cited in J. D. Brown, *Henry Miller* (New York: Ungar Pub. Co, 1986), 2.
56 Edmund Wilson, "Twilight of the Expatriates," in *Critical Essays on Henry Miller*, ed. Ronald Gottesman (New York: G. K. Hall, 1992), 25.
57 George Orwell, "Inside the Whale," in *Henry Miller and the Critics*, ed. George Wickes (Carbondale: Southern Illinois University Press, 1963), 33.
58 Brown, *Henry Miller*, 1.
59 Ibid., 3.
60 Ibid., 4.
61 Ibid.
62 Jeffrey Bartlett, "The Late Modernist," in *Critical Essays on Henry Miller*, ed. Ronald Gottesman (New York: G. K. Hall, 1992), 317.
63 Ibid., 324.
64 Decker, *Henry Miller and Narrative Form*, 153.
65 Ibid., 7.
66 Ibid., 150.
67 David Hopkins, *Dada and Surrealism: A Very Short Introduction* (Oxford University Press, 2004), 4 and 9.
68 Robert Short, "Dada and Surrealism," in *Modernism: 1890-1930*, eds. James W. McFarlane and Malcolm S. Bradbury (Harmondsworth: Penguin, 1976), 299.
69 Bartlett, "The Late Modernist," 319.

70 Short, "Dada and Surrealism," 293.
71 Ibid., 295.
72 Tristan Tzara, "Manifesto of Mr. Antipyrine," in *The Dada Painters and Poets: An Anthology*, ed. Robert Motherwell (Cambridge, MA: Belknap Press of Harvard University Press, 1989b), 75.
73 Ibid.
74 Tristan Tzara, "Dada Manifesto, 1918," in *The Dada Painters and Poets: An Anthology*, ed. Robert Motherwell (Harvard University Press, 1989a), 77.
75 Hopkins, *Dada and Surrealism*, 16.
76 Ibid., 17. Hopkins also points out that Breton's and Freud's meeting in Vienna showed that Freud himself was not in the least interested in these artistic adoptions of his theories.
77 Short, "Dada and Surrealism," 302.
78 Hopkins, *Dada and Surrealism*, 17.
79 André Breton, "First Surrealist Manifesto," in *Surrealism*, ed. Patrick Waldberg (New York: McGraw-Hill, 1971), 68.
80 Ibid., 69.
81 George Wickes, *Americans in Paris* (Garden City, NY: Doubleday, 1969), 253.
82 Bartlett, "The Late Modernist," 321.
83 Gwendolyn Raaberg, "Surrealism in the Works of Henry Miller and Anaïs Nin," in *Proceedings of the 7th Congress of the International Comparative Literature Association/Literatures of America: Dependence, Independence, Interdependence*, eds. Milan V. Dimić and Juan Ferraté (Stuttgart: Bieber, 1979), 253.
84 Chiefly in Raaberg (1979) and Kent Ekberg's "Studio 28: The Influence of the Surrealist Cinema on the Early Fiction of Anaïs Nin and Henry Miller," in *Deus Loci: The Lawrence Durrell Quarterly* 4, 3 (1981): 3–4.
85 Cited in Raaberg, "Surrealism in the Works of Henry Miller and Anaïs Nin," 254.
86 Blinder, *A Self-Made Surrealist*, 2.
87 Ibid., 3.
88 See Jane Nelson's study for an in-depth Jungian reading of Miller's works. She claims, for example, that Archetype Feminine images are the most crucial in Miller. Jane A. Nelson, *Form and Image in the Fiction of Henry Miller* (Detroit: Wayne State University Press, 1970), 14.
89 Bartlett, "The Late Modernist," 322.
90 Ferguson, *Henry Miller: A Life*, 226.
91 Ibid., 227–8.
92 See James Gifford, "Surrealism's Anglo-American Afterlife: The Herbert Read and Henry Miller Network," *Nexus: The International Henry Miller Journal*, 5 (2008): 36–64.
93 Cited in Gifford, "Surrealism's Anglo-American Afterlife," 36–64.
94 Branko Aleksic, Karl Orend, "The Unpublished Correspondence of Henry Miller & André Breton, the 'Steady Rock', 1947-1950," *Nexus: The International Henry Miller Journal* 5 (2008): 150–72.
95 Ibid., 157.
96 Blinder, *A Self-Made Surrealist*, 9.
97 Martin Heidegger, *Being and Time*, trans. John Macquarrie and Edward Robinson (New York: HarperPerennial/Modern Thought, 2008), 24.

2

Apocalypse Now: The End of History and the Twofold Present

History is a meaningless décor for the show we never put on.

—Henry Miller

Modernists' dialectical visions of concurrent destruction and renovation, the decreation and creation of modern man and society have been thought to express an apocalyptic and crises-centered view of their reality.[1] Since the interplay of *death* and *rebirth* has been demonstrated to play an important role in Miller's thinking as an integral part of the quest for one's authentic self[2] he, too, seems to exhibit strong apocalyptical tendencies.[3] Such a view ties Miller tightly to other modernists, for the often-shared desire "to regenerate a decadent society" has been taken to be essential to the modernist spirit.[4] These apocalyptic tendencies in Miller also seem to go hand in hand with his view of himself as a "modern day Christ figure"; someone who wishes not only to transform himself but also wants to "save as many people as he can from the perils of modernity."[5] Since these apocalyptic descriptions of the modern age seem to deal predominantly with the *moods* or *feelings* of the age, they provide only limited explanatory power regarding the complexity of modernity in its entirety. While perhaps acknowledging the overall apocalyptic mood, there are usually more specific instances or phenomena of modernity that modernists rejected or welcomed. For this reason, my aim in this chapter is precisely to reveal the content of Miller's "perils of modernity" that permeates his thinking, and only the overcoming of which seems to make possible his further philosophical evolution as a modern artist. I argue in this chapter that at the bottom of Miller's interpretation of the modern age as "dying" lies, to a certain extent, the sense of a fixed historical destiny of man. Indeed, the modern crisis,[6] while it has other elements, for Miller seems to make itself known, first and foremost, as the crisis of history or the crisis of man as entrapped within history. Holding scientifically rewritten concepts of time and history as responsible, in part, for creating the unsavory modern condition, and realizing that these rigidly construed notions are unable to offer meaningful avenues for the "creating" and "renovating" of himself as a modern artist, he decidedly repudiates the *linear view* of history.

I suggest that Miller's abandonment of the traditional notions of time and history is absolutely crucial to his philosophical transformation. First, it enables him to formulate his idea of two presents, the *traditional present* and the *full present*, which he sees as a major division between the "vulgar reality" of the "dying" modern age and the emerging artist's realm. Unlike the largely abstract dichotomic pair of *death* and *rebirth*, with which apocalyptic explanations operate, the divide I emphasize has a more specific ground and as such it not only describes Miller's goals better but also organically leads Miller to further distinct features of the modern age. Second, I point out that the rejection of a *linear conception of history* distinguishes Miller and his view of the modern crisis from several other literary moderns whose engagements with history can be seen as ambiguous at times. Furthermore, I will show that in Miller's views on history we find perhaps the strongest traces of the ideas related to the discussions of history by Nietzsche, Jung, and Spengler in mid-1930s' Anglo-American literature. While the exact relations between philosophical accounts of history and modernist literature are indistinct elsewhere, in Miller's works they are rich and inseparable. This philosophical basis in Miller, in turn, can be said to have contributed to his overcoming of the *transitional view* of the crisis of (the history of) the age. To anticipate the account below, the *transitional view*, which was held by several senior moderns such as Yeats and Woolf, meant construing the historical present as the threshold to a new age or a new world soon to appear. The *ahistorical* dimension of the type of life that Miller comes to defend, however, rules out this view.

Apocalypse and modern consciousness

Even if modern apocalypse is not our main interest here, we need to explain some of its key features since they help us to understand the spiritual climate in which Miller's ideas on history were situated. While apocalyptic theories have imposed themselves for many centuries on our attitude to history, social organization, and sexual behavior, the reoccurrence of the apocalypse-theme in modernist discourse marks the beginning of a significantly different construal of the concept. Traditionally, apocalypticism is a view of universal history. Most often the term is used to designate

> . . . eschatological (end-time) views and movements that focus on cryptic revelations about sudden, dramatic, and cataclysmic intervention of God in history; the judgement of all men, the salvation of the faithful elect, and the eventual rule of the elect with God in a renewed heaven and earth.[7]

The traditional Judeo-Christian view of history, thus, depends upon an omnipotent God who is above history and who at certain points in time intervenes directly in the temporal journey of mankind. The modernist perspectives of history and the sense of the apocalypse as, for example, put forth in the works of D. H. Lawrence, have been characterized, however, as attempting to "retain a vision of destruction and renovation in a godless universe."[8] Thus in modernist consciousness, both the individual and the cosmic process of salvation have been importantly transferred from God to man.

Indeed, it is precisely in this vein that commentators often consider modernists as having "associated notions of the artist's freedom . . . with notions of cultural apocalypse and disaster."[9] David Trotter, a noted commentator on modernism, confirms that modernists "saw themselves as inhabitants of a social and cultural system which had stagnated to the point where it was no longer susceptible to reform, but could only be renewed through total collapse or violent overthrow."[10] Other well-known modern writers who, like D. H. Lawrence, placed themselves and their generation at the very center of such apocalyptic upheaval and change are, for example, W. B. Yeats, Ezra Pound, Wyndham Lewis, and T. S. Eliot.

Modernist writers, however, were not alone in voicing these dramatic visions regarding their historical and cultural situation. As we saw in the previous chapter, corresponding worries can be detected already in the late-nineteenth-century philosophies of Max Stirner and Friedrich Nietzsche. In the first decades of the twentieth century, Oswald Spengler and Arnold Toynbee importantly carried forward Stirner's and Nietzsche's skeptical views concerning the condition of modern man in their philosophical accounts of history. In different ways, modern literature and modern philosophical interpretations of history were both stressing the declining nature of the age and pointing out its disillusionment with the past, and its need for the new. Both literature and philosophy at the time were, thus, deeply concerned with modern man and his destiny. Still, the relationship between the works of literary moderns and the ideas of the philosophers of history is by no means self-evident or direct. Indeed, there were only a handful of writers who explicitly expressed the existing philosophies of those who "rejected the progressively linear interpretations of historical process and assumed either a cyclical, creatively rhythmical, eschatological, or Messianic form."[11] D. H. Lawrence was certainly one to subscribe to such a repudiation of the linear view of history. "Our idea of time," Lawrence wrote, "as a continuity in an eternal straight line has crippled our consciousness cruelly."[12] While other moderns such as Yeats, Eliot, and Woolf also verbalized their disaffection with the age, we will see shortly that their views regarding history and their own role in it often remained ambiguous, traditionally linear, or even historicist. Miller, however, positioned himself directly "above history" and was, thus, able to adopt a sort of hands-on approach for solving the modern crisis.

Toward the ahistorical

Miller's discontent regarding the age finds ample manifestation in his *Tropic of Cancer* (1934). "The cancer of time is eating us away. Our heroes have killed themselves, or are killing themselves. The hero, then, is not Time, but Timelessness," wrote Miller in the very first pages of the book (CAN, 9). While "time" can be read here both as history and as a temporal category in a metaphysical sense, in either case the failure is evident for Miller. In the sense of history, time has failed to produce the better man and world that "our heroes" dreamt about. Miller is also fighting against a notion of time that is embedded in the very metaphysics of the age, a metaphysics that is commonly taken to support a linear conception of history. Time's role, commonly construed as rigid, it seemed to Miller, served to a great extent merely for the purpose of justifying historical developments as necessary and inevitable. Since this very notion of history has produced only madness, then, Miller reasons, the exact opposite of time and history is needed, namely *timelessness* and *ahistoricity*.

In order to fully grasp the nature of Miller's apparent frustration with a particular concept of time and history, the historical background of the view he quarreled with needs to be further explained. Miller, it is clear, did not position himself against any particular individual or view but rather against a general trend of the modern Western world, which saw its main purpose in human progress. The idea of progress, being one of the most dominant ideas of the Occident, reached "its zenith in the Western mind in popular as well as scholarly circles" in between 1750 and 1900.[13] Robert Nisbet, a distinguished scholar in the field, observes quite rightly that throughout this period "system after system in philosophy and social sciences was concerned primarily with demonstration of the *scientific reality* of human progress and the laws and principles which make progress necessary."[14] In addition, the idea of progress is often based on an interpretation of history "which regards men as slowly advancing in a definite and desirable direction, and infers that this progress will continue indefinitely."[15] Accordingly, it was believed that "a condition of general happiness will ultimately be enjoyed."[16] While there are several prominent defenders of this *progressive view* (e.g. Turgot, Condorcet, Macaulay, Maine etc.), Auguste Comte (1798–1857) and G. W. F. Hegel (1770–1831) represent, in our context, the most important features of this highly influential *Weltanschauung*, and as such, help us to explain Henry Miller's positioning himself directly against such a world view.

It was precisely Comte, who, in his monumental *Positive Philosophy* (published in 1830–42) put forward an overtly progress-laden approach for explaining the human condition. He argues that historically the human mind has progressed through three stages: the theological, the metaphysical, and the positive or scientific. Comte claims that in the first stage all explanations are made in terms of deities and in the second with the help of some abstract spirits (or entities without empirical foundation). In the crucial third "advanced state of social life," however, the rationally more developed human mind will employ genuinely scientific explanations, rooted in the study of nature and the discovery of her laws.[17] Comte believes that all major sciences (astronomy, physics, chemistry, and biology) have passed through these three stages. Thus, his proposed study of society, which he first calls *social physics* and later labels *sociology*, must also enter into its final, positive stage. Sociology as a discipline Comte sees as divided into two broad areas: *statics* and *dynamics*. It is only the latter that interests us here since it consists in the study of progress: its laws, stages, causes, and manifestations. Comte considers progress to be the "main resource of every genuine political system."[18] He pairs progress importantly with "order" since "no real order can be established [in a society] . . . if it is not fully compatible with progress."[19] Crucially, then, his "positive social science," which is meant to become *the* science of explaining human society, would combine the two: order and progress. Clearly, Comte's basis for this belief is his firm faith in the natural sciences, which he sees as an important ideal, and indeed the basis, for his sociology. He explains:

> The ideas of order and progress are, in social physics, as rigorously inseparable as the ideas of organization and life in biology; from whence indeed they are, in a scientific view, evidently derived.[20]

The terms "progress" and "evolution" are evidently equated in Comte's thinking. Progress in human affairs corresponds to evolution in biology and the animal kingdom. Comte was convinced that the progress of the human mind is continuous and that humans can only become more refined as a result of this. "It is unquestionable that Civilization leads us on to a further and further development of our noblest dispositions . . .," Comte writes.[21] The conception, or rather the phenomenon, of progress, then, is an inevitable scientific law for Comte. Explaining human society, therefore, without the notion of "progress" is not possible according to Comte's view.

Hegel's philosophical account of history highlights another crucial dimension of the *progressive view*. Hegel thinks that human beings are thoroughly historical creatures. Our history—the events that have happened to us and led to our present condition—creates the possibilities of what we might become. Our historical nature shows itself in all our endeavors (legal, moral, social, economic), according to Hegel.[22] In his *Lectures on the Philosophy of World History* (delivered between 1822 and 1830), Hegel presents a linear account of *world history* as an intelligible process moving toward the realization of human freedom or the Idea of Freedom.[23] This desire for freedom is definitive of all humanity and throughout the development of humanity (from Asia to Greece to modern Germany) the realization of freedom has gradually become greater, according to Hegel. "The aim of the world spirit in world history is to realize its essence and obtain the prerogative of freedom," writes Hegel.[24] By "spirit" [*Geist*] Hegel means something like ultimate or absolute self-consciousness. This self-consciousness, however, is meant to be universal and concerns nations and not individuals.[25] To a smaller or greater degree, "spirit" shows itself in all nations, according to Hegel. The stronger the national self-awareness, the clearer the manifestation of "spirit" and its freedom. Hegel's conception of "freedom" is a pivotal aspect of his philosophy, to which avant-garde movements and modernists (Miller included) would later stand up against. For it is clear from the analysis of Hegel's "spirit" that he is not concerned with individuals' liberal freedom (as their rights against state) as, for example, in J. S. Mill's widely accepted sense. On the contrary, Hegel's vision of freedom, which "spirit" must realize, means every individual's full participation in a free and meaningful society. Arguably, Hegel saw precisely this happening in Germany at the time.

Comte and Hegel, then, reveal the core of the *progressive view* the essence of which Miller decidedly rejects in his works. Although he was not directly exposed to the foregoing views, he learned them via the works of later critical commentators of modernity (Stirner, Nietzsche, Spengler, and others) and the purported results the ideas described above had on the modern society of his day. We will learn (throughout the book) that Comte's insistence on solely scientific descriptions of the human condition is one of the fundamental errors of the modern day for Miller since it completely disregards the artist's perspective. In like manner, Hegel's linear account of history and the universal notion of freedom Miller considers not a victory but indeed the defeat of humanity. Miller certainly could not have accepted Hegel's view that mankind has (in the realization of its "spirit") reached its authentic or ultimate goal. On the contrary, Miller saw the present condition of mankind precisely as deluding itself about having reached any such state. In addition, since Hegel's influence was still felt in some other modernists' works, Miller rejects these authors with the charge of historicism.

In passing, it deserves to be noted that Hegel's views, in turn, were the starting point for Karl Marx (1818–83). Marx saw the "key to the riddle of history" in the rise of the proletariat and classless civil society, which would liberate men from their *alienation* (due to their labor being exploited by capitalists). Miller, thoroughly anti-political, had no illusions about human betterment through class struggle. While he would agree, to an extent, with Marx about the horrid condition of modern workers, the social (and revolutionary) dimension of Marx's solution had no appeal for him. For Miller, "the solution" to the crisis of man and history had to start with inward reflection and not with "outward struggle" (DML, 18).

Having seen the impact Stirner, Nietzsche and Spengler made on Miller in the previous chapter, it is no great surprise that it is precisely under their influence that Miller starts to "solve" the "riddle of history." Stirner, we saw, attacked the state, government, law, private property, and everything else that imposed limits on the individual freedom that he perceived (contrary to Hegel) as being under threat. Nietzsche can be seen as importantly continuing Stirner's revolt against modernity and it is precisely his writings, as we shall see shortly, which helped to shape a great part of Miller's philosophy, including his view on the role of history. In addition to Nietzsche, Miller builds heavily on Spengler who famously rejected the linear view of history in favor of a cyclical one. This then concludes the sketchy detour into the "genealogy" of Miller's dispositions toward history. In what lies ahead, we will continue to unpack Miller's position and explore its affinities with Nietzsche and Spengler in detail.

Linear history rejected

Miller declares in *Tropic of Capricorn* that "the world I knew is no more, it is dead, finished, cleaned up. And everything that I was is cleaned up with it. I am a carcass getting an injection of new life . . ." (CAP, 204). In this decidedly apocalyptical description, he seems to fix the past, as historically dead. He also marks the end of his past self understood within the limits of the wardship of history. Yet, Miller sees this as a thoroughly positive event. He welcomes the abandonment of his life from the indifferent flow of linear time, which seems not to bother most of the people around him. Miller distances himself, as it were, from the general *human* history altogether.

It is, it seems, precisely with the help of Oswald Spengler's distinctions between "two possibilities of world formation" that Miller saw the potential for rejecting the historical and time-bound view of himself.[26] In asking "for whom is there History?," Spengler concedes that while "history is obviously for everyone," it makes a great difference

> ... whether anyone lives under the constant impression that his life is an element in a far wider life-course that goes on for hundreds and thousands of years, or conceives of himself as something rounded off and self-contained. For the latter type of consciousness there is certainly no world-history, no world-as-history.[27]

Furthermore, Spengler argues that a whole culture can "rest on this ahistoric spirit" and uses Hellenic culture as an example, in which "all experience, not merely personal but the common past, was immediately transmuted into a timeless, immobile, mythically-fashioned background for the particular momentary present . . .."[28] Spengler claims that the historical sense of Western Culture is "an exception not a rule" and that, therefore,

> ... world-history is our world picture and not all mankind's. Indian and Classical man formed no image of a world in progress, and perhaps when in due course the civilization of the West is extinguished, there will never again be a Culture and a human type in which 'world-history' is so potent a form of the waking consciousness.[29]

It is evident Spengler directly opposes himself to the *progressive view* of the history of the Enlightenment, as introduced earlier. In his quest for "timelessness," in both its metaphysical and ahistorical meaning, Miller exhibits similar anxieties to Spengler. Miller, being an individualist, clearly saw himself as being "self-contained" in Spengler's terminology and, as noted above, he needed no "world-history." Miller seems to echo Spengler's distinction when he separates the "objective" time that people ("historical men" in Spengler's terms) measure with clocks and calendars from the time of one's own "inside chronometer." In a letter to Michael Fraenkel, he elaborates this view:

> Are times out of joint? Then look to the clock! Not the clock on the mantelpiece, but the chronometer inside which tells when you are living and when you are not. I should say blandly — throw away all existing clocks! We don't want to know what time it is by sun or moon, but by past and future. Now we are swamped with time — Western Union time, sidereal time, Einsteinian time, reading time, bedtime, all kinds of time which tell us nothing about what is passing inside us, or even outside us. We are moving on the escalator of time . . .. (HAM, 19–20)

Consequently, Miller moves toward the establishment of his own notion of time on the basis of his individual experiences, not on those of natural laws and science. He steps off, as it were, from the "escalator of time" because it has nothing to do with his personal life and feelings. To illustrate this even more, he states:

> In winding up this salutation I notice that the calendar says November 7th! I just want to point out to you how false and unreliable the calendar is, because according to my chronology it is still November 2nd and I have not moved an inch from the terrasse at Ècole-Militaire. It may be that everything I have to say will be written from this terrace which is particularly pleasant and soothing to the senses. (20)

Since time is now measured, or rather directed, by his own "inside chronometer," Miller can, it seems, uphold certain moments and sustain their aura as long as he pleases. The moment is over when one no longer wishes to dwell on it, not when the clock or calendar says it's another minute or day. Time for Miller becomes something essentially psychological or phenomenological. Capitalizing on David Hoy's insight, it could be even argued that Miller makes a salient distinction between *time* and *temporality*. *Time*, according to Hoy, refers to "universal time, clock time, or objective time," whereas *temporality*, however, is "time insofar as it manifests itself in human experience."[30] Temporality is "lived time" and thus, quite literally, Hoy suggests, "time of our lives." It is this thoroughly personal view of time *as* temporality that Miller draws our attention to. Tacitly adopting the distinction between time and temporality, Miller seems to come very close to Spengler's conjecture that "we ourselves are Time, inasmuch as we live."[31] According to Spengler, the word "time" had no meaning for primitive men. They *had* time, but they *knew* nothing of it. Time didn't exist before "higher Cultures," Spengler claims, "created it as an idea or notion." He also attacked Immanuel Kant's view of time as a *pure intuition*, which apparently "must precede and structure all experience of individual outer objects and inner states."[32] Spengler criticizes Kant for not saying anything about time's "character of directedness" the result of which is that time becomes identified with "motion" [*Bewegung*] as understood by physicists.[33] Spengler thinks, however, that everything living "has life direction, impulse, will, a movement-quality [*Bewegtheit*]" which is "entirely indeterminable by mechanics."[34] Life, Spengler writes, is "indivisible and irreversible, once and uniquely occurring"[35] and as such it cannot be subordinated to the universal or rigid concepts of time.

Evidently, Spengler's discussions of time and history had an enormous effect on Miller. He, in a true modernist spirit, refused to dance "to the cracked tune that Chronos sings,"[36] that is, to the music of the *progressive view* of time, which, among other things, is susceptible to Spengler's charge of being "mechanical" in nature. If one continues to be moved by physicalistically construed time, nothing can change. "More obscene than anything is inertia. More blasphemous than the bloodiest oath is paralysis," Miller concurs (CAN, 251). Similarly to Joyce's Stephen Dedalus, Miller wants to awake from the "nightmare of history."

The idea of the *ahistorical*, which we have started to unpack and which we saw making an impression on Miller, can be traced even further back than Spengler to Nietzsche's early text "On the Uses and Disadvantages of History for Life" (1874). There are no explicit references to this particular Nietzsche text in Miller's writings, but the similarities are too great to ignore the possibility that he had read it. In this second *Untimely Meditation*, Nietzsche set out to reveal that we are all "suffering from a consuming fever of history and ought at least to recognize that we are suffering from it."[37] To explain the value of the unhistorical, he uses the example of cattle who "do not know what is meant by yesterday or today, they leap about, eat, rest, digest, leap about again, and so from morn till night and from day to day fettered to the moment and its pleasure or displeasure, and thus neither melancholy nor bored."[38] Nietzsche goes on to say that man envies the life of animals for their happiness because "a life neither bored nor painful, is precisely what he wants, yet he cannot have it because he refuses to be like animal."[39] Having no sense of past or future, Nietzsche claims that

> . . . the animal lives unhistorically: for it is contained in the present . . . it conceals nothing and at every instant appears wholly as what it is; it can therefore never be anything but honest. Man, on the other hand, braces himself against the great and ever greater pressure of what is past: it pushes him down or bends him sideways, it encumbers his steps as a dark, invisible burden which he can sometimes appear to disown and which in traffic with his fellow men he is only too glad to disown so as to excite their envy.[40]

Thus, it is the "honesty of the present," the recognition of the present not as a means but a goal in itself that makes Nietzsche criticize the past which is nothing but "the gravedigger of the present."[41] There is no need, Nietzsche seems to suggest, to construe the role of the past as something essentially necessary for understanding the present. For Nietzsche, the recognition of this is also a condition for happiness, for "he who cannot sink down on the threshold of the moment and forget all the past . . . will never know what happiness is . . . ."[42] We will see shortly how these views influenced Miller to reach very similar conclusions regarding the present. The main difference between Nietzsche's and Miller's attitudes toward history is that, while both give prevalence to the present, Nietzsche still acknowledges the need for a certain degree of the past and history, a "healthy balance" of the unhistorical and the historical, whereas Miller fervently and completely rejected historicity as such.

Away from the "middle"

In radicalizing the present but denying its position in the linear course of events construed as history, Nietzsche and Miller both refused to be "in the middle of events" because it seemed to marginalize the uniqueness of individual human life, its own sense of time, in the path, and for the sake of some kind "monumental" history imagined by the supporters of the Hegelian *progressive view*. It is no accident that the epigraph for the third chapter of Miller's book on D. H. Lawrence reads: "Unless from us the future takes place, we are death only" (WOL, 85). With this, Miller confirms once more that history and time are not something predetermined by the past. If one is not involved in one's own future, one might as well be dead, seems to be Miller's message.

The phenomenon of refusing one's position as situated in the middle of the series of historical events has received attention from several commentators. "Men, like poets," Frank Kermode writes, "rush 'into the middest,' *in medias res,* when they are born; they also die *in mediis rebus,* and to make sense of their span they need fictive concords with origins and ends, such as give meaning to lives and to poems."[43] According to the Kermodian reading, then, rejecting the in-the-middle-of-history thesis, Miller can be said to draw our attention to the fact that one can indeed choose one's own beginning by means of artistic practices. Since no objective or teleological history has relevance any longer for Miller, one's rendition of one's own life within one's own chosen form of temporal and historical narrative becomes imperative. Everybody creates his or her own history, as it were.

This sense of (a new) beginning in the present and the possibility of transcending *progressive* history are characteristic of much of the modernist spirit. Carl Gustav Jung (1875–1961), clearly echoing Nietzsche, opined that the refusal of the typical pre-twentieth-century threefold notion of history (past, present, and future) is something that essentially characterizes modern man. The modern man, Jung writes, is "aware of his immediate present" and it is he who "stands upon a peak, or at the very edge of the world, the abyss of the future before him, above him the heavens, and below him the whole of mankind with a history that disappears in primeval mists."[44] Modern man, according to Jung, "becomes unhistorical" precisely in rising above the values and strivings of "those past worlds" and by "leaving behind him all that has been discarded and outgrown."[45] Jung's insistence on a present with future possibilities left open and past restrictions forgotten is an affirmation of the present as a possible beginning for those who seek it. As with Miller, for Jung, man can do and be anything because he "stands before a void out of which all things may grow."[46]

Two presents uncovered

Miller, unquestionably, was influenced by Jung's ideas since he quoted several of the very same passages to Michael Fraenkel in his letters. While their discussion revolved loosely around Shakespeare's Hamlet, Miller invoked the Jungian notion of the present, reading it both into Hamlet's relationship with his time and into his own and Fraenkel's relationships to the modern era: ". . . we stand to Hamlet," Miller wrote,

> . . . as Hamlet stood to his age. It was the very exactitude of his relation to the age which permitted Hamlet as a 'projection' of the modern man . . . he was so neatly socketed in time that he burns eternally. The ghost, then, becomes the traditional present; that dead slag of the past which refuses to stay buried, which burrows into the present and corrodes it like a cancer. (HAM, 73–4)

On Miller's reading, then, the main enemy both for Hamlet and for himself becomes the *traditional present.* For him personally, as for others who also shared the emerging modernist consciousness, the *traditional present* was to be understood as the *progressive* present, which started with the Enlightenment and had developed, with the help of the Industrial Revolution and its multiple mutated manifestations (positivism, totalitarianism), to his day.

Let us investigate Miller's notion of the present further. There clearly seems to be two ways of understanding the present according to Miller. One of them, as we saw before, is the *traditional present* as brought about by "historical men" "with ourselves as the culmination of all that has gone before" (50). This is essentially a species of the *progressive view* that sees history as ever evolving, with the present being merely a point in time in the course of it. It sees history as being necessary, linear, and teleological. The present according to such a view is always seen as being "in the middle." This "delusion of historical destiny," Miller responds, "is merely the counterpart of our picture of scientific planetary destinies" (61). He, thus, rejects this view of the present describing it as

> . . . a vacuum, a painful frozen state, a sort of gloomy vestibule in which we lie suspended, ready to explode with the least barometric change. In a way we are like those wonderfully preserved objects which are found in the Egyptian tombs; we crumble away upon exposure . . . A static, sanitary eternity of the present . . . That's us today. With this reality I have no concern. (50)

This condition of the present, Miller seems to suggest, is only due to the misplaced belief in the power of the linear nature of history and time. Once we give that view up, the present, too, becomes something else. "There is another reality," Miller wrote,

> . . . of which the vivid dream is composed, and this reality is the very plasma of life. Rimbaud recognized it, and Proust, and Dostoyevsky, and Lawrence. Van Gogh knew it too. Every tree, every hand, every stone or chair or flower he painted testified to the act of revelation. (50)

One of the manifestations of the "revelation" of this reality is precisely the realization of the arbitrariness of time and history. As an artist is unwilling to "adapt himself to what is vulgarly called 'reality'" (i.e. the *traditional present*), he is always, Miller claims,

> . . . acting against the time-destiny movement. He is always ahistorical. He accepts Time absolutely, as Whitman says, in the sense that any way he rolls (with tail in his mouth) is direction; in the sense that any moment, every moment, may be the all; that there is nothing but the present, the eternal here and now, the expanding infinite moment which is flame and song. (63)

We see that Miller, very much in the spirit of Spengler, "frees" his understanding of time from scientific rigidity and by doing so he also frees the artist from the static and ultimately passive view of the *traditional present.*

The Walt Whitman reference is of no arbitrary significance here, for it plays a crucial role in the formation of what Miller calls the *full present.* The *full present*, as opposed to the *traditional present*, is not the highest point of man historically; it is also not betwixt past and future. Rather, it is the present in which man can be and do anything. The *full present* for Miller is fundamentally a possibility, a beginning. It is the absolution of time and the salvation of the modern artist. Miller explains:

> We are all going forward, some of us faster than others, that is all. None of us are going back, except in the mind, which is delusion and an illusion. Some of us have liquidated the past, most of us will never liquidate the past. And finally, it is not the past which matters at all, because when we come into the full present the past is there and the future too and neither of them are frightening or bewildering. In the full present which is the living moment, we join forces with past and future . . . we forget and enjoy, and remember everything. (112)

Whitman's influence on Miller becomes particularly evident when he coins the notion of the *full present* in the passage above. In his *Leaves of Grass*, Whitman stressed the similarity and continuity of all the time tenses in an open universe in saying that

> A vast similitude interlocks all . . .
> All lives and deaths, all of the past, present, and future . . .
> And shall forever span them
> and compactly hold them
> and enclose them.[47]

The present is still the focal point of all time to Whitman as it is to Miller. The important thing is that while the *traditional present* is bound to the historical view of time and thus, to Miller, covers only a "short span of human behaviour, human evolution" (HAM, 123), the *full present* seems to accord with what Miller labels the "anarchic" view "in which we move not within definite cultural limits but within unlimited human ones based on the realization of our own potentialities" (*ibid*). Miller, thus, rejects time qua *historical time*, but welcomes it universally as "the earth time" (93). Miller sees only this "earth time" as thoroughly authentic and as something in which he can truly be himself. "It is only when I am in no hurry to go anywhere," Miller writes,

> . . . that I can forget and enjoy, and that means living in the present, I take it. That means that the past is liquidated, my own past and the world's past too. Because in those moments I am not standing before a date and place but before all time, from the beginning to end, and there's no more time because it is all time. (112)

Like Whitman, then, Miller participates in all three time tenses simultaneously; or rather the distinction between the tenses is now rendered meaningless. Miller feels time neither "historically" nor "progressively" but "absolutely":

> Every day I live in three times — the past, the present and the future. The past is the springboard, the present is the melting pot, and the future the delectation . . .

> I gloat over the past, I revel in the present and I make merry in the future. What it takes the ordinary man a number of incarnations — supposing there are such things — to live out, I live out in a lifetime. I have the accelerated rhythm which goes with genius . . . . (151)

Against the "transitional" moderns

As mentioned in the introduction to this chapter, Miller, with his call toward being ahistorical and paving the way to the *full present*, differs in his approach from several fellow modernists. When, for example, W. B. Yeats claimed that a crucial period would come to an end in 1927, or Virginia Woolf thought that "on or about December, 1910 human character changed," or D. H. Lawrence wrote that "it was 1915 the old world ended," they all, as has been noted, "attempted to discern a moment of transition."[48] Moreover, largely due to these authors, modernists are quite commonly regarded as "participating in a profound transition."[49] What interests us particularly in the current context, however, is that their statements concerned history. According to Harvey Gross, the above statements were "prophetic" in the sense of speaking from a "heightened historical consciousness," from an "awareness of living in the stream of events and the turbulent currents which are history."[50] Thus, the aim of these moderns, it seems, was, via prophetic claims, to inform their readers of (what they thought to be) the exceptional events or developments taking place in their time and to regard them as history. All of the above claims stating the apocalyptic upheaval, were, as we can see, expressed in the language of history, for they made use of chronological categorization, using particular dates. As Frank Kermode has usefully explained, "a crisis date gives history structure, and provides ways of talking about it."[51] The rationale for these "prophetic moderns" using such historical markers to verbalize the change or crisis seems to rest on the power they believed to exist in chronological matter-of-factness. The appeal to chronological and historical unquestionability makes Woolf's alleged change in the human character in 1910 look like a genuine world historical event. Indeed, as every significant event in history—upheavals, crises, and apocalypses—has had a date, it was widely believed they needed one in order to have happened at all. It is easy enough to understand the above writers' fear that if they didn't report premonitions, including particular years, the distingué and unparalleled events of their time would pass unnoticed. Consequently, they quite literally wanted to *make* or *be* history.

From Miller's perspective, however, this approach seems to have several irresolvable problems. First of all, it is hard not to notice the apparent *historicist* assumption embedded in this view: the notion that man is a product of historical development and that history plays a crucial role in making sense of man's life. Eliot, Woolf, and Pound have all been said to exhibit somewhat historicist tendencies at times (I will discuss this shortly). In their case, historicism mainly took the form of a historical explanation with a heightened role given to the past. While understanding perfectly well that historical explanations based on the *progressive view* did not exactly accord with their generation, they (especially

Woolf and Eliot) were still fascinated by history; they still had hopes for historical explanations. Modern ideas, for Miller, however, needed a newer temporal framework than the worn-out model of world history, which he associated only with the *traditional present*, and the *progressive view* of history. According to my reading of Miller, Woolf and others did not need to explain, let alone justify, their new modern experiences within the language of history; thus, they should have abandoned such language altogether. With their "year statements," they didn't need to say that moderns, too, were part of history; rather that historical explanations are altogether inconsequential if they don't capture the new realities organically. History for Miller was precisely one of those "cultural limits," discussed earlier, that he declared himself to have escaped. This escape manifested itself in his notion of the *full present*, as this was essentially ahistorical and thus a different way to describe one's being. While the older moderns expressed their anxieties regarding the age still in terms of history, Miller, giving up the old cultural modes of self-description, also gave up the historical dimension and thus also the vocabulary of it. One is tempted to say on this point that Miller far exceeds the "radicalism" of the early moderns who appeared to be somewhat blinded by the lure of the power of history.

In addition to being trapped in unnecessary historical modes of self-explanation, the above "year games," and the "transitional view" of the present, effectively show that one is, again, thrown back into the *middle* of history. The belief that their historical reality was transitional became for Yeats and several other modernists "an age, a saeculum" itself.[52] As such, the transition stage seems to become endless as the prophesized end or change, being always present, or "just around the corner," never actually "arrives." In either case, one's attitude in relation to one's surroundings seems utterly passive. If the transition is imagined to last for a long period of time, then one's role merely seems to lie in waiting until the transition has taken place and a "new order" has emerged. If the transition has a more definite time frame, such as Yeats's 1927 premonition, then again one's hope is placed in a certain future event before which nothing really seems to need to be done. Throwing oneself upon the mercy of mysterious historical forces, however, one exhibits a great sense of naïveté as if history, by itself, could take care of human problems. It even mattered little whether the apocalypse actually occurred or not in 1927, or any other year, for it is a characteristic of transitional thinking that "the end is immanent rather than imminent."[53] Accepting the present as in transition in the Yeatsian sense meant that the end was embedded in one's temporal projection of oneself in any case. Since the end "immanently" is always on the horizon as a possibility, there will always be good reasons to pick another year in case it doesn't arrive "imminently" on a particular date because, as Kermode writes, "any date can be justified on some calculation or other."[54] It is important to notice that both the "immanent" and "imminent" construal of oneself are examples of historical thinking, for they appeal to some kind of fixed temporal *directedness* in one's interpretation.

We can now see more clearly why Miller couldn't possibly accept the "transitional view" of the present. We saw that he separated the *traditional* and *full present*. The modernists above, however, seemed to view the present, and presumably reality in general, only one-dimensionally, as some state which is now expected to transform into something else. This is then viewed as a transition from state *A* to state *B*. What Miller seems to be implying, however, is that the present is only a matter of perspective. There is no ultimate historical or temporal reality, a universal state *A*, to change from in the first place. This is an illusion deriving from the ideologies of the scientifically inclined *progressive view*. Similarly to Nietzsche, necessity (including historical necessity) for Miller, too, is not a fact but an interpretation. Time and history are neither objective nor significant attributes of reality for Miller. Thus, instead of the transition from one state to another, Miller changes his perspective on the present which he then calls the *full present*. Seeing the *full present* as a beginning, Miller takes an essentially active view of himself as an artist in regard to his possibilities. The "transitional view" of the present, however, remains passive as it upholds the old threefold model of history with the beginning projected either into the past or far ahead into the future and thus, in both cases, out of reach for the man of the present. That seems to reduce the present into being "a mere foothold either on the past or on the future," Miller writes (WOL, 81).

Yeats, for example, is perfectly capable of seeing that things are not exactly the best in the present, for he says in *The Second Coming* that

> Things fall apart;
> the centre cannot hold;
> Mere anarchy is loosed upon the world.[55]

Yet, he seems to form this negative judgment by making a comparison to the imagined past state of *Arcadia* (an idyllic paradise where people led simple yet happy lives), which, he feels, is no longer accessible to the modern consciousness:

> The woods of Arcady are dead, and over is their antique joy.[56]

Meanwhile, Yeats undoubtedly sees a possibility for things to change since he also expresses a belief in *The Second Coming:*

> Surely some revelation is at hand,
> Surely the Second Coming is at hand.[57]

Then again this belief in the "second coming" is projected into an abstract future without involving himself as an artist and active force that would make this happen. This leaves Yeats in Miller's *traditional present*, to dream about the past, hope for the future, or simply try to forget about the present by leaving the modern city and living the life of a hermit with "nine bean rows" and "a hive for the honey-bee"[58]; or else to keep inventing more fictive ends like that of 1927. Yeats, it is clear, didn't approve of the current events of history, but he saw no way out of its conceptual web. Indeed, in his poetic world, it has been noted, there was no "salvation *from* history."[59] He accepted the world *as* history.

Let us now also juxtapose Woolf's, Pound's, and Eliot's views on history with Miller's. Virginia Woolf, it has been observed, exhibited somewhat mixed feelings toward history. Her views have been said to be a "combination of a modern view of history and a traditional concept of history as story and particularly as English story."[60] She had a "lively interest in the past, a fascination with history which she inherited from the Victorians," one commentator notes.[61] Woolf's relation to history has been described as "existential": Woolf was "in search of something meaningful" and "in search of a tradition."[62] Another commentator also points out that Woolf showed "conscious and constant awareness of the historical past" and "a quest for a belief in history as pattern and continuity."[63] Importantly, even if her own age seemed to her "strangely deficient in itself," she still saw it as a part of "history as a whole" and as a "link between past and future."[64] On the one hand, she "felt repressed by the bonds of a tradition hostile to women," yet, the commentator concludes, "her constant preoccupation with the English past, her plans for a 'complete' history reflect an unreflective need to reassure herself of and within some sort of historical tradition."[65] This is enough in order to see the clash with Henry Miller's views. Woolf upheld an ultimately "historical view" of man and society. Like Yeats (although, perhaps, for different reasons), she couldn't deny the past and its role in the present. Accordingly, she maintained the traditionally rectilinear view of the present as being in the middle of the past and the future. Miller, as we have seen, denied the need for any kind of history as such.

Ezra Pound, whom a fellow modernist, Wyndham Lewis, called "a sort of revolutionary simpleton,"[66] should also be considered as embracing history. His *Cantos*, "the longest, most complex and most ambitious poem of our time,"[67] has been described as "a didactic poem about history" in which "he exhorts the reader to consider the *Cantos* as part of history itself. They intend not only to instruct our memories but also to involve us in events; we "become" history as we immerse ourselves in Pound's discourse."[68] While "involving" one effectively in the present may be seen at least as a less passive perspective than the one Yeats held, regarding one's possibilities and role in the present, "becoming history"—as should be evident by now—is something that one shouldn't want to become, according to Miller's thoroughly ahistorical approach. In addition, Pound's treatment of the "historical substance" of the *Cantos* and the belief in "the validity of the printed matter, of forgotten scandal, and the detritus of personal memory" has been described as naive and uncritical.[69] Pound's view that by accumulating historiographical knowledge and, by means of his *Cantos*, "retelling the history" the "achievements of the past" can be "rescued" is thoroughly at odds with that of Miller, who on more than one occasion exhibited ill-feelings toward the power of knowledge and its imagined positivist results. "I am against knowledge," Miller wrote to Lawrence Durrell, in the fall of 1936, "I abhor it. I loathe it. I want to become more and more ignorant, more quiet, more vegetative, more ruminative, more omnivorous, carnivorous, herbivorous. I want to stand still and dance inside . . ." (DML, 22). All the knowledge in the world, in Miller's view, had not hitherto helped man to make better decisions about his condition. Why believe that it would change now? He had little patience for the "untold" promises of history because one cannot redeem history by retelling it, but only by unceremoniously destroying it.

T. S. Eliot, too, was a modernist with strong historicist dispositions which, according to Gross's authoritative interpretation, amount to the view that "man is a product of historical development, totally determined by an unredeemed past and a chaotic present."[70] Gross has suggested that Eliot saw history "through Hegelian lenses" and that he "knew that there is no escape from time or avoidance of history."[71] Indeed, in his essay "Tradition and the Individual Talent" (1922), Eliot emphasizes the need for an artist to have a "historical sense" which involves "a perception, not only of the pastness of the past, but of its presence; the historical sense compels a man to write not merely with his own generation in his bones, but with a feeling that the whole of the literature of his own country has simultaneous existence and composes a simultaneous order."[72] This kind of "historical sense" makes a writer "traditional" according to Eliot. Again, this alone suffices to show the difference between Eliot and Miller in regard to history. Miller had no interest in Eliot's historically bolstered "traditional" literature; on the contrary, he considered "literature" as such to belong to the *traditional present* and not to his artistic *full present.* "Everything that was literature has fallen from me," declared Miller in *Tropic of Cancer* (CAN, 10). Making things even worse for Miller, Eliot insists that a poet should surrender himself completely to the "consciousness of the past," which he sees as "more valuable" than the "expression of personality" and which ultimately results in the poet's "continual self-sacrifice, a continual extinction of personality."[73] Evidently, this view is at variance with Miller's notion of the ahistorical artist who should, contrary to Eliot, transcend the cultural limits both of his past and traditionally construed present. "The man of genius," Miller writes, "is he who makes his own laws, his own reality . . . he alienates himself from the rest of the men" (WOL, 53). He had seen enough of the "pastness" of Eliot's present.

It should be noted that, despite these different views on history, and as surprising as it may sound, Miller felt affinities with several of the aforementioned modernists. He spoke highly of Pound's verse and also corresponded with T. S. Eliot, who, as we saw in the previous chapter, felt sympathetic toward Miller's *Tropic of Cancer.* As critics of their era, they all essentially shared similar anxieties with one another. It is in the proposed "solutions" to the present situation that they differ and, as we saw, they differ quite diametrically. It should be apparent now that history played a very important role for the modernists whose consciousness (especially in case of Yeats and Woolf) was perhaps still strongly influenced by the Romanticist era. To Miller, imbued with Nietzsche's nihilism and Spengler's ahistoricity, the "solutions" of those moderns seemed no doubt weak or even naive. Looking back to these earlier days, Miller intimated later that "I was sick to death of the lack of substance in English literature with its portrayal of a truncated, partial man. I wanted a more substantial diet, the whole being . . ." (CHM, 83). Miller, it seems, felt the need to break with the other moderns doctrinally, to bring something new to the game. And this he achieved in his contrasting view of history. For Miller, human life cannot be changed by means of history. The traditional linear model and views yearning for the lost past, it seemed to Miller, rest on the assumption that there is nothing really to be done about history. That to him seemed wrong and he set out to demonstrate this. The beginning of the twentieth century had already seen too many manifestos, too many words, too much "literature" such that Miller had little faith in the power of the "year statements" of other moderns. By "playing" with history, one indeed becomes a part of it and that is the securest way to be forgotten, Miller thought.

Dealing with the crisis

Miller's distinction between the *traditional* and *full present* importantly enabled him to localize and then deal, in his own way, with the unbearable present. The ills of the epoch for Miller were always first manifested in relation to his own life. He as an individual represented the ongoing doom. "The world is the mirror of myself dying. . .," he said (BS, 26). In this, Miller once again reflects a disposition common to modern artistic types who "carry within themselves profound anxieties (as a mirror of their 'civilization'), yet have the power to transform, to transmute them into symbols of spiritual strength, integrity, and plenitude."[74] Since Miller has importantly qualified his understanding of the present, it is clear that he was "dying" only in so far as he construed himself to be part of the *traditional present.* The *full present* is where he would be reborn. This is precisely what people do not see when entangled in the game of one-directional history. Miller writes:

> To spit on the past is not enough. To proclaim the future is not enough. One must act *as if* the past were dead and the future unrealizable. One must act *as if* the next step were the last, which it is. Each step forward is the last, and with it a world dies, one's self included. We are here on the earth never to end, the past never ceasing, the future never beginning, the present never ending. (BS, 26)

What Miller is trying to say is that if we continue to think in terms of past, present, and future, we will never get out of the web of history; we will be stuck in the *traditional present* and at the mercy of its historical dictates (whatever happens to be in fashion at the moment). Thus, we have to "kill" the past and future, and embrace ourselves in the "present never ending," which is the *full present;* an ahistorical approach to one's life and its surroundings. This liberates us to being reborn in the current moment. It frees us from the foot race with time. "There is never anything but the present," says Miller.

> The past is a word for something lost; the future is a word for something unattained. Why do we ignore or despise the present? Why do we yearn to be in another place, another time, why do we strive to become something other than we are? Is it because we do not realize that heaven is here and now? (WOL, 81)

It looks, according to Miller, as though we need to understand ourselves and our world as dying and as being resurrected at the same time. In the *traditional present* we die and in the *full present* we are reborn. There are no temporal sequences between these events, for the situation would become historical again if there were. It all happens *now.* If the apocalypse is *now,* so is redemption. For Miller, as for Walter Benjamin, "that things 'just go on' *is* the catastrophe. It is not that which is approaching but that which is. Strindberg's thought: Hell is not something which lies ahead of us, – but *this life here.*"[75] The end *is.* As opposed to Yeats, however, the end, according Miller, looks "imminent" only to those with the historical sense of the *traditional present.* "We are all alone here and we are dead," Miller announces in the first paragraph of *Cancer* (CAN, 9). This is a voice *from* and *of* the *traditional present.* For him, that realization also meant a goodbye. Miller needed to leave the *traditional present* and to step into the *full present.* "I am a man without a past and without a future. I am that is all," he wrote in *Black Spring* (BS, 23). Miller saluted his ahistorical self. He became a man of the *full present.* "I don't give a fuck any more what's behind me, or what's ahead of me . . . No past no future. The present is enough for me. Day by day. Today!" (CAN, 57). History for Miller ended here.

The need to make a clean break with one's past and become a man of the *full present* was not merely an artistic slogan but very much a principle of action for Miller. This view will only become fully evident in the chapters ahead. Being an anti-intellectual, ideas for Miller were always related to living. Philosophies, necessarily, had to be "wedded to action" (243). Miller clearly seems to have demonstrated this attitude by applying his view of the present and history to an important personal event: leaving his first wife Beatrice and their daughter. In leaving his wife, Miller saw, to a great extent, an act of artistic liberation from the bonds of tradition and society. To Miller, the continuation of the unhappy marriage would have meant subordination to the status quo of the time and the *traditional present.* Thus, the task of leaving his family came as a test or initiation for Miller: a condition of the possibility of his further emancipation as an artist and also as a human being. "I want to pass beyond the responsibility of fatherhood to the irresponsibility of the anarchic man who cannot be coerced nor cajoled nor bribed nor traduced," he said (CAP, 131). We notice here the element of the "anarchy" that Miller earlier associated with the *full present.* By cutting loose from the past, Miller ended the "things which are no longer alive to us, which no longer have meaning to us" (HAM, 110). This to Miller applied equally to personal relationships and the condition of the *traditional present.*

Leaving his family, of course, was only a first step in Miller's life toward stepping out of the dying part of the *traditional present* and beginning life in the *full present.* As Miller's struggles of the 1920s indicate, the true break with his past also needed a physical relocation on a grander scale than just moving to another part of New York. That "great escape" became possible only when he moved to Paris. Not only did he find it necessary to free himself from his personal relationships but also more than anything else he needed to free himself from America: the embodiment of the failure of the past and his former self. New York for Miller was the end of the *traditional present,* and Paris became the beginning of the *full present.* "I did not open my eyes wide and full and clear until I struck Paris . . . because I had renounced America, renounced my past," Miller recalled (CAP, 45). Indeed, moving to Paris provided Miller with his much-needed chance for "rebirth" after feeling himself continuously "dying" in America. "Before I could make a proper start I had to go through my 'little death.' The false start, which lasted ten years, enabled me to die to the world. In Paris, as everyone knows, I found myself," Miller wrote (WOS, 66). This overwhelming experience of "rebirth" in Paris Miller expresses excitedly in *Black Spring*: "Born and reborn over and over. Born while walking the streets, born while sitting in a café, born while lying over a whore. Born and reborn again and again" (BS, 185). And thus Miller escaped from his American destiny, his former life, time, and history.

> According to the map, I am in Paris; according to the calendar I am living in the third decade of twentieth century. But I am neither in Paris nor in the twentieth century. I am in China and there are no clocks or calendars here. (191)

This is where Miller seems to have entered into the timeless *full present.* Having diagnosed the illness of the *traditional present,* Miller chose not to be "ill" and created a different and crisis-free present. When he left America, Miller understood himself as stepping out of world time and world history and into *China.* He became *ahistorical.* We will continue to unpack Miller's philosophy through the notions of the *traditional* and *full present* in Chapter 3 and will elucidate the important notion of *China* in Chapter 4.

En route to Philosophia Milleriana via the *traditional* and *full present*

Where then do things now stand with our inquiry? We saw in this chapter that Miller rejected the traditional notion of time and history. By this rejection, he created a ground for the division between the *traditional* and *full present.* We then saw how this "ahistorical" view of Miller shaped his understanding of the modern crisis. In fact, this distinction helped him to localize the crisis, often described in apocalyptical terms, in the *traditional present.* Now, using this important distinction and Miller's rejection of history as a philosophical basis, we can venture a further and more detailed elaboration of the realms of the *traditional* and *full present.* For Miller, the crisis at hand was the crisis of the things that "go on" in the *traditional present.* By identifying, then, which particular things (besides the linear conceptions of history and time) Miller saw as a threat to himself as a modern artist, we should be able to come gradually closer to the essence of Miller's philosophy. Furthermore, I suggest that it is precisely the detailed criticism of the *traditional present* that forms the important center from which Miller's philosophy springs forth toward the *full present.* In proposing the *traditional present/ full present* divide as a basis for the categorization of Miller's ideas, I certainly hope to somewhat ease the worries of those skeptics who, like John Parkin, believe that systematic philosophical approaches to Miller are bound to fail. While it may be true that Miller did not aim to build a system of thought as such, there are still recognizable patterns in his thinking, explicit enough, that focusing on the *traditional* and *full present* in their entirety helps us to reveal them.

By way of Miller's idiosyncratic notions of the *traditional* and *full present,* we have already brought some clarity to the nature of modern society and artistic controversy, with which our inquiry began. Keeping a tight focus on this axis, we will continue to analyze Miller's two modes of time and related ideas more closely below. Since we have already begun to unpack Miller's negative philosophy of the "death" of the *traditional present*, it is natural to continue with that first and then gradually move on to his more positive "rebirth" philosophy of the *full present* and the artist. This methodological strategy is even more justified in light of the fact that the *full present* and Miller's conception of art is a direct response to decline both on the personal and on the literary-philosophical plane. It is imperative then that the *traditional present* should be fully unveiled first. For this reason, we continue with Miller's views on *modern technology* and *work* which, as defining features of the *progressive view*, have completely overtaken the *traditional present,* according to Miller.

Notes

1 Malcolm Bradbury, "The Name and Nature of Modernism," in *Modernism: 1890–1930*, eds. James Walter McFarlane and Malcolm Bradbury (Penguin Group, 1976), 20.

2 Thomas Nesbit, "Death, Rebirth, and the Self in *Tropic of Cancer*," *Nexus: The International Henry Miller Journal* 1, 1 (2004): 149.

3 Since modern apocalypse-discourse is an enormous topic in its own right, I will not in any way attempt to enter into its endless battlefields here or to make a compelling case for Miller as a possibly overlooked apocalyptical modernist. Instead, the topic of modern apocalypse should be understood here only as a general intellectual framework to which some of Miller's ideas call attention.

4 David Trotter, "Modernism and Empire: reading The Waste Land," *Critical Quarterly* 28, 1 (2008): 143.

5 Nesbit, "Death, Rebirth, and the Self in *Tropic of Cancer*," 149.

6 To avoid possible ambiguities by "modern crisis," I mean something more general than its apocalyptic description. While most of the modernists considered their age to be going through some sort of crisis, not all of them necessarily expressed their feelings through apocalyptic imagery. It would be best then, when appropriate, to talk only of apocalyptic moods, feelings, or descriptions of the crisis, catastrophe, upheaval, and such, as these can all be described as "apocalyptic" when necessary but do not require nor exclude the idea of the "apocalypse" *per se*.

7 This is how Frank Kermode summarizes his view on apocalypse in his *Foreword* to Peter Fjågesund, *The Apocalyptic World of D. H. Lawrence* (London: Norwegian University Press, 1991), vii. We will come to the in-depth discussion of his works shortly.

8 Ibid., 1.

9 Roger Fowler, *A Dictionary of Modern Critical Terms* (London: Routledge & Kegan Paul, 1987), 151.

10 David Trotter, "The Modernist Novel," in *The Cambridge Companion to Modernism*, ed. Michael H. Levenson (Cambridge: Cambridge University Press, 1999), 77.

11 Pitirim Sorokin, *Modern Historical and Social Philosophies* (New York: Dover Publications, 1963), 8.

12 D. H. Lawrence, *Apocalypse*, ed. Richard Aldington (London: Heinemann, 1972), 97–8.

13 Robert Nisbet, *History of The Idea of Progress* (New Brunswick, NJ: Transaction Publishers, 1994), 171.

14 Ibid., 172.

15 John Bagnell Bury, *The Idea of Progress: An Inquiry into its Origin and Growth* (New York, Cosimo Classics, 2008), 6.
16 Ibid., 18.
17 Auguste Comte, *The Positive Philosophy of Auguste Comte*, Vol. 2, trans. H. Martineau (New York: Cambridge University Press, 2009), 149.
18 Ibid., 4.
19 Ibid., 5.
20 Ibid.
21 Ibid., 150.
22 Georg Wilhelm Friedrich Hegel, *Lectures on The Philosophy of World History*, trans. H. B. Nisbet (Cambridge: Cambridge University Press, 1998), 52.
23 Ibid., 46.
24 Ibid., 63
25 Ibid., 51.
26 As we saw from Miller's quotations in Chapter 1, he had already adopted Spengler's notion of history as seasons.
27 Oswald Spengler, *The Decline of the West*, trans. Charles Francis Atkinson (New York: Knopf, 1926), 8.
28 Ibid., 8.
29 Ibid., 14.
30 David Couzens Hoy, *The Times of Our Lives: A Critical History of Temporality* (Cambridge, MA: MIT Press, 2009), xiii.
31 Spengler, *The Decline of the West*, 122.
32 Paul Guyer, "Immanuel Kant," in *Routledge Encyclopedia of Philosophy*, ed. E. Craig, (2004), url: http://www.rep.routledge.com/article/DB047.
33 Spengler, *The Decline of the West*, 122.
34 Ibid.
35 Ibid.
36 W. B. Yeats, "The Song of the Happy Shepherd," in *The Collected Poems of W. B. Yeats* (London: Macmillan, 1958c), 7.
37 Friedrich Wilhelm Nietzsche, "On the Uses and Disadvantages of History for Life," in *Untimely Meditations*, trans. R. J. Hollingdale (Cambridge: Cambridge University Press, 1997), 60.
38 Ibid.
39 Ibid.
40 Ibid., 61.
41 Ibid., 62.
42 Ibid.
43 Frank Kermode, *The Sense of an Ending: Studies in the Theory of Fiction* (New York: Oxford University Press, 1967), 7.
44 Carl Gustav Jung, *Modern Man in Search of a Soul* (London: Routledge & Kegan Paul, 1961), 227.
45 Ibid.
46 Ibid., 228.
47 Walt Whitman, "Leaves of Grass," in *The Portable Walt Whitman*, eds. Malcolm Cowley Mark Van Doren and Gay Wilson Allen (New York: Viking, 1985), 169.
48 Bradbury, "The Name and Nature of Modernism," 51.

49 Ibid., 33.
50 Harvey Seymour Gross, *The Contrived Corridor: History and Fatality in Modern Literature* (Ann Arbor: University of Michigan Press, 1971), 74.
51 Frank Kermode, "D. H. Lawrence and the Apocalyptic Types," in *Modern Essays* (London: Fontana, 1990), 172.
52 Kermode, *The Sense of an Ending*, 101.
53 Ibid.
54 Ibid., 98.
55 W. B. Yeats, "The Second Coming," in *The Collected Poems of W. B. Yeats* (London: Macmillan, 1958b), 211.
56 W. B. Yeats, "The Song of the Happy Shepherd," in *The Collected Poems of W. B. Yeats* (London: Macmillan, 1958c), 7.
57 Yeats, "The Second Coming," 211.
58 W. B. Yeats, "The Lake Isle of Innisfree," in *The Collected Poems of W. B. Yeats* (London: Macmillan, 1958a), 44.
59 Gross, *The Contrived Corridor*, 93.
60 Sabine Hotho-Jackson, "Virginia Woolf On History: Between Tradition And Modernity," *Forum for Modern Language Studies* XXVII, 4 (1991): 296.
61 Ibid., 297.
62 Ibid., 305.
63 Werner J. Deiman, "History, Pattern, and Continuity in Virginia Woolf," *Contemporary Literature* 15, 1 (1974): 50.
64 Hotho-Jackson, "Virginia Woolf On History, 296.
65 Ibid., 310.
66 Wyndham Lewis, *Time and Western Man* (Boston: Beacon Press, 1957), 38.
67 Leland D. Peterson, "Ezra Pound: The Use and Abuse of History," *American Quarterly* 17, 1 (1965): 33.
68 Gross, *The Contrived Corridor*, 100.
69 Ibid., 105.
70 Ibid., 44.
71 Ibid., 44 and 72.
72 T. S. Eliot, "Tradition and the Individual Talent," in *Selected Prose of T. S. Eliot*, ed. Frank Kermode (London: Faber, 1975b), 38.
73 Ibid., 40.
74 David Stephen Calonne, "Euphoria in Paris: Henry Miller Meets D. H. Lawrence," *Library Chronicle of the University of Texas* 34 (1986): 95.
75 Walter Benjamin, "Central Park," trans. Lloyd Spencer, *New German Critique* 34 (Winter 1985): 50.

3

The Anxiety of *Enframing*: Miller, Modern Technology, and Work

Hard, hard on the earth the machines are rolling, but through some hearts they will never roll

—D. H. Lawrence

Having seen Miller discard two important features of the *traditional present*—time and history—we will continue in this chapter by examining his further criticism regarding modern technology and work, as both of these characterize the aversive essence of modern society for Miller. While this chapter's specific focus concerns technology and work, its wider task is to shed an important new light on the whole realm of Miller's *traditional present.*

The philosophical role that modern technology plays in Miller's texts has not yet been emphasized to the degree it deserves. The reason for this may well lie in the fact that it is only due to our highlighting of Miller's notion of the *traditional present* that this special relevance of technology now unveils itself with such clarity. Now, as indicated above, modern notions of technology and work, as well as those of time and history, belong to Miller's *traditional present.* I will interpret the *traditional present*, however, as expressing similar anxieties with Martin Heidegger's *metaphysical ground* of the modern age. Since such an all-encompassing *ground* "holds complete dominion" over the age, this poses a problem for Miller as an emerging radical artist. Thus, in criticizing modern technology and work as vital but mistaken aspects of the everyday life of the *traditional present*, Miller implicitly pushes us forward to his theory of art, which he envisions as a kind of release. Consequently, in rejecting modern technology, Miller in fact rejects the entirety of modern metaphysics.

The notion of technology will be construed rather broadly in this chapter; most commonly not as a particular technical device, or machine, but, similarly to Martin Heidegger, as a *technological way of thinking*, which characterizes both the modern age and industrialism. Miller's notion of technology is also fairly similar to Georg Henrik Von Wright's *techno-system*, which is an umbrella term for the alliance of science, technology, and industry.[1] Thus, the *progressive view* and *techno-system* are taken to designate more or less the same phenomenon here and they are used interchangeably below.

One of the crucial aims of this chapter is, through Miller, to do justice to the (by and large) two main types of readings of modern technology: as a part of social and political criticism and as *ontological*, that is, as emerging from and concerning our very being. These are descriptions relating to different levels of the same phenomenon and both perspectives, I think, have legitimate application in examining Miller's views.

In the first part of this chapter, we will go over a very short summary of the formation of the "problem of modern technology" as it has historically been raised. We will then go on to discuss Miller's early memories of his industrial surroundings through which modern technology first began to permeate his consciousness. Following this, we familiarize ourselves with Miller's sympathy to Spengler's criticism of technology and the "Faustian culture" of the machine age. Subsequently, we will analyze Miller's views on progress, to be followed by a close reading of Miller and the theorists of the Frankfurt School, all of whom accentuate technology's role with consumerism and "false needs." We will then move on to a discussion of Heidegger where I show, based on his conceptual insights, that Miller's *traditional present*, to which modern technology belongs, should be read as precisely manifesting the *metaphysical ground* of our age. This in turn will suggest the possibility of a deeper philosophical reading of Miller's *traditional* and *full present* in the light of Heidegger's distinction between *ontic* and *ontological* as well as his notion of *Enframing*.

In the second part of the chapter, we will discuss work as a part of the very same *traditional present*, which Miller resists. While Miller's unease with work is well known, there has been little in the way of scholarly research to explain this peculiar disposition—aside from laziness. I would argue that work plays an important role in Miller's resentment of the *traditional present* because, as with technology, it expresses the *metaphysical ground* of the age for him. In addition, Miller rejects work as an ideological obsession with "making a living" which he construes to be the opposite of play and art. Miller's abandonment of his working career should hence be seen as an important step in overcoming the false consciousness typical of the age.

The rise of modern technology

Oswald Spengler famously suggested that technology as such became a cultural problem for the first time "only in the nineteenth century."[2] "The eighteenth century," Spengler writes, "the age of Robinson Crusoe and of Jean Jacques Rousseau, of English park and of pastoral poetry, had regarded 'original' man himself as a sort of lamb of the pastures, a peaceful and virtuous creature until Culture came to ruin him. The technical side of him was completely overlooked, or, if seen at all, considered unworthy of the moralist's notice."[3] It is only after Napoleon, Spengler goes on to claim, that "the machine-technics of Western Europe grew gigantic and, with its manufacturing towns, its railways, its steamships, it has forced us in the end to face the problem squarely and seriously."[4]

It is no secret that in the 1890s and 1900s a series of key developments were produced which, according to one commentator, "remain the foundation of the technology of the twentieth — as distinct from that of the nineteenth — century."[5] Some examples of technologies that originated at this time are the internal combustion engine, the diesel engine, the stream turbine, electricity, oil, and petroleum as new sources of power, the automobile, the motor bus, the tractor, the aeroplane, the telephone, the typewriter, the tape machine, the foundations of modern office organization, and the production of synthetic materials—dyes, man-made fibers, and plastic—by the chemical industry.[6] Lewis Mumford, in his seminal study, *Technics and Civilization* (1934), points out that while many important instruments of modern technology (clocks, printing presses, water mills, magnetic compasses, looms, lathes, gunpowder, paper etc.) already existed in other cultures, the fact remains that although "they had machines they did not develop 'the machine.'" "It remained for the peoples of Western Europe," Mumford holds, "to carry the physical sciences and the exact arts to a point no other culture had reached, and adapt the whole mode of life to the pace and the capacities of the machine."[7]

These rapid and radical advances in technology instigated ambivalent feelings in people's everyday lives: on the one hand, it is said to have "provoked enormous pride" being able to "exert such control over their environment," but at the same time it also resulted in "enormous anxiety that technology was changing the nature of what it meant to be human."[8] Many modernist writers exhibited, consciously and unconsciously, both sorts of feelings in response to the appearance of new technologies. Sara Danius rightly points out that modernist classics such as Andrej Belyi's *Petersburg* (1922), James Joyce's *Ulysses* (1922), Thomas Mann's *The Magic Mountain* (1924), John Dos Passos's *The 42nd Parallel* (1930), Herman Broch's *Sleepwalkers* (1930–32), and Robert Musil's *The Man Without Qualities* (1930–32), among other things, "chronicle the advent of modern technology, each in its own way."[9] Stephen Kern adds in his study that, for example, James Joyce was fascinated by the cinema, and in *Ulysses* "he attempted to recreate in words the montage techniques used by early film makers."[10] It is clear, however, that while many modernists most certainly drew on means of representation inherent in photography, phonography, and cinematography, they nonetheless remained skeptical about many other, less benign aspects of the arrival of technology. As we will see shortly, it is not so much with particular technical inventions that modernist anxiety lies (with the important exception of modern weapons) as with calculative or technological thinking.

Not all artistic schools, and not even all modernists, saw the appearance of new technologies, at the turn of the twentieth century, as universally appalling or as a matter of necessary rejection. On the contrary, Ezra Pound in his *Machine Art* reflects on the formal beauty of machines, their plastic as well as their sonorous qualities and concludes that "you can no more take machines out of the modern mind, than you can take the shield of Achilles out of Iliad."[11] The Futurists, too, celebrated speed, machinery, violence, youth, and industry and sought both modernization and cultural rejuvenation (in Italy). In "The Founding and Manifesto of Futurism" (1909), Filippo Marinetti writes:

> We affirm that the world's magnificence has been enriched by a new beauty: the beauty of speed. A racing car whose hood is adorned with great pipes, like serpents of explosive breath—a roaring car that seems to ride on grapeshot is more beautiful than the Victory of Samothrace.[12]

Such views can be read as versions of the idea labeled as technological determinism. Technological determinism is the contention that "social progress is driven by technological innovation, which in turn follows an 'inevitable' course."[13] This idea of social progress, in turn, is oriented around the idea that the human condition can be improved by technological advancement, and this is the way in which society moves "forward." According to this outlook, technical inventions "have made modern man and the modern condition."[14] We will associate this determinative or decisive aspect of technology upon human history, and our modern identity, with the *progressive view* of modernity, which has been discussed previously. For Miller, to be clear on this, this is one of the essential features of the *traditional present.* On the surface, he, like several other modernists, resists this technological way of thinking "as a common sense or obvious way of doing things which requires no discussion."[15] America, particularly, Miller saw as technologically obsessed and he continually singled it out as providing abundant empirical evidence of the dreadful nature of the modern age. In this he preceded later commentators who likewise found that America, throughout the twentieth century, had characteristically "mistaken technology for the answer, rather than the question" and that Americans "attached so much of their national and personal identity to technology."[16]

Technological America and Miller's youth

We can see America's infatuation with technology through the eyes of the young Miller since, having grown up in Williamsburg, a more remote part of Brooklyn in New York, images of industrial surroundings, and the desolate feelings they invoked, belong to his earliest memories. In *Black Spring*, reflecting on his youth, Miller writes:

> Where others remember of their youth a beautiful garden, a fond mother, a sojourn at the seashore, I remember, with a vividness as if it were etched in acid, the grim, soot-covered walls and chimneys of the tin factory opposite us and the bright, circular pieces and gleaming, others rusted, dull, copperish, leaving a stain on the fingers; I remember the ironworks where the red furnace glowed and men walked toward the glowing pit with huge shovels in their hands, while outside were the shallow wooden forms like coffins with rods through them on which you scraped your shins or broke your neck. (BS, 5)

In this early reminiscent picture, Miller opposes the natural warmth of motherly love and the beauty of places like garden and seaside to the cold and indifferent presence of factories, so characteristic of both the era and his personal environment. Evidently, he also remarks on the consequences of the Second Industrial Revolution (1870–1914), which saw its success particularly in the advancement of the steel and chemical industry.[17] It is known that Miller witnessed plenty of construction and production-related activities taking place in the area. Brooklyn, at the time Miller lived there, was one of the fastest developing areas and is said to have "changed character almost from decade to decade."[18] In *Sexus*, we find another of Miller's descriptions of industrial Brooklyn that conforms to the grim imagery presented above of his nearby surroundings as a child. These images seem to have cut deeply into Miller's everyday experiences and his self-image:

> On the way home we always rode through dreary, somber patches of land studded with gas tanks, smoking chimneys, grain elevators, car barns and other biochemical emulsions of our glorious civilization. The way home bore in on me the fact that I was just a shit, another peace of stinking offal like the burning garbage piles in the vacant lots. (SEX, 81)

In the passage above, we are brought close to the essence of the antagonism between the young Miller and technology. The use of grand-scale technology, Miller suggests, is in modern cities taken to such a dominating level that people are completely ignored in the midst of it. Miller as a human being feels humiliated and downgraded for being unimportant amid this process of industrialization.

Miller describes the manifestation of modern technology, which persistently makes itself felt in his surroundings, in several other places. We find, for example, a colorful and humorous, yet effectively sad, juxtaposition of the pastoral idyll of country life and that of the modern city, bearing all the technical signs of its time:

> Looking out on the contemporary landscape. Where are the beasts of the field, the crops, the manure, the roses that flower in the midst of corruption? I see railroad tracks, gas stations, cement blocks, iron girders, tall chimneys, automobile cemeteries, factories, warehouses, sweat-shops, vacant lots. Not even a goat in site. (11)

While Miller at that time was not a great admirer of country living, the above passage is a good example of a typically early modernist (perhaps even especially Yeatsian) blenching, as if suddenly having discovered oneself within industrialist surroundings. In these kinds of sudden realizations, the tacit and creeping nature of technology has only been detected after the fact. Once one notices the change in one's altogether altered surroundings, it already has happened: the technology has already risen to prevalence.

Spengler, the machine and the Faustian man

Miller's critique of modern technology is unquestionably influenced by Oswald Spengler's philosophy. Miller, for example, quotes his view, word for word, on the dominance of the machine straight out of *The Decline of the West* toward the end of his *Plexus*:

> For the sake of the machine, human life becomes precious. Work becomes the great word of ethical thinking; in the eighteenth century it loses its derogatory implication in all languages. The machine works and forces the man to co-operate.

> The entire Culture reaches a degree of activity such that the earth trembles under it . . . And these machines become in their forms less and ever less human, more ascetic, mystic, esoteric . . .. (PLEX, 626)[19]

In his *magnum opus*, Spengler calls our Western, machine-oriented culture "Faustian" and modern man "Faustian man." He explains the parallel between the tragic figure of Goethe's Faust and the Western world as follows: just as Faust sold his soul to the devil to gain greater power, the Western man sold his soul to the Technics. "The decisive turn in the history of the higher life," Spengler writes, "occurs when the determination of Nature (in order to be guided by it) changes into a fixation — that is, a purposed alteration of Nature."[20] While in earlier times Nature had "rendered services," in the modern era, it is "tied to the yoke as a slave" with her work being "measured by a standard of horse-power," Spengler adds. The angst that Miller exhibited earlier now appears to have an affinity with these very words of Spengler:

> . . . Faustian man has become the slave of his creation. His number, and the arrangement of life as he lives it, have been driven by the machine on to a path where there is no standing still and no turning back. The peasant, the hand-worker, even the merchant, appear suddenly as inessential in comparison with the three great figures that the Machine has bred and trained up in the course of its development: the entrepreneur, the engineer, and the factory worker.[21]

In *Tropic of Cancer*, Miller seems to touch on Spengler's Faustian type: the inhabitants of modern cities "whose last drop of juice has been squeezed out by the machine" and who appear to be "martyrs of modern progress" (CAN, 166–7). Miller, similarly to Spengler, sees technological thinking as completely overtaking the age and envisages an unfeeling picture of its success:

> A new ice age is setting in, the transverse sutures are closing up and everywhere throughout the corn belt the fetal world is dying, turning to dead mastoid. Inch by inch the deltas are drying out and the riverbeds are smooth as glass. A new day is dawning, a metallurgical day, when the earth shall clink with showers of bright yellow ore. (169)

We find Miller making a mockery of the machine-obsession of the "Faustian man" and his naive hopes in the following ironic passage from his anti-war essay "Murder the Murderer" (1941):

> . . . It is quite possible that in the next few hundred years we shall see everybody turning artist. An hour or two at the machine each day, and the rest of the day for art! . . . Suddenly, thanks to the ubiquity and the domination of the machine, we will become again as the primitives, only wiser, happier, conscious at last of our blessedness. Everybody dancing, singing, painting, carving, fiddling, drumming, strumming . . . so marvellous! All due to the machine. How simple! (MM, 459)

Against false progress

Stephen L. Starck has claimed that with "Miller's attack on modernity, his critique has been implicitly, when not explicitly, an attack on the notion of progress."[22] While modernity and progress should not be equated, the statement seems to be correctly describing a major aspect of Miller's wider discontent with technology. Sharing Spengler's fears over the "alteration of Nature," Miller writes in "An Open Letter to Surrealists Everywhere": "back of the idea of progress, which is the false idea underlying all civilizations — and the reason why they perish — is the notion of conquering over Nature" (OLSE, 192). In *Black Spring*, Miller presents us with an interesting list (making such lists is a part of his style) of the atrocious things that he thinks the progress of modern technology has brought to his era:

> The Plague of modern progress: colonization, trade, free Bibles, war, disease, artificial limbs, factories, slaves, insanity, neuroses, psychoses, cancer, syphilis, tuberculosis, anemia, strikes, lockouts, starvation, nullity, vacuity, restlessness, striving, despair, ennui, suicide, bankruptcy, arterio-sclerosis, megalomania, schizophrenia, hernia, cocaine, prussic acid, stink bombs, tear gas, mad dogs, auto-suggestion, auto-intoxication, psychotherapy, hydrotherapy, electric massages, vacuum cleaners, pemmican, grape nuts, haemorrhoids, gangrene. No desert isles. No Paradise. Not even relative happiness. (BS, 47)

In the above prolix list of ills of the age, Miller manages to compress an impressive amount of the history of the results of the Second Industrial Revolution. Similarly to several pre- and early modernist authors, Miller, for example, verbalizes worries about "colonization," which was a direct result of this industrialization, especially in Great Britain, with its need for new resources and labor at the beginning of the twentieth century. In some measure, Miller echoes Joseph Conrad who condemned colonization in his *Heart of Darkness* (1902) by criticizing Europeans for their cruel treatment of the natives in Africa.[23] Miller also included "stink bombs" and "tear gas" in his list, which were first used in World War I in 1915, to express his negative attitude toward the "advancement" of modern technology. It is precisely World War I which is said to have exploded the "myth of progress" and to have demonstrated that the "West's obsession with technological advance . . . leads to destructive megalomania."[24] Advancement, yes; but toward making more efficient weapons to be used in wars. Miller, literally only days before the start of World War II, was sadly forced to admit that the previous one had taught virtually nothing to mankind: "In our world the blind lead the blind and the sick go to the sick to be cured. We are making constant progress, but it is a progress which leads to the operating table, to the poor-house, to the insane asylum, to the trenches" (COM, 82). The modern need for more "artificial limbs," which Miller points out above, is yet another matter related to wars due to a large number of amputees, already dating back to the Napoleonic Wars in Europe and the American Civil War. Miller blatantly mocks the belief in peace and happiness promised by the ideologies behind the technological inventions of warfare.

Not all unwanted technological developments on Miller's list are war-related, however. While the vacuum cleaner (the first electric one was produced 1910 in Europe) may seem to be an innocent and even very practical device, it too, Miller seems to suggest, has failed to bring happiness, let alone Paradise to people. Many such technical appliances, in Miller's view, while they may not exactly bring death, do not seem to enhance life either—at least not to the degree that many seem to have expected. Miller's fight, which we can see everywhere in his writings, is foremost against the age-specific belief that the progression of machine technology somehow will lead people to a better life.

It is evident from Miller's early descriptions of Brooklyn, as well as from *The Air-Conditioned Nightmare* and most of his other texts, that he deemed America to be particularly enthralled by the lure of modern technology and the belief in its everlasting progress. It is, thus, precisely the opposite that he had hoped to find in Paris and in Europe. In *Nexus*, we find Miller's plea for a "non-progressive" Europe:

> Do not, O faithful Europe, do not, I beg you, show me the polished surface of a continent devoted to progress, I want to see your ancient, time-worn visage, with its furrows carved by age-long combat in the arena of thought. (NEX, 284)

Years later, at the age of 79, Miller, when asked whether technological progress was not just the inevitable "consequence of the Industrial Revolution," and also whether there is "a way to turn back time," answered:

> That's what they would like to have us believe, the powers-that-be. But I can think of going back. Sure. Why not go back as well as forward . . . You don't have to belong to the Establishment and follow this way of life that's laid out for you. (CHM, 149)

As we can see, Miller remained convinced throughout his life that the *traditional present* with its ideologies and superficial goals can and should be surpassed. This, we will see, is to be achieved precisely by way of his concept of art in the *full present*, wherein one is able to "go back as well as forward" without selling one's soul to technological progress.

Miller, technology, and the Frankfurt School

Miller's sentiments toward the hegemony of machine technology not only accord with Spengler's views but also express, to some extent, views of some neo-Marxist thinkers—also Miller's contemporaries—belonging to the Frankfurt School. It should be noted, however, that here we concern ourselves mainly with the social (and to a lesser degree political) aspects of (machine) technology and its relatedness to consumerism which the Frankfurt School theorists famously called attention to. It goes without saying, however, that while being *anti-progressivist* Miller could not have shared, for example,

Herbert Marcuse's Hegelian Marxist perspective of history.[25] Since it is, by and large, the same age in which they both lived, Marcuse's opinions on technology are valuable in assessing Miller's thoughts on the same subject historically, too. He, for example, sounds extremely close to Miller's thinking when he writes:

> Today political power asserts itself through its power over the machine process and over the technical organization of the apparatus. The government of advanced and advancing industrial societies can maintain and secure itself only when it succeeds in mobilizing, organizing, and exploiting the technical, scientific, and mechanical productivity available to industrial civilization.[26]

Marcuse expresses similar fears to Miller in the sense that it is through technology that the "Establishment" controls most of what is going on in the *traditional present.* Modern technology, which on the surface seems to be inventing better tools, offering new commodities, and easing man's work load by our growing reliance upon machines, is, in effect, a crucial part of the techno-system, which in the modern age plays an increasing role of social control. In his "Some Social Implications of Modern Technology" (1941), Marcuse observes:

> Technology, as a mode of production, as the totality of instruments, devices and contrivances which characterize the machine age is thus at the same time a mode of organizing and perpetuating (or changing) social relationships, a manifestation of prevalent thought and behaviour patterns, an instrument for control and domination.[27]

Indeed, there's no sense of talking about the evolvement of human values or the "bettering" of man when "the prevalent thought" is concerned with technological progress. Miller certainly vindicates Marcuse's point when he says:

> If one takes a sweeping glance at the paraphernalia which distinguishes our civilization from those of the past — I mean our battleships, factories, railways, torpedoes, gas-masks, etc. — one realizes that this is our civilization and not something else which we imagine civilization to be. (OLSE, 177)

The individual of the modern age (the *traditional present* in Miller's vocabulary) seems both to Miller and Marcuse to be left without a chance to contemplate his real needs, wants, and desires because of the overwhelming scope of the techno-world which produces, in Marcuse's terminology, "false needs." "Today," Marcuse writes, "this private space [of the self] has been invaded and whittled down by technological reality. Mass production and mass distribution claim the entire individual, and industrial psychology has long ceased to be confined to the factory."[28] We can certainly sense Miller's bipolarity and a sense of conflict similar to his *traditional* and *full present* in Marcuse's techno-world and "private self." In both instances, technology covers up the more meaningful senses of self. Miller highlights his epoch's specific obsession with mass-produced goods and "false needs" when he recalls meeting a Turk, a Syrian, and an Argentine on his way to Greece in 1939. "They said," Miller writes,

> . . . there was no life for them in their own country. When would life begin? I wanted to know. When they had all the things which America had, or Germany, or France. Life was made up of things, of machines mainly, from what I could gather. Life without money was an impossibility: one had to have clothes, a good home, a radio, a car, a tennis racquet, and so on. I told them I had none of those things and that I was happy without them, that I had turned my back to America precisely because these things meant nothing to me. (COM, 8–9)

Miller also shares Marcuse's fears about the modern means of mass communication and the commodity fetish which, according to Marcuse, "soothe and prolong the stupefication" of individuals.[29] In *The Colossus of Maroussi*, we find Miller echoing Marcuse's worries:

> Newspapers engender lies, hatred, greed, envy, suspicion, fear, malice . . . We need peace and solitude and idleness. If we could all go on strike and honestly disavow all interest in what our neighbor is doing we might get a new lease of life. We might learn to do without mines, without explosives, without battleships, without politicians, without lawyers, without canned goods, without gadgets, without razor blades even or cellophane or cigarettes or money. This is a pipe dream, I know. People only go on strike for better working conditions, better wages, better opportunities to become something other than they are. (COM, 46)

Owing to that disposition, Marcuse argues, people in a modern society start to "identify themselves with the existence which is imposed upon them and have in it their own development and satisfaction."[30] This is precisely the mentality of the age in which Marcuse's famous "one-dimensional man" and Miller's man of the *traditional present* is born:

> The means of mass transportation and communication, the commodities of lodging, food, and clothing, the irresistible outputs of the entertainment and information industry carry with them prescribed attitudes and habits, certain intellectual and emotional reactions which bind the consumers more or less pleasantly to the producers and, through the latter, to the whole. The products indoctrinate and manipulate; they promote a false consciousness which is immune against its falsehood. And as these beneficial products become available to more individuals in more social classes, the indoctrination they carry ceases to be publicity; it becomes a way of life. It is a good way of life — much better than before — and as a good way of life, it militates against qualitative change. Thus emerges a pattern of one-dimensional thought and behaviour . . ..[31]

The one-dimensionality, which Marcuse establishes in the foregoing passage, characterizes the experience of Miller's *traditional present*. It is precisely the fact that it seems "a good way of life" which prevents the average man from seeing the vacuity of the *traditional present*. Miller captures this nauseating essence of the modern consumerist in an image when visiting *Bloomingdale's*:

> There is a condition of misery which is irremediable — because its origin is lost in obscurity. Bloomingdale's, for example, can bring about this condition. All department stores are symbols of sickness and emptiness, but Bloomingdale's is my special sickness, my incurable obscure malady. . . . In Bloomingdale's I fall apart completely: I dribble on to the floor, a helpless mess of guts and bones and cartilage. There is the smell of, not of decomposition, but of misalliance. Man, the miserable alchemist, has welded together in a million forms and shapes, substances and essences which have nothing in common. (CAP, 186)

Hannah Arendt, a philosopher who shares sympathies with the Frankfurt School thinkers, has also observed of the era that "the spare time of the *animal laborans* (modern laboring man) is never spent in anything else but consumption, and the more time left to him, the greedier and more craving his appetites" and that "these appetites become more sophisticated, so that consumption is no longer restricted to the necessities but, on the contrary, mainly concentrates on the superfluities of life . . .."[32] Max Horkheimer, similarly, argued that "the more intense an individual's concern with power of things, the more will things dominate him, the more will he lack any genuine individual traits."[33]

Overthrowing metaphysics with Heidegger: *Traditional present* and the *metaphysical ground*

Ever since Chapter 2, we have stressed Miller's opposition to modernity that we more precisely labeled as the *progressive view*. The *progressive view*, by and large, was taken to have risen to prominence since the Enlightenment and its main characteristic was the belief in the progress of the arts, science, technology, economic welfare etc. The *progressive view* also insisted that history was *linear*. We have already seen that for Miller the *progressive view* still very much dominated in mundane everyday reality, which he named as the *traditional present*. We also saw that Miller sought ways to repudiate the latter by creating the ahistorical *full present*. Now, I believe that with the help of Martin Heidegger's philosophical acumen, we can venture to interpret Miller's rejection of the *progressive view* qua *traditional present* as, in effect, a partial overthrowing of modern metaphysics.

It appears that our *progressive view*, by and large, characterizes something which Heidegger calls the *metaphysical ground* of the modern age.[34] According to Heidegger, every age has its specific metaphysical conception of itself which fundamentally determines all the ways of understanding it. "Metaphysics grounds an age," Heidegger explains, "in that through a specific interpretation of what is and through a specific comprehension of truth it gives to that age the basis upon which it is essentially formed. This basis holds complete dominion over all the phenomena that distinguish the age."[35] Heidegger further suggests that it is precisely "the essence of modern technology, which is the essence of modern metaphysics."[36] Besides modern technology, science, loss of the gods, the emergence of culture, and the rise of esthetics are also part of this modern metaphysics, or modern "world picture," for Heidegger.[37] It seems that for the most part Heidegger's *metaphysical ground* and Miller's *traditional present* both identify and then reject similar features of the *progressive view*, namely science, technology, and esthetic art.[38] From the previous chapters, Miller's antipositivistic stance is obvious. The life which "the men of science have covered with the wallpaper," Miller calls "the grand whorehouse" (CAN, 170) and he also describes the modern age elsewhere as a "benighted scientific age" (COM, 82). It can be said, then, that the scientific world picture for both Heidegger and Miller covers up something more essential about man and his relation to the world and himself. We will see in later chapters that both Miller and Heidegger also reject the *esthetic* notion of art, which they situate in the *traditional present* and *metaphysical ground*, respectively. When Miller condemns modern man for having "lost something in their soul"(CHM, 179) due to their infatuation with progress and thinks that due to mass media and modern work people increasingly "become something other than they are," he seems to parallel Heidegger's deep conviction that "... nowhere does man today any longer encounter himself, i.e. his essence."[39] While undoubtedly expressed in different forms and vocabularies, Miller and Heidegger stand close mostly in their similar *mood* regarding modern man and his surroundings. They see corresponding faults with the "destitute times."

Heidegger's contribution to our discussion of technology and modern man is an important one. While Spengler and the Frankfurt School thinkers brought out the more descriptive and socio-political aspects of modern technology, science, and progress, Heidegger stresses their metaphysical dimension, and thus their essentially more fundamental and all-encompassing role in the modern age. The modern scientific thinking or *progressive view* is not simply an ideology or some political agenda but it in fact concerns man's being in the most profound sense. Revealing this metaphysical basis, then, offers a new way of reading Miller's *traditional present*, which we likewise may interpret as representing the age's *metaphysical ground* and can, in the light of Heidegger's theory, treat as covering up man's being in some more meaningful sense. This interpretation will become even more credible when we come to a closer examination of Miller's *full present*, *China*, and art's transcendent role in the next chapter.

Traditional present ontic, *full present* ontological?

There is a further component in Heidegger's analysis of the modern scientific world view which may prove to be helpful in interpreting Miller's project. Principally, I suggest that Heidegger may provide us with important qualifiers for Miller's *traditional* and *full present*, which, if true, would clarify the philosophical underpinnings of his conceptual apparatus considerably.

We saw in the last chapter that Miller made the initial distinction, by which he separated the *traditional* and *full present*, based on the current, that is, *progressive* notion of time and history. He rejected these notions because they offered only a narrow perspective on what it meant to experience oneself temporally. Time and history, we can now say, are part of modern metaphysics, which along with technology, progress, and science define the essence of the *traditional present* for Miller. He called the life of the *traditional present* "vulgar reality" and a "sanitary eternity of the present" with which he himself "had no concern" (HAM, 50). The antithetical *full present* Miller described as ahistorical, ecstatical and he saw it as fitting for artists as "the very plasma of life" (*ibid*). The *full present* is where one defies "definite cultural limits" and realizes one's innermost potentialities. Since we can sense that it is precisely the *traditional present* which constitutes "the loneliness of the creative individual" and is the basis for the "modern neurosis" (30), Miller's aim throughout his texts seems to be to transcend this reality, which he endeavors to achieve through the "creative process" and, according to my reading, also through his *China* experience.

Although evidently lacking the depth of Heidegger's demanding philosophy, we can interpret, naturally in some very limited measure, Miller's *traditional present* as predominantly exhibiting *ontic* treatments of the world since in this reality man is preoccupied, and in fact determined, by the elements of modern metaphysics, that is, history, technology, science, esthetics, etc. Ontic for Heidegger concerns the world of everyday appearances and experience. Ontic is to do with entities and facts about them.[40] Importantly, ontic inquiries of the "world" are "concerned with beings, not with their being."[41] Consequently, an ontic construal of the world is concerned with the world only as much it appears as a configuration of entities within our particular world picture, quantified and measured in the sciences and in our everyday lives. From numerous examples we have already seen that this propensity, for Miller too, thoroughly characterizes modern man. It is also evident, especially in the light of Miller's later views on the role of art, that the *traditional present* and the anguish it causes for Miller himself, and which we read here conceptually, is always to do with practical life and everyday living. Thus, we could say that the conflict between the facets of the ontical *traditional present* and Miller's strivings as an artist, to some degree, describe positively a conflict of *being*. Miller believes that the conflict of *being* in this sense can be solved by way of "creative life": by forming a new reality called the *full present*. This, however, seems to correspond to Heidegger's *ontological* "world-forming" capability which manifests itself through *ek-stasis*. Crucially, since the artist according to Miller releases himself from the everyday of the *traditional present* as described by modern metaphysics and maintained by the dominant world view, the new world he strives toward seems to concern ontology in the sense that it is in his quest that the artist is concerned with his *being*, as opposed to being treated merely as "a being" according to the ontical approach of the *traditional present*. The ontological relation to the world is more fundamental precisely because it concerns the "being of beings" as such.[42] It is "more primordial, as over against the ontical inquiry of the positive sciences," writes Heidegger.[43] In applying Heidegger's jargon to Miller's spiritual journey, we could say that his *full present* arises out of a deeper need for experiencing one's "selfhood" which is not yet completely concealed by the *traditional present.* Art, we remember, was precisely one of the ways in which one can be ontologically open and transcend the ontical, according to Heidegger.[44] In traversing the *traditional present*, Miller, then, could be said to overthrow modern metaphysics, and in his insistence on transcendence via art he seems to force us in the direction of a transcendental view of *being.* Precisely such transcendence-ability has also been said to be "one of the hallmarks of the modernist movement in poetry."[45] The plausibility of this reading is particularly pertinent when Miller says that "art is always about and around whereas metaphysics tries to answer, science tries to answer" (CHM, 73). Clearly, Miller ascribes to art an essentially all-encompassing and liberating essence, which he sees as thoroughly different from the guiding and prescribing "answers" of metaphysics and science of the *traditional present.* I will return to some related issues of this reading in the discussions of Miller's notion of art and *China* in the next chapter.

Modern technology as *Enframing*

While Heidegger's idiosyncratic and complex notion of technology may seem, at first blush, as having little in common with Spengler or the Frankfurt School of thinkers, the warning or fear that Heidegger believes to underlie modern technology is in fact fairly similar to these thinkers' views and Miller's alike. Given the limited nature of our inquiry, only a few of Heidegger's key concepts concerning technology are worthwhile stressing here, for they add a new dimension to our discussion.

We saw above that modern technology, for Heidegger, is an exemplification of modern metaphysics. In fact, it is perhaps the biggest and most pervading aspect of it. As such, technology is one of the main culprits in the forgetting or fragmentation of being, which Heidegger thinks rules in the modern age. The main problem of modern technology lies in the fact that its meaning, or essence, has become severely corrupted since Greek times. Technology for Heidegger is *revealing. Revealing* means that something is being brought forth by an artisan: "Bringing-forth brings hither out of concealment forth into unconcealment."[46] Artists or craftsmen "let what is not present arrive into presencing."[47] The Greek notion for this kind of revealing nature of technology Heidegger calls *aletheia* [*unconcealment, truth*]. Modern technology, Heidegger says, is similarly a mode of *revealing.* The modern mode of *revealing*, however, has changed its meaning from the former Greek notion of it as *poiesis* [*making, bringing-forth*]:

> ... the revealing that holds sway throughout modern technology does not unfold into a bringing-forth in the sense of *poiesis.* The revealing that rules in modern technology is challenging [*Herausforden*], which puts to nature the unreasonable demand that it supply energy that can be extracted and stored as such.[48]

As we can see, the difference between the Greek and modern notions of technology lies predominantly in the respect, or lack thereof, given to the material or resource which the technology exploits: technology in this Greek sense "brings-forth" from the material, whereas modern technology demands or "challenges-forth" from it. Owing to this fact, modern technological thinking starts treating everything as *orderable resources*. "The earth now reveals itself as a coal mining district, the soil as a mineral deposit," Heidegger writes.[49] Modern man treats nature as something he can order around and use for his pleasure and comfort. The essence of modern technology then is to "set itself upon nature," says Heidegger. While in earlier times a peasant took care and maintained the land by only watching over and nurturing what he grew, modern means of agriculture *set* themselves upon land in the sense of *challenging* and demanding the harvest (energy, power) out of it. At this point, Heidegger's view is not entirely dissimilar to Spengler's, for the latter too saw modern technology as having reached the point at which the "earth trembles" and which had as its main goal the "purposed alteration of Nature." Heidegger goes on to describe this fundamentally changed relationship between modern man and the world as giving rise to a particular human attitude he calls *Enframing* [*Ge-stell*].[50] The German word *Gestell* [from *stellen*, to set or place] has a number of meanings: bookrack, skeleton; the basic sense is of an armature or framework. Heidegger, however, develops a new application of this term to describe how human beings have come to relate to the natural world.

> Enframing means the gathering together of that setting-upon which sets upon man, i.e. challenges him forth, to reveal the real, in the mode of ordering, as standing reserve. Enframing means the way of revealing which holds sway in the essence of modern technology and which itself is nothing technological.[51]

Enframing is the most important feature of modern technology for Heidegger. Its pivotal characteristic is that it depicts the type of thinking which is carried out in the technology but which itself is nothing technological. First and foremost, modern technology, as we saw above, concerns nature "as the chief storehouse of the standing energy reserve."[52] *Enframing*, however, does not simply endanger man in his relationship to himself and to everything that is. Technological thinking is not limited to natural resources. Indeed, to a certain extent, Heidegger argues, technology transforms humanity itself into *standing-reserve* [*Bestand*]. Heidegger's *standing reserve* is closely related to the idea of instrumentality. He elaborates:

> The forester who, in the wood, measures the felled timber and to all appearances walks the same forest path in the same way as did his grandfather is at the mercy of the paper industry, which in turn is at the mercy of the print industry, which in turn transforms the reading public into a source of its own profits.[53]

Heidegger also points out that our use of the expression "human resources" aligns human beings with raw materials such as coal or petroleum. He concludes:

> The threat to man does not come in the first instance from the potentially lethal machines and apparatus of technology. The actual threat has already affected man in his essence. The rule of Enframing threatens man with the possibility

> that it could be denied to him to enter into a more original revealing and hence to experience the call of a more primal truth.[54]

What is paramount is that while *Enframing* indeed sets itself upon man's thinking in such an all-encompassing way, there is still, according to Heidegger, a "more original revealing" and a "more primal truth" which man, at least in theory, is able to pursue.

Heidegger's concepts of *standing reserve* and *Enframing* certainly prompt us to search for more depth in Miller's *traditional present.* We saw in several places before that Miller's disquietude with technology manifested itself in his growing sense of alienation as a human being in the midst of the technological "wonders" of the modern age. Miller, it can be said, anticipated Heidegger's warnings about technology's direction as having already materialized by the 1920s. People's naive belief that technology was a mere means in the hands of man was indeed the other way round: man was now being ordered forth to lend a hand to the coming to presence of technology.[55] Miller, similarly, depicted the man of the *traditional present* as "a cog in a machine over which he has no control" (WOS, 92). The most alarming thing for both Heidegger and Miller was perhaps the fact that modern man is in fact proud of having become such a "deified robot," which Miller saw as "the end product of the machine age" (92). Being "the man of long-range calculation," modern man is prevented from seeing a "more primordial truth" and pursuing a more meaningful relationship with himself and the world. That, however, can change, at least in principle, when man, according to Miller, starts to think less and feel more and, by means of art, transcends to the *full present.*

Modern work as part of the *traditional present* and its metaphysics

The discussion of the *metaphysical ground* and the industrial nature of the modern age directs us to the next crucial feature of the *traditional present*, namely work. Those familiar with Miller's texts and life are well aware of his unenthusiastic disposition toward working, or more precisely, with his open unwillingness to steadily engage in any kind of work. While he has been blamed for being lazy, manipulative, and for using people's goodwill to get by in life, his notion of the *traditional present*, and work's specifically metaphysical relation to it, opens up a far more plausible explanation for this lifelong peculiarity. There are two major senses in which Miller can be said to resist work and working. First, as hinted above, Miller dismisses work because it belongs to the *traditional present*, and since it then augments its *metaphysical ground*, it falls prey to the same criticisms as modern technology. Indeed, the modern notion of work, according to Heidegger, is closely related to modern technology since they both concern "production processes." In this context, the character of the work people do becomes mechanized and meaningless for Miller. Also, work in this modern sense exhibits an apparent threat similar to technology: it makes workers appear as *raw material* to be used for expanding the scope of technological power.[56] Second, working as merely "making a living" for Miller is the opposite of *play* and, as *play* and art are essentially related, work and art become enemies. Similarly, then, Miller thinks that work in this sense contributes to the status quo of the *progressive view* and will not let people strive for the freedom which artistic ways of life would offer. "Every new job I took," Miller recalls in *Big Sur*, "was a step further in the direction of 'murder, death, and blight.' I think of them still as prisons, whorehouses, lunatic asylums . . ." (BSOHB, 117–8). These intense feelings alone should deliver the sense of importance of the whole issue for Miller. Indeed, as I suggest below, Miller, by firmly sticking to his vagabond lifestyle, used his own life to exemplify the uncompromising nature of becoming an artist. Since the transformation process required overthrowing the entire *metaphysical ground* of the *traditional present*, he needed to dispense with work, too.

Before finally freeing himself for writing, Miller worked, among others, as a field laborer in California, an employment manager in New York, a gravedigger in Queens County, and a proofreader in Paris.[57] In 1909, Miller had left City College in New York after only one semester and, instead of joining his father in the garment trade, took his first job as a filing clerk at the Atlas Portland Cement Company. "It was dull work," a biographer suggests.[58] In 1912, Miller was heading out on a spiritual journey to California where he also needed to take several casual jobs at a cattle ranch, a lemon grove, etc. By around 1914, Miller was still unaware of what to do with his life, and the increasing pressure from his family to settle down and join his father's tailor shop on a full-time basis was ever so immanent. After marrying his first wife Beatrice Sylvas Wickens (1917) and the birth of their daughter Barbara (1919), Miller found himself under real pressure to find a job and to provide for his family.

In 1920, Miller started to work as an employment manager for Western Union Telegraph. Before long, however, as his awareness of the nature of the modern age deepened, the work he was expected to perform daily, and the emerging artistic strivings, became markedly at variance with one another. Miller became disillusioned not only with his own work but also with work *per se.* How many people, Miller asked, actually like what they are doing day in and out? "Most of them," he answered, "look upon their work as stultifying and degrading. Few ever find a way out" (BSOHB, 268). The "way out" for Miller stood for more than just leaving one's job. It meant overthrowing the entire flock of existing presuppositions of modernity: it meant dethroning the entire existing life of the *traditional present.* Quitting his job, then, became Miller's first plain act against modern metaphysics. This step marked a definitive turn in his life. On the surface, and in the eyes of his friends and family, Miller lost his job. Philosophically, however, he deliberately lost not only his job but also the entire realm of thinking to which it belonged. In a certain passage, where Miller is ruminating about the idea of withdrawing from his job and pursuing the life of a writer, we notice the significance Miller ascribes to this tremendous step in his life.

> I had the comfortless excuse that by my labors I was supporting a wife and child . . . The part of me which was given up to work, which enabled my wife and child to live in the manner they unthinkingly demanded, this part of me which kept the wheel turning — a completely fatuous, egocentric notion! — was the least

> part of me. I gave nothing to the world in fulfilling the function of breadwinner; the world exacted its tribute of me, that was all. (SEX, 188)

Fundamentally, the passage expresses a deep inner conflict between Miller as still partly a man of the *traditional present* and Miller as an emerging artist. We can see that, as with technology, work is not just a theoretical notion for Miller. It cuts deeply into his sense of self: the expected breadwinner side of him, while important, perhaps, for the people around him, for himself feels existentially the smallest and most inferior one. Since work visibly affects his *being*, the full potential of which, he feels, has become hindered, Miller's engagement with work can be said to express genuinely ontological concerns. Consequently, for him, there really was an irreversible decision to be made here: if he indeed truly wanted to become an artist, he would have to go all the way: he must go beyond the very essence of the "false being" of his present life. "The world would only begin to get something of value from me," Miller explains, "the moment I stopped being a serious member of society and became — myself" (188). Most people, according to Miller, remain "serious members" of society and only "repeat the mistakes of their forefathers. They are caught in the wheel from birth and they keep at it till death — and this treadmill they try to dignify by calling it 'life'" (188–9). Miller was determined not to make the same mistake and decided to leave this treadmill "life" of the *traditional present* once and for all by attacking one of the predominant features of its ideological and metaphysical core: work.

Becoming a machine

Let us have a closer look at Miller's work in the Western Union and see how exactly he came to his conviction about its thoroughly "evil" nature. It was around 1922 that Miller seems to have become particularly tired and bored with working under the false pretences of providing for his family. In *Plexus*, Miller describes his utter boredom this way:

> I had lost all interest in my job. All I thought of was to begin writing. At the office I did less and less, grew more and more slack . . . As often as possible I would clear out of the office on the pretext of inspecting the branch offices. I would call on one or two in the heart of town — just to establish an alibi — then duck into a movie. After the movie I would drop in on another branch manager, report to headquarters, and then home. (PLEX, 19)

Miller's sentiments reflect the feelings of one who has completely lost personal connection with his job. Borrowing from Heidegger, we may call this connection *relatedness*. Having lost the relatedness to one's work is, according to Heidegger, a major characteristic of the modern worker as opposed to, say, an old cabinet maker, whose craft was precisely maintained by his close relatedness to the material of his handcraft and its specific qualities. Heidegger raises an important question for the modern age: "where in the manipulations of the industrial worker is there any relatedness to such things . . .?"[59] The important thing about Heidegger's observation is that not having or knowing such relatedness is not, as may be expected, a matter only for "a worker in the sense of the worker at the machine";[60] rather it concerns "every handicraft, all human dealings": "writing of poetry is no more exempt from it than is thinking."[61] What is critical about this idea is that "without that relatedness, the craft will never be anything but empty busywork, any occupation with it will be determined exclusively by business concerns."[62] Again, this should be read as applying most widely: "all human dealings are constantly in that danger," says Heidegger.[63] Miller vividly points out that the anguish which many feel in the modern age is precisely due to having lost this personal relatedness to the objects of their labor:

> . . . don't forget that we WORK to make things easy. This is what we are all working at — making these gadgets, improvements, and so on. But we make ourselves miserable doing it. Nobody makes shoes any more — alone — does he? Or a suit of clothes? Or builds his own house? He makes part of a shoe. (CHM, 149)

While the reference above may have been aimed to criticize predominantly the mass production in which modern workers lose their relatedness, it applies to Miller's own job just as well. Inasmuch as the modern worker in an assembly line is only responsible for making a "part of a shoe" and thus lacks relatedness to the finished product, Miller felt the same sense of modern fragmentation, an awareness of lost wholeness, by only being a small part of the massive corporation, a "cog in the machine." A "cog," however, can never have a deeply meaningful relationship with the whole "machine" of which he is only a miniscule and impersonal part. Describing his job in *Tropic of Capricorn*, Miller says that the Telegraph Company was "a slaughterhouse, so help me God. The thing was senseless from the bottom up. A waste of men, material and effort" (CAP, 18). This alone goes to show the level of detachment Miller had begun to feel toward his work. According to Brown, the company, as a whole, increasingly became for Miller, a "symbol of American inhumanity and heartless organization."[64] Since Miller's job was to "hire and fire like a demon," he felt that the "slaughterhouse"-like work mentality completely overtook his sense of self. Moreover, he became disgusted with himself for helping to "slaughter" more and more people every day: for sacrificing them on the altar of the *traditional present*. Miller recalls the situation in *The Books in My Life*:

> They wept, they knelt at my feet, they snatched my hand to kiss it. Oh, to what lengths did they not go? And why? In order to get a job, or in order to thank me for giving one! As if I were God almighty! As if I controlled their private destinies . . . And so every day I found myself averting my gaze. I was in turn humiliated and exasperated. Humiliated to think that anyone should regard me as his benefactor, exasperated to think that human beings could beg so ignominiously for such thing as a job . . . . (BIML, 245)

Ferguson has observed that Miller now saw himself as forced to act as "a censor of experience" and "a shield against spontaneity" toward the people he had to deal with professionally.[65] Indeed, we can see that Miller felt positively torn for being seen as a "benefactor" because he had already seen the deep cracks at the very core of the organization he still officially represented.

The way Miller was expected to deal with people at his work every day reminds us of Heidegger's notion of *standing reserve*. Since Miller's job consisted of hiring and firing messengers, in other words, of humans *as* a resource, he sensed, to an extent, that he was treating people as *standing reserve*: as raw material, which can be ordered and manipulated. It became increasingly clearer to Miller that in modern working relations individuals are shaped by the need of the "machine" and not vice versa. In this Miller echoed Karl Marx who observed that "it is a common characteristic of all capitalist production that the worker does not make use of the working conditions. The working conditions make use of the worker . . .."[66] Since modern productionist ideology was overrun with the "will to make and be effective"[67], everything was to be sacrificed for that goal. The American worker, Miller appropriately illustrates in *The Air-Conditioned Nightmare*, "delivers himself body and soul to the most stultifying labor a man can perform" and that "even when one works under the best possible conditions" he "forfeits all rights as a human being" (ACN, 23). Miller goes on to explain that "the best possible conditions (in American lingo) mean the biggest profits for the boss, the utmost servitude for the worker, the greatest confusion and disillusionment for the public in general" (*ibid*). The same applied to Miller's own work: he felt that he had lost himself as a human being by not treating others as human beings. Moreover, using people daily as *raw material* was expected by his very job description: it belonged to the essence of his job. The realization of this made any further complicity impossible for Miller.

Work vs. play

In addition to the reasons described above, Miller repudiates work and working in another sense. In *Sexus*, he expresses a view that significantly explains his growing sense of disgust with work in this other sense. Work, Miller says, is opposed to creativity and freedom:

> Work, it seemed to me even at the threshold of life, is an activity reserved for the dullard. It's the very opposite of creation, which is play, and which just because it has no *raison d'être* other than itself is the supreme motivating power in life. (SEX, 116)

In the foregoing passage, Miller distinguishes between work and *play*. As we will come to see even more clearly later, *play* for Miller means a "childlike yet profound attitude towards life" (HAM, 35) and as such it is a vital component of art. In valuing *play* over work, Miller, once more, steps against the *progressive view* of the *traditional present.* Since the ideology of the *traditional present* is predominantly concerned with economic growth and progress, the working man clearly becomes more valuable for the modern age than the artist. In his appeal for *play*, then, Miller wants to counterbalance and reinstate art's role in man's life. More importantly, as art is supposed to free man to a qualitatively new way of being, *play* qua a part of art, can again be said to exhibit an ontological concern for Miller. Work, however, directly obstructs such endeavors as it is expected to prevail and undergird everything modern man does. We saw before that Miller considered most of the jobs he had had as "dull" as well as obstructive for his creative nature. A sociological commentator, Schumacher, has documented the negative side of modern labor practices, commenting that work by many was experienced then as

> . . . mechanical, artificial, divorced from nature, utilizing only the smallest part of man's potential capabilities; it sentences the great majority of workers to spending their working lives in a way which contains no worthy challenge, no stimulus to self perfection, no chance of development, no element of Beauty, Truth or Goodness . . .[68]

Miller's feelings seem to be similar. Perhaps what is most horrifying for him is that people were voluntarily agreeing to comply with their "mechanical" and "artificial" jobs because they thought it was somehow inevitable: that they needed to "make a living." Precisely this prevailing attitude of the *traditional present* of modern society, "whatever we do, we are supposed to do it for the sake of making a living,"[69] seemed to disgust Miller. Hannah Arendt has shed some light upon this age-specific phenomenon. In modern conditions, Arendt explains, artists came to be seen as the only exceptions to the former principle that most of human activities are to be done in order to sustain life or to make a living. Since all serious activities were associated with making a living, labor was defined as the opposite of play. "As a result," Arendt concludes, "all serious activities, irrespective of their fruits, are called labour, and every activity which is not necessary either for the life of the individual or for the life process of society is subsumed under playfulness."[70] This view that a "serious activity" means "making a living" was in nobody as deeply rooted as in that of Miller's mother who never seemed to understand his aspirations to become a writer, especially at the cost of constantly being broke. In a scene in *Nexus*, she speaks her mind:

> Times have changed. When I was a girl my father sat on the bench from morning till night. He earned the money. He didn't need inspiration . . . nor genius. He was too busy keeping us children alive and happy . . . But this fellow, and she nodded in my direction, this genius, as you call him, he's too lazy to take a job. He expects his wife to take care of him — and his other wife and child. If he earned anything from his writing I wouldn't mind. But to go on writing and never get anywhere, that I don't understand. (NEX, 92)

Since Miller was not making any money from his writing, he was automatically only *playing* according to his mother. He was not a "serious member" of society. That, however, was exactly what Miller wanted to be. What was essentially at stake here for him was the opposition of necessity and freedom, which work and play, respectively, represented to him. Miller was striving to show that his mother's (and modern society's) understanding that work was necessary is just another ideological expedient of the *progressive view.* Instead, it is precisely through artistic activities that one comes to see behind the trivialities and political agendas of the everyday and discover the true, ecstatic sense of oneself.

Free at last

In certain passages from Miller's *Plexus*, we can sense the magnitude of the degree of freedom which he feels when, with the support of his now second wife June Mansfield, he eventually came to quit his job at Western Union:

> Finally it came about that I remained away from the office three days handrunning. It was just a sufficient break to make it impossible for me to return. Three glorious days and nights, doing exactly what I pleased, sleeping long, enjoying every minute of the day, feeling immeasurably rich inside, losing all ambition to battle with the world, itching to begin my own private life, confident of the future, done with the past, how could I go back into harness? (PLEX, 44–5)

It was precisely then that Miller "made a vow never to work for anyone again." Firm in his decision Miller was destined to "become a writer or starve to death" (46). He was thoroughly delighted about having gained his freedom at last:

> It was over with. Like a surgical operation. It didn't seem possible to me that I had spent almost five years in the service of this heartless corporation. I understood how a soldier must feel on being mustered out of the army. Free! Free! Free! (*ibid*)

From then on, Miller and his wife June lived off whatever she earned as a taxi dancer and, more importantly, what she could sponge off from her numerous male admirers. June insisted that Miller should not think of getting a job and must solely dedicate himself to writing. The reality was that they were constantly broke and, with rent often overdue, they were forced to move around New York constantly. In *Tropic of Capricorn, Sexus, Plexus,* and *Nexus*, Miller documents their situation with brutal honesty without diminishing their willingness to utilize their friends and family, let alone strangers, whenever they could. As we saw from the reactions of Miller's mother, his family and friends did not readily accept his attitude that he, at the time only as a self-appointed writer, didn't need to work. They often drew Miller's attention to their disapproval via (sometimes funnily) sarcastic reactions. McGregor, for example, says in *Sexus* of Miller:

> He thinks we ought to support him, nurse him along until he writes his masterpiece. He never thinks that he might look for a job meanwhile. Oh no, he wouldn't soil his lily-white hands that way. He's an artist. Well, maybe he is, for all I know. But he's got to prove it first, am I right? Did anybody support me because I thought I was a lawyer? It's all right to have dreams — we all like dreams — but somebody has to pay the rent. (SEX, 112)

In a similar vein, Cronstadt, a character in *Black Spring*, makes fun of the romantic view of those writers who seem to idealistically think that their art is all they need to keep them alive:

> You people live in a fairyland. You think literature is everything. You eat literature. Now in this house we eat goose, for instance. (BS, 126)

In 1930, Miller moved to Paris with a little money June was able raise from yet another admirer. That money quickly spent, Miller had to take a job as a proofreader for the *Paris Tribune*. For a couple of months, Miller "enjoyed" again the awfulness of work. In a letter to his friend Emil Schnellock, Miller wrote of the experience:

> Although the job is very unimportant it seems that everything centers about it. It forms the very core of my life, shapes it, directs it, permeates all my activities, my thoughts, etc. . . . The very atmosphere of the place has gotten into my blood . . .. (LE, 81)

This again confirms the pervading and all-encompassing nature of the working world, which Miller feels, forces itself upon man once he becomes trapped in it. The gloomy essence of his proofreader days, no doubt reminiscent of his experiences in Western Union Telegraph, finds its expression by way of an image of a machine in *Tropic of Cancer.* In a certain scene, Miller and his friend Van Norden pick up a prostitute, but then they discover that the banal practicality of the transaction suddenly kills the "mood." "As I watch Van Norden tackle her," Miller writes, "it seems to me that I'm looking at a machine whose cogs have slipped. Left to themselves, they could go on this way forever, grinding and slipping, without ever anything happening. Until a hand shuts the motor off" (CAN, 148). Miller watches the couple "with a cool, scientific detachment" and finds that watching Van Norden having sex with the prostitute "is like watching one of those crazy machines which throw the newspaper out" (148). In this scene, Miller, in effect, precisely remarks upon a trend in the modern age, which, based on the automatic and mechanistic nature of work, manifests itself also in the casualness of sexual relationships. Solomon has perceptively described the phenomenon by commenting on the very same Miller scene:

> This is a vision of sexual activity as a reflection of the routinized drudgery of everyday life in modernity, of the elimination of physical desire, even when engaged in erotic pursuits, due to one's adaption to the regularized, monotonous rhythms of the work process. So powerful is the force of rationalization that leisurely fornication becomes the mirror image of rationalized labour, both boring, serialized operations devoid of human affect or purpose: automatized screwing.[71]

Even Van Norden, whom Miller describes as an incurable womanizer, in reality wants to step out of this life of "automatized screwing." He wants to step out of the metaphysics of the age that has turned him into a senseless fucking machine. He wants to leave the life he currently leads but paradoxically "completely surrender to a woman" who is supposed to, Miller has him say, "take me out of myself" (135). Clearly, Van Norden's initial "self" is meant by Miller to be a false notion: the self of the man of the *traditional present*, which he needs to surpass in order for him to encounter his authentic self and enter into more meaningful relationships.

In his early Paris years, Miller also worked out a cunning rotating scheme, whereby he would be invited to meals by his acquaintances on a daily basis. He describes this humorously in *Tropic of Cancer.* As Ferguson notes, Miller "spread the responsibility for his welfare over as many people as possible so that he would not wear out a welcome in one home."[72] An important turning point in Miller's relative financial security during the Paris years began when he met Anaïs Nin in 1931. After starting a love affair with Miller, Nin, similarly to June, thought that "Henry's value to her and to others must be preserved by shielding him from responsibility and by allowing him to play his way through life."[73] In addition to paying for his rent and food, Nin even put 5000 francs of her own money toward the publication of *Tropic of Cancer* in 1934.

Even after the Paris era, when Miller had become relatively well known as a writer, but not yet wealthy like he was to become in the mid-60s when the *Tropic* books were finally allowed to be sold in the United States, he had no problem with asking for financial support from his readers, publishing a note every once in a while in a newspaper and asking for help. In his essay "Artist and Public" (1947), Miller even defends a view according to which society should make a conscious decision to put in place an extensive funding system for artists. This further illustrates Miller's view that there is something essentially wrong with a society where artists are forced to beg, or do dull jobs, in order to survive. I will come back to these issues in Chapter 5.

Hopefully, the discussion above has managed to give at least some reason to question the common criticism that Miller didn't like work simply because he was lazy. However martyr-like or selfish his actions in regard to working may have been on an everyday level, his revolt in the deeper sense was decidedly directed against the purportedly false foundation of the modern age.

Toward the *inhuman* and the *full present*

In this and the previous chapter, we have been dealing with the clarification of Miller's philosophical notion of the *traditional present.* We have established that modern conceptions of time, history, technology, and work all belong there, and since these together form a kind of metaphysical *Enframing* of the modern age, this causes problems for those who are more artistically inclined.

In the following chapter, we will sharpen our focus on certain additional concepts which arise organically from Miller's texts and which continue to reveal Miller's philosophical journey from the *traditional* to the *full present.* Most importantly, the rebellious figure who resists the *traditional present,* and who thus far in our analysis has been mainly restricted to Miller himself, will be explained philosophically through his notion of the *inhuman.* This slight shift from Miller's persona to a more theoretical *inhuman artist*, while the two remain always connected, helps to differentiate Miller's wider intellectual ambitions that arise from his critique of the modern age. Indeed, through an analysis of the *inhuman* we will move toward Miller's ideas on art and *China*, which will disclose an exhilarating and meticulously envisioned world of the artist of the *full present.* This, together with what has been already said, is Miller's *inhuman philosophy.*

Notes

1 Georg Henrik von Wright, "The Myth of Progress," in *The Tree of Knowledge and Other Essays* (Leiden: E. J. Brill, 1993), 222.
2 Oswald Spengler, *Man and Technics: A Contribution to a Philosophy of Life* (London: G. Allen & Unwin, 1933), 3.
3 Ibid., 5.
4 Ibid.
5 Alan Bullock, "The Double Image," in *Modernism: 1890-1930,* eds. James Walter McFarlane and Malcolm Bradbury (London: Penguin, 1976), 59.
6 Ibid.
7 Lewis Mumford, *Technics and Civilization* (London: Routledge & Kegan Paul, 1934), 4.
8 Leigh Wilson, "Historical Context of Modernist Literature," in *The Modernism Handbook,* eds. Philip Tew and Alex Murray (London: Continuum, 2009), 40.
9 Sara Danius, "Technology," in *A Companion to Modernist Literature and Culture,* eds. David Bradshaw and Kevin J. H. Dettmar (Malden, MA: Blackwell Publishing, 2006), 69.
10 Stephen Kern, *The Culture of Time and Space 1880-1918* (Cambridge, MA: Harvard University Press, 1983), 6.
11 Cited in Danius, "Technology," 69.
12 Filippo Marinetti, "The Founding and Manifesto of Futurism," in *Futurism: An Anthology*, eds. Lawrence Rainey, Christine Poggi, and Laura Wittman (New Haven: Yale University Press, 2009), 51.
13 Michael Smith, "Recourse of Empire: Landscapes of Progress in Technological America," in *Does Technology Drive History? The Dilemma of Technological Determinism,* eds. Merritt Smith and Leo Marx (Cambridge, MA: The MIT Press, 1994), 38.
14 Raymond Williams, *Television: Technology and Cultural Form* (London: Routledge, 2003), 5.
15 Albert Borgmann, *Technology and the Character of Contemporary Life: A Philosophical Inquiry* (Chicago: University of Chicago Press, 1984), 35.

16 Smith, "Recourse of Empire," 38.
17 Joel Mokyr, "The Second Industrial Revolution 1870-1914," faculty.wcas. northwestern. edu/~jmokyr/castronovo.pdf, 1.
18 Robert Ferguson, *Henry Miller: A Life* (New York: Norton, 1991), 2.
19 The original quote is on page 503 in *The Decline of the West*. See the next entry.
20 Oswald Spengler, *The Decline of the West*, trans. Charles Francis Atkinson (New York: Knopf, 1926), 499.
21 Ibid., 504.
22 Stephen L. Starck, "Hacking Away with an Ax: Henry Miller and Modernity" (PhD diss. University of Oklahoma, 1999), 282.
23 Miller refers sympathetically to Conrad in several places. For example, CAN, 206 and BIML, 317.
24 Robert Short, "Dada and Surrealism," in *Modernism: 1890-1930*, eds. James Walter McFarlane and M. S Bradbury (Harmondsworth: Penguin, 1976), 293.
25 I am indebted to Dr Geoffrey Boucher for this observation.
26 Herbert Marcuse, *One Dimensional Man: Studies in the Ideology of Advanced Industrial Society* (Boston: Beacon Press, 1964), 3.
27 Herbert Marcuse, "Some Social Implications of Modern Technology," in *The Essential Frankfurt School Reader*, eds. Andrew Arato and Eike Gebhardt (New York: Urizen Books, 1978), 138.
28 Marcuse, *One Dimensional Man*, 10.
29 Ibid.
30 Ibid., 11.
31 Ibid., 12.
32 Hannah Arendt, *The Human Condition* (Chicago: University of Chicago Press, 1958), 133.
33 Max Horkheimer, *Eclipse of Reason* (New York: Continuum, 1985), 129–30.
34 By the modern age Heidegger does not mean so much a specific historical era, but a way of thinking which he similarly associates with Enlightenment thinkers such as Voltaire and nineteenth-century positivists. For him, however, the modern age and the downfall of Western metaphysics had already begun with Plato and Aristotle. The modern technological age, and its peculiar thinking, for Heidegger still persist; we are still very much overtaken by it.
35 Martin Heidegger, "The Age of The World Picture," in *The Question Concerning Technology, and Other Essays*, trans. William Lovitt (New York: Harper & Row, 1977a), 115.
36 Ibid., 116.
37 Ibid.
38 The only important feature which Heidegger does not reject in the *progressive view* is the importance of history. On the contrary, as opposed to Miller, Heidegger is a full-blown *historicist*.
39 Martin Heidegger, "The Question Concerning Technology," in *The Question Concerning Technology, and Other Essays*, trans. William Lovitt (New York: Harper & Row, 1977b), 27.
40 Martin Heidegger, *Being and Time*, trans. John Macquarrie and Edward Robinson (New York: Harper Perennial/Modern Thought, 2008), 31.
41 Michael Inwood, "Ontology and Fundamental Ontology," in *A Heidegger Dictionary* (Oxford, UK: Blackwell Publishing Ltd, 1999), 147.
42 Ibid.

43 Heidegger, *Being and Time*, 31.
44 According to Heidegger, we experience the ontological in moments of ecstasy, intense religious experience, and in encounters with art. In these moments, one no longer takes the things around oneself for granted but begins to see them as miraculous expressions of *being* itself. It is precisely this sense of wonder that Heidegger feels we have lost in modernity because we see all things around us either as products of humanity or as raw materials for future human production rather than as expressions of *being* itself.
45 Jonathan Derr, "The Poet's Place in Modernity: Heidegger, Eliot and Pound," (PhD diss. Chicago: Loyola University, 2002), 15.
46 Heidegger, "The Question Concerning Technology," 10.
47 Ibid., 10–11.
48 Ibid., 14.
49 Ibid.
50 Veronique M. Fóti has suggested an alternative translation of *Ge-stell* as "posure" in her *Heidegger and the Poets: Poiesis/Sophia/Techne* (New Jersey: Humanities Press International, 1992), xvii.
51 Heidegger, "The Question Concerning Technology," 20.
52 Ibid., 21.
53 Ibid., 27.
54 Ibid., 28.
55 Martin Heidegger, "The Turning," in *The Question Concerning Technology, and Other Essays*, trans. William Lovitt (New York: Harper & Row, 1977c), 37.
56 Michael E. Zimmerman, *Heidegger's Confrontation with Modernity: Technology, Politics, and Art* (Bloomington: Indiana University Press, 1990), xiii.
57 Leon Lewis, *Henry Miller: The Major Writings* (New York: Schocken, 1986), see Chronology.
58 Ferguson, *A Life*, 16.
59 Martin Heidegger, *What Is Called Thinking?* trans. J. Glenn Gray (New York: Harper & Row, 1968), 23.
60 Ibid., 25.
61 Ibid., 14–15.
62 Ibid., 15.
63 Ibid.
64 J. D Brown, *Henry Miller: Literature & Life* (New York: Ungar Pub. Co, 1986), 45.
65 Ferguson, *A Life*, 89.
66 Cited in Walter Benjamin, *Illuminations*, ed. Hannah Arendt (New York: Schocken Books, 1986), 171–2.
67 Heidegger, *What Is Called Thinking*, 25.
68 Cited in A. R. Gini and T. Sullivan, "Work: The Process and the Person," *Journal of Business Ethics* 6, 8, (1987): 649–55.
69 Hannah Arendt, *The Human Condition* (Chicago: University of Chicago Press, 1958), 127.
70 Ibid.
71 William Solomon, "Laughter and Depression: Henry Miller and the Emergence of the Technocarnivalesque," in *Literature, Amusement, and Technology in the Great Depression* (New York: Cambridge University Press, 2002), 80.
72 Ferguson, *A Life*, 180.
73 Ibid., 235.

4

Behold, I Teach You the *Inhuman*!: *Inhuman Artist, Übermensch, and China*

I want to declare that I am a traitor to the human race

—Henry Miller

In *Tropic of Cancer*, Miller introduces the term *inhuman*. As it unfolds, we see that his *inhuman* stands for a creative artist type. On the basis of this idiosyncrasy and the distinction between the *traditional* and *full present*, I argue in this chapter that the *inhuman* or *inhuman artist*, associated with Miller's *full present*, is meant to be read as the antithesis of the *human* of the *traditional present*. After presenting the intellectual evolution of the *inhuman* term, I introduce its essentially twofold nature, which Miller expressed in assigning a *Beelzebub* and a *St. Anthony* side to the *inhuman artist*. Then, due to the prevailing similarities, I analyze the affinity between Miller's *inhuman* and Nietzsche's *Übermensch*. It appears that while there are many overlapping aspects between Miller's and Nietzsche's concepts, the two thinkers seem to have been connected more by their respective criticism of the *human* and *last man* rather than by some clear-cut congruity between the philosophical tasks of the *inhuman* and *Übermensch*. In the second half of this chapter, I discuss the ultimate task of the *inhuman*: freeing oneself to *China*. *China* is another Miller-specific term, which designates the realm where the *inhuman artist* finally "creates a reality of his own" (CD, 4). I argue that *China* is an important further qualification of the meaning of the *full present* which replaces the Western *traditional present* for Miller. Under the *China* concept, Miller also importantly manifests his philosophy of art. While several biographers and critics have mentioned the *China* notion, its origin and relation to other tenets of Miller's theory have been only superficially investigated. I provide an extensive reading of the origin and symbolic significance of *China* and its prominence in Miller's thought. In the last section, I reflect most widely on Miller's approach to art and argue that his ideas on art can be seen as a species of ethics. I also demonstrate how the approach taken in this book helps to explain several issues regarding Miller's notion of art, which hitherto have been found problematic by several critics and commentators.

The appearance of the *inhuman*

The notion of the *inhuman*, in its Miller-specific meaning, finds its first "doctrinal" expression in *Tropic of Cancer*. He does not, however, use the term exclusively or consistently in its technical sense, even after coining it in the *Cancer*-book. Indeed, when Miller uses the word in several other books, or letters, it is mainly meant to be read in the usual orthodox way, as "not having the qualities proper or natural to a human being" or "brutal, cruel and barbarous."[1] But there are passages where Miller's use of the term defies standard usage.[2] The fact that most of his other published books were written after *Tropic of Cancer* adds to the possible ambiguity, leaving it up to the reader to determine whether a particular use of the *inhuman* represents its usual, or its specific, post *Tropic of Cancer*, sense. It has been suggested that Miller, becoming "fond of the flexibility of the word," may have even deliberately left it unclear.[3]

My research shows that chronologically the *inhuman* term can be traced back to a couple of letters between Anaïs Nin and Miller in 1932–33, which coincides with the period during which Miller was working on the *Tropic of Cancer*. Nin's usage of the term, it will become clear, is fairly similar to Miller's: that is, that *inhuman* is some esoteric notion of the artist. In the creative *inhuman life*, Nin writes, one is able to "surpass the petty human being" (LP, 102). Nin seems to take the *inhuman* to be some sort of transcendence from "just human life" since she also claims that in her writings she writes against herself, "against what you call my imperfections, against the woman, against my humanness . . ."(103). She elaborates that humanly she has "no strength" and that the only strength she has comes from her writing. She evidently opposes the creative *inhuman life* and the dull everyday *human life*. This meaning is noticeable also in another letter where she suggests that Henry and herself should go on a vacation to Spain because, she tries to convince Miller, "You need a human life . . . in between" (142). This plainly suggests that everyday human life is only something where the artist occasionally rests from his *inhuman* activities. It is hard to tell, however, whether Miller adopted the *inhuman* from Nin and turned it into his own concept.[4] Since Miller and Nin reviewed and commented on each other's works extensively in that period, it could have been equally possible that Nin picked the term up from Miller's draft of *Tropic of Cancer*. Their correspondence does not give enough information to decide this matter one way or the other.

Let us now proceed with Miller's own treatment of the *inhuman* as he voiced it in *Tropic of Cancer*. The explicit discussion of the *inhuman* term takes place on only two pages. There Miller writes:

> Once I thought that to be human was the highest aim a man could have, but I see now that it was meant to destroy me. Today I am proud to say that I am inhuman, that I belong not to men and governments, that I have nothing to do with the creaking machinery of humanity — I belong to earth! I say that lying on my pillow and I can feel the horns sprouting from my temples. I can see about me all those cracked forebears of mine dancing around the bed, consoling me, egging me on, lashing me with their serpent tongues, grinning and leering at me with

> their skulking skulls. I am inhuman! I say it with a mad, hallucinated grin, and I will keep on saying it though it rain crocodiles. (CAN, 255)

We can see that Miller defines *inhuman* here very similarly to Nin's usage before. The *inhuman* is meant to represent the exact opposite of the *human* of the day. The passage clearly signals the failed ideals of humanism in modernity. Moreover, we can now say that these false hopes in certain ideals that were taken to promote humanism or human life have resulted precisely in the "creaking machinery" of the *traditional present* as described in the previous chapters. *Human* for Miller, then, becomes an essentially derogatory notion. His *inhuman*, thus, is not somebody who lacks "qualities proper" of a *human* but is rather somebody who wishes to be "not human in nature or character." Miller's *inhuman* deliberately lacks the apparently negative qualities of the *human*. It is also distinct, in that, in terms of our ongoing categorization, *humans* for Miller seem to occupy the sphere of the *traditional present* and the *inhumans* that of the *full present*.

In a passage shortly following the one just cited, Miller qualifies the notion of the *inhuman* and reveals that he is, in effect, a certain type of artist:

> Side by side with the human race there runs another race of beings, the inhuman ones, the race of artists who, goaded by unknown impulses, take the lifeless mass of humanity and by the fever and ferment with which they imbue it turn this soggy dough into bread and the bread into wine and the wine into song. Out of the dead compost and the inert slag they breed a song that contaminates. I see this other race of individuals ransacking the universe, turning everything upside down, their feet always moving in blood and tears, their hands always empty, always clutching and grasping for the beyond, for the god out of reach: slaying everything within reach in order to quiet the monster that gnaws at their vitals. (255–6)

The *inhumans* Miller then equates with a breed of artists who, while living "side by side" with humans, pursue an entirely different life. The passage importantly also reveals the twofold nature of the *inhuman artist*. While on the one hand he is "turning upside down" the life of the *humans* in the *traditional present* and therefore moves "in blood and tears," on the other hand, the *inhuman* "sings" and "grasps for the beyond."[5] To anticipate, it is precisely in the latter that the *inhuman artist* manifests his striving toward the ahistorical *full present*, in which he leaves behind "men and governments" and "the lifeless mass of humanity." This essentially diverse and seemingly, perhaps, even contradictory nature of the *inhuman artist* Miller calls on more patently in the following passage:

> I know that I spring from the mythological founders of the race. The man who raises the holy bottle to his lips, the criminal who kneels in the marketplace, the innocent one who discovers that all corpses stink, the madman who dances with lightning in his hands, the friar who lifts skirts to pee over the world, the fanatic who ransacks libraries in order to find the Word—all these are fused in me, all

> these make my confusion, my ecstasy. If I am inhuman it is because my world has slopped over its human bounds, because to be human seems like a poor, sorry, miserable affair, limited by senses, restricted by moralities and codes, defined by platitudes and isms. (CAN, 257)

Miller affirms above that he is indeed a first member of the *inhuman* artist race which possesses the ecstatic, mixed qualities of a holy man, a criminal, a madman, a child, and a scholar and which is opposed to the "miserable humans" who have restricted their lives in the *traditional present* with "moralities and codes." Continuing with his elaboration of the *inhuman* in *Tropic of Cancer*, we find Miller emphasizing the uncompromising and exploding nature of the *inhuman* as artist:

> A man who belongs to this race must stand up on the high place with gibberish in his mouth and rip out his entrails. It is right and just, because he must! And anything that falls short of this frightening spectacle, anything less shuddering, less terrifying, less mad, less intoxicated, less contaminating, is not art. The rest is counterfeit. The rest is human. The rest belongs to life and lifelessness. (256)

Here, Miller, in addition to the condemnation of the typical ills of the *traditional present*, which the *inhuman artist* should remedy, also signals the need to question the art of the humans. Indeed, the "age demands violence" (19) for Miller at all levels, and perhaps especially so in literature. The "lifeless art" which *humans* produce may only be an "abortive explosion," but what is needed is a revolution. That is exactly why Miller on several occasions opposed his own writings to "literature": "literature" was something *humans* busied themselves with in the *traditional present*, whereas Miller himself, as the *inhuman artist*, was "singing" (10). In producing *Tropic of Cancer*, he "never wrote a novel" but revealed "a slice of life" (CHM, 146). The *inhuman art* for Miller, we can venture to say, "consists in going the full length. If you start with the drums you have to end with dynamite, or TNT," declares Miller (CAN, 83). These remarks reveal importantly that Miller's *inhuman*, with his art, rails not only against the modern concepts of history, technology, and morality but also perhaps even more so against his own "colleagues." Furthermore, as we will see later, *human* art as esthetics for Miller belongs to the same mistaken *metaphysical ground* of the modern age.

The *inhuman* revolution

It is worthwhile reflecting, based on what we know thus far, on what sort of "doctrine" Miller's *inhuman* revolution is exactly supposed to propound. As we saw above, Miller seems to look to the *inhuman* to provide a cure for pretty much everything that causes him unease both in his personal life and in society. Miller's main concern all along—which is already suggested by his very distinction between *traditional* and *full present*—seemed to be with art and artists. Indeed, Miller is convinced that "an age such as ours is the most difficult one of all for an artist. There is no place for him" (OLSE, 158). One of the major goals for Miller, then, seems to be protecting the noncommercial artist from the metaphysics of the *traditional present*. "To-day with the mass of mankind completely under the hypnotic sway of the scientific-minded, art is fighting for its life, for its very right to exist," Miller announces (166). While Miller's main unease may lie with art and the artists, it is evident that the role of the *inhuman artist* is not only to protect his own kind from the *humans* but, through his actions, also to influence the *traditional present*. Indeed, the *inhuman artist* is expected to "revive the primitive anarchic instincts which have been sacrificed for the illusion of living in comfort . . ." (156). The task of the *inhuman artist* then is very much also the enlightening of the *human*.

This *inhuman reform* for Miller, however, does not seem to mean a socio-political movement but is entirely directed through art and artistic practices, which for Miller are decidedly individual. In the Surrealists, we saw in Chapter 1, Miller had already witnessed the failure of conjoining art with political goals. The true artist, therefore, "knows that the transformation must proceed from within outward, not vice versa . . . It is a process of expropriating the world, of becoming God" (193). Thus, the *inhuman revolution* for Miller begins necessarily within a person, and once it has made its effect internally in many individuals, the grand outcome will appear also externally or socially. The *inhuman reform*, therefore, seems to be intersubjective rather than collective. The result of this metamorphosis, toward which the *inhuman* is directed, is then the *inhumanized human*, "the new man, the real human type who will put an end to the culture cycle of history," Miller explains (WOL, 142). This "real human" will then have defeated his false being and destroyed the *traditional present*.

The *inhuman* was born in *Tropic of Cancer* in the same way Miller himself was reborn in Paris by writing about it. This inward revolt had doubtlessly started in New York; he simply did not have a proper term to fully capture what he felt and thought before the early Paris-era. In Chapter 2, we saw how, by moving to Paris, Miller rid himself of history and time. The *inhuman* is the continuation and further qualification of the same process. In Paris, Brown confirms, he freed himself "of the false American selves he had acquired. He had to destroy himself to become his genuine self."[6] The *inhuman* then became the label for something that intimately characterized Miller's life up to this point. In the *inhuman*, he had found a term that expressed everything he denied but also everything he stood for. The *inhuman* adequately conveyed the dialectics of the *traditional* and *full present* for Miller. It also worked both as a personal narrative and as a vision for a modern artist.

More or less organically, then, the *inhuman* then grew out of Miller's life. In addition to quitting his job and moving to Paris, he later identified leaving his first wife, too, as one of the first *inhuman* acts. In his identification, we also find the closest usage of the term *inhuman* in its decidedly technical, *Tropic of Cancer*, sense because the passage appeared in Miller's *Tropic of Capricorn*, published 5 years after *Cancer*. There, Miller describes the situation of leaving his first wife, Beatrice, thus:

> I walked right out of the old life and into the new. There wasn't the slightest effort involved. I was thirty then. I had a wife and child and what is called a 'responsible' position. These are the facts and facts mean nothing. The truth is my desire was

> so great it became a reality. At such a moment what a man does is of no great importance, it's what he is that counts . . . I was pure inhuman, I was detached, I had wings. I was depossessed of the past and had no concern about the future. (CAP, 309)

The reader notices that Miller pinpointed the event as that of breaking free from the *traditional present* and *humans*. Since his wife and family life had become a part of what *traditional present* represented to Miller, they had to be abandoned. He had become *inhuman*. According to Leon Lewis, one of Miller's commentators, "his first marriage and the responsibilities it brought . . . changed Miller's outlook radically and permanently."[7] His leaving that life, it should be emphasized, changed Miller no less radically. Getting away from that old way of living marked the first steps toward the artistic life, the first steps toward becoming fully *inhuman* in Paris.

Less sympathetic readers may, of course, accuse Miller of simply attempting to justify, in retrospect, his marital failure with some "larger-than-life" theory. For Miller, however, this is precisely what is expected from "those who remain behind" (HAM, 172).

Two sides of the *inhuman artist*: *Beelzebub* and *St. Anthony*

By invoking the *inhuman*, Miller, in addition to his former *traditional* and *full present* dichotomy, has now importantly qualified the sense of the inhabitants of these respective realms. Establishing the *inhuman* enables Miller to distance himself and the artist kind firmly from the *traditional present* and the *humans*. The *inhuman* is now importantly defined against the *human* as the "other." We saw before that the *inhuman's* task is largely twofold: he should wreak havoc on the *traditional present* and also build up a new world—the *full present*. The *inhuman* then has both negative and positive qualities. The duality of this peculiar *essentia* of the *inhuman* is perhaps best captured when we find Miller writing that he has "St. Anthony on one side of me, Beelzebub on the other" (BS, 196). The symbiosis of these two apparently contradictory figures—a religious hermit[8] and "the prince of the devils," then, is how Miller seems to construe the antagonistic nature of the *inhuman artist*. He seems to refer to this opposing combination also in *Tropic of Capricorn* when he says that he is a "most suave silky, cunning animal — and at the same time what might be called a holy man" (CAP, 207). Through the *inhuman artist* as *Beelzebub*, it seems, Miller was able to bespeak the destructive component of his philosophy and to deal unceremoniously with all the superfluities of *human* life in the *traditional present*. It is Miller himself as the *inhuman* qua *Beelzebub* who walks in "blood and tears" and who seeks to bring the "life of illusion" to an end. In this regard, the *inhuman artist*, Miller seems to indicate, is "a maggot in the corpse which is the world" (HAM, 152). The *inhuman artist* as *Beelzebub* "feasts on the death" of the *traditional present*, as it were: "the more death there is the stronger I become," Miller writes (152). The *Beelzebub* side of the *inhuman artist* is then an authoritarian one; he gives orders and punishes. It is Miller's hands-on approach to the *human problem*.

Although the two are intimately related, the *St. Anthony* side of the *inhuman artist* Miller associates predominantly with the building up and nurturing of the *full present*. As such it is best to return to a discussion of this side of the *inhuman* alongside Miller's notion of art, which we will do in a little while.

Inhuman = Übermensch?

Miller's division between *inhuman/human* and his metaphorical use of *St. Anthony* and *Beelzebub* as representing the *inhuman's* tasks of "good and evil," which he must carry out, seem to warrant immediate comparisons between Miller's *inhuman artist* and Nietzsche's *overman* [*Übermensch*]. Indeed, given Miller's copious sympathies with Nietzsche's philosophy, it seems to be thoroughly justified to compare the two and see to what extent the *inhuman* can be shown to echo the *overman*'s qualities and agenda.

The *inhuman*, as we saw from the descriptions in the previous section, just like Nietzsche's *overman*, is qualitatively different from an ordinary man or *human*. To be *human* to Miller seemed "like a poor, sorry, miserable affair, limited by senses, restricted by moralities and codes, defined by platitudes and isms" (CAN, 257) against whom he, as the *inhuman*, set out to struggle. This deeply conflicting relationship between the *human* and the *inhuman* can be read as importantly similar to Nietzsche's distinction between the *last man* and the *overman*. Who is this *last man* whom Nietzsche regards as the antithesis of the *overman*? The *last man* represents a degraded, weak-willed individual of Western civilization, one who is tired of life, takes no risks, and seeks only comfort and security. For Nietzsche, the *last man* is the "most contemptible" because "the time is coming when man will no longer shoot the arrow of his longing beyond man, and the string of his bow will have forgotten how to whir!"[9] The *last man* is too complacent to follow his own desires; he is thoroughly determined by mainstream views of morality, tradition, and history. This results in a noncritical way of living, in being incapable of initiating something new and original. "Alas, the time is coming," Nietzsche writes, "when man will no longer give birth to a star. Alas, the time of the most despicable man is coming, he that is no longer able to despise himself. Behold, I show you the last man . . . The earth has become small, and on it hops the last man, who makes everything small," Nietzsche writes.[10]

As vehemently as Nietzsche condemns the *last man* in relation to the *overman* for doing little in order to follow his own course in life, Miller, as we have seen throughout the book, denounces *humans* for being lethargically passive about the horrifying developments of the modern age. Miller's *human*, who occupies the sphere of the *traditional present*, appears to be very similar to the *last man* in Nietzsche's sense. The *human* to Miller, as we've established, has done nothing to stand against the progressive sense of history, time, work, science, art, morality, and the like. Very likely influenced by Nietzsche, Miller, thus, exclaims that to "run with the herd, and die with the herd, is the natural animal instinct which man shares with other beasts" (OLSE, 156). It is rather obvious that by "man" he really means modern man as *human*. In this Miller seems to resemble the Nietzschean idea that "the unphilosophic and inartistic mass remain animalic."[11] One remains a part of the "herd" if one does not "become who one is": a famous slogan of Nietzsche.[12] The term "herd" also occurs extensively in Nietzsche's works; if in Miller it is meant to denote *human*, in Nietzsche, respectively, that of *last man*. The terms *human* and *last man*, therefore, bear remarkably similar referents in Miller's and Nietzsche's systems. They designate a similar kind of individual who ill-defines himself in the modern age.

Nietzsche's *overman*, in the contrast, and as the word suggests, is somebody who is capable of overcoming [*überwinden*] himself when he identifies his situation as that of conformity and "mediocricy and stagnation."[13] Man who overcomes himself becomes literally over (*über*) his false notion of himself as predefined by modern society: he becomes *overman* (*Übermensch*). *Overman* for Nietzsche designates "a type of supreme achievement" as opposed to "modern men, good men and Christians," he explains in *Ecce Homo*.[14] *Overman* creates his "own new table of values"; he is driven by a wish to become who he is: "the new, the unique, the incomparable."[15] *Overman*, thus, gives himself his own law; he creates himself anew. He is his "own judge and avenger of his own law."[16] *Overman* does not accept the world as it is offered to him. Every man, if he wishes to become *overman*, must create by himself "what you have hitherto called the world." The world, Nietzsche explains, "should be formed in your image by your reason, your will, and your love! And truly, it will be your happiness, you enlightened men!"[17] Through his Zarathustra, Nietzsche, thus, declares: "I teach you the overman. Man is something that shall be overcome. What have you done to overcome him?"[18] He explains further:

> All beings so far have created something beyond themselves; and do you want to be the ebb of this great flood and even go back to the beasts rather than overcome man? What is the ape to the man? A laughing stock or a painful embarrassment. And man shall be just that for the overman: a laughing stock or a painful embarrassment. You have made your way from worm to man, and much in you is still worm. Once you were apes, and even now, too, man is more ape than any ape.[19]

In a similar fashion, modern man, or the *human* of the *traditional present*, is an "embarrassing laughing stock" to Miller for his overall complacency with the status quo. What distinguishes the majority of men from the few, Miller writes, "is their inability to act according to their beliefs. The hero is he who raises himself above the crowd" (OLSE, 155–6). An allusion to the respective pairs of *inhuman/overman* ("the few") and *human/last man* ("the majority," "the crowd") can be read as expressed by Miller. Miller's worry in *Tropic of Capricorn* that—"man is not even able to destroy himself; he can only destroy others. I am disgusted" (CAP, 82)—also parallels Nietzsche's overall contempt toward the *last man*'s inability to overcome himself.

The similarities between *overman* and *inhuman* seem to go even further. Nietzsche has even used the word "inhuman" himself, which certainly may have played a role in Miller's choosing this particular word for his purposes. Talking about the asserted differences between humanity and nature, Nietzsche dismisses the need for such a division at all. Natural and human qualities should be construed as something "indivisibly grown together":

> Man, in his highest and most noble capacities, is wholly nature and embodies its uncanny dual character. Those of his abilities which are awesome and considered inhuman are perhaps the fertile soil out of which alone all humanity . . . can grow.[20]

Nietzsche sees the "inhuman abilities and qualities" then as natural, which in conjunction with his declaration that *overman* "shall be the meaning of the earth"[21] can be seen as having influenced Miller in his earlier exhortations that he as the *inhuman* "belongs to earth" and not to "men and governments" (CAN, 255). The *last man* and *human* wrongly oppose themselves to nature, whereas the *overman* and *inhuman* recognize themselves as springing from it. They gather power from it. In order to become Miller's *inhuman*, one has to be

> . . . wiped out as a human being in order to be born again as an individual. You have to be carbonized and mineralized in order to work upwards from the last common denominator of the self. You have to get beyond pity in order to feel from the very roots of your being. (CAP, 33)

In Nietzsche's *Zarathustra*, we find a remarkably similar suggestion:

> You must wish to consume yourself in your own flame: how could you wish to become new unless you had first become ashes.[22]

How similar this sounds to Miller's earlier visions of "dying" in America and "resurrecting" in Paris. By leaving his job and wife Miller "became ashes" in order to become a flame again in Paris. Miller as a *human* or *last man* overcame himself and resurrected as the *inhuman* by creating himself anew in *Tropic of Cancer*. Becoming the *inhuman* was such a tremendous struggle for Miller in his early days because it was hard to break with one's convictions and traditions. He admitted being taken in by so many aspects of civilized *human life* before becoming the *inhuman*. In *Tropic of Capricorn*, he writes:

> I realize quietly what a terribly civilized person I am — the need I have for people, conversation, books, theatre, music, cafes, drinks, and so forth. It's terrible to be civilized, because when you come to the end of the world you have nothing to support the terror of loneliness. To be civilized is to have complicated needs. And a man, when he is full blown, shouldn't need a thing. (CAP, 280)

Yet, the *inhuman artist* should resist these "pleasures" of the *traditional present* and "break the evil spell which has been put upon him":

> But when you drive a man almost crazy and when, to his own surprise perhaps, he finds that he still has some resistance, some powers of his own, then you are apt to find such a man acting very much like a primitive being. Such a man is apt not only to become stubborn and dogged, but superstitious, a believer in magic and a practicer of magic. Such a man is beyond religion — it is his religiousness he is suffering from. Such a man becomes a monomaniac, bent on doing one thing only and that is to break the evil spell which has been put upon him. Such a man is beyond throwing bombs, beyond revolt; he wants to stop reacting, whether inertly or ferociously. This man, of all men on earth, wants the act to be a manifestation of life. If, in the realization of his terrible need, he begins to act regressively, to become unsocial, to stammer and stutter, to prove so utterly unadapted as to be incapable of earning a living, know that this man has found his way back to the womb and source of life and that tomorrow, instead of the contemptible object of ridicule which you have made of him, he will stand forth as a man in his own right and all the powers of the world will be of no avail against him. (263)

The above description could be easily read as some sort of manifesto of the *inhuman artist*. It is a call for breaking loose from *humans* and the *traditional present*.

Miller's twofold division of *the inhuman artist* as both *Beelzebub* and *St. Anthony* can be seen as expressing some other important qualities of Nietzsche's *overman*. The *Beelzebub* side, which Miller associated with destruction, seems to echo *overman's* warrior side and the "evil" dimension. Modern man, according to Nietzsche, must "grow better and more evil"[23] because it is as much through evilness as it is through goodness toward himself as the *last man* that he can become the *overman*. *Overman's* evil side, just as Miller's *inhuman's Beelzebub* side, gathers together this enormous anger toward the moderation of the *last man/human*. *Overman*, thus, brings "lightning and madness" with which *last man* "should be cleansed."[24] It is part of *overman's* nature to be "warlike," it is "among his instincts" to attack, writes Nietzsche.[25] *Inhuman's St. Anthony* side resembles perhaps even more Nietzsche's Zarathustra than that of the *overman*. We will see later that the *St. Anthony* side of *inhuman* is construed very much as that of the old sage, or seer, who preaches overcoming of oneself not via violence and hatred but through kindness, and most idiosyncratically to Miller, through art.[26] I will then come back to these extrapolations with Nietzsche's *overman* and other related points as they arise in later sections.

Critics on Miller and *Übermensch*

Nietzsche's influence on Miller's work in general has been acknowledged by most critics and commentators. The relation of Miller's narrator to Nietzsche's *overman*, however, has not yet been established. William Gordon, for example, seems to neglect this connection, although he says in his *The Mind and Art of Henry Miller* (1967) that

> Nietzsche became for Miller, as for many others who dreamed of a better world, a prophet of the future direction of salvation for mankind. Salvation was to come through internal liberation. Restraints and institutions would fall, not by external attack, but from their own weight. Nietzsche and the anarchists whom he influenced looked forward to a new man who would be the complete antithesis of Western man as he had been up to then.[27]

While avoiding commitment to any explicit claims regarding kinship between Miller's "new man" and *overman*, Gordon's reading of Nietzsche's relation to Miller can be taken, by and large, to be supportive to our interpretation of Miller's *inhuman* as "the complete antithesis of Western man." In addition, Gordon says that "Nietzsche's response to the new biology, as we have seen, was to place the individual entirely on his own, to remove God from the cosmos, then to seek life enhancement in the individual himself."[28] This is similar to the approach taken in this book, which states that as a response to the progressive world view in its entirety, Miller's enlightened individual, the *inhuman*, builds his own realm in the *full present*. Thus, Gordon and I seem to largely agree on at least some important basic attunements which characterize Miller's *inhuman*.

Eric D. Lehman, another critic, decidedly rejects the idea that Miller's *inhuman* is a version of the *overman*. In a recent essay, he opines that "the presence of Nietzsche's philosophy in Miller's work remains undeniable" and that "Miller's philosophy mirrors many aspects of Nietzsche's mostly because they both believe that freedom comes with self-liberation. For both authors, this freedom leads to transcendence of the condition of human being."[29] Lehman, however, insists that "Miller's narrator certainly does not fit most of the qualities of Nietzsche's Übermensch" because (a) "the narrator never believes for one moment that he has evolved into some sort of higher being" and (b) "he does not make his own laws, or take control of anything at all."[30] It is to be noted, however, that Lehman wants to defend Lyotard's reading of the *inhuman* against Nietzsche's reading, and this means endorsing Lyotard's "reject[ion of] the Übermensch and the dialectic of the Apollonian and Dionysian."[31] As such, Lehman is inclined from the start to downplay similarities between Miller's *inhuman* and Nietzsche's *overman*.

As a response, it could be said that Lehman seems to have a somewhat restricted view since he bases his analysis only on a few of Miller's texts and therefore disregards whatever evidence can be found from numerous others. His first claim (a) seems to be, at best, only partially true. As we saw earlier in several places, Miller describes a true *artist/inhuman* life as *summum* (e.g. in BSOHB, 193) which can be taken to be short for *summum bonum*, meaning the highest good. The idea of a complete or highest good is defined as "what will wholly satisfy the complete need and destiny of humans."[32] Now when Miller places the *artist/inhuman* life on such an ultimate pedestal, surely he sees those practicing that kind of life as, to some extent, enlightened or higher beings. Indeed, Miller openly expresses this propensity, for example, when he has Ulric say in *Sexus* that he envies the true artist's life "because I know that he is infinitely richer than any other kind of human being" (SEX, 129). Additionally, Lehman's insistence on the present perfect tense, that Miller's narrator "has not evolved" into some higher being, is somewhat ill-positioned, for the good life that the *artist/inhuman* is pursuing is, in the course of Miller's writing, still very much a process of shifting from the *traditional present* to the *full present*. Ultimately, it is only in light of the evolution of Miller's concept of *China*[33] that the *inhuman artist* will make full sense. We then must come back to these questions in the sections where we elaborate these interrelated concepts.

To Lehman's second charge (b) that Miller's artist doesn't "take control of anything at all" one could respond that while Miller's *artist/inhuman* striving toward a better life may, perhaps, not be comparable to *overman*'s "will to power," it nonetheless exhibits an attitude of complete autonomy. The accusation that Miller's *inhuman* does not "take control" in some politically charged sense is to miss the point completely, because Miller's task is individual self-liberation through the artist's life and not world domination. In a way, Miller's *artist/inhuman* does indeed "take control" in the most profound sense—he takes a control of his life in the *full present*. The same could be said in response to Lehman's law requirement: Miller's *artist/inhuman* is the law unto himself.

Finally, the affinity between Miller's *inhuman* and Nietzsche's *overman*, as we have previously discussed, seems to be strong not because they can be shown to be particularly similar in every possible respect but rather because their similarity is manifested through the mutual contempt of "Western man." Thus far we can say rather confidently that the *inhuman* for Miller, as our reading has shown, stands to *human* as Nietzsche's *overman* stands to the *last man*. Further possible similarities and differences will be discussed ahead after we have introduced the other crucial aspects of Miller's *inhuman artist*.

Miller: A king of allusion or a poor man's Nietzsche?

Despite the historical evidence and Miller's rather unhidden sympathy to Nietzsche's philosophical legacy, virtually no research has been conducted on the (more or less) direct intertextual connections between the works of the two. In light of many possibly overlapping metaphors and other literary and philosophical peculiarities, it is still very much an open question as to what extent, if at all, Miller deliberately took to echo Nietzsche's ideas and to what end. A close reading of Miller's usage of possible Nietzschean symbols offers then a priceless source for anyone interested in allusion, reference, accidental association, and parallel. In view of the immense complexity of ongoing discussions regarding what in fact constitutes an allusion and in the face of arrays of proposed taxonomies of references, answering this question adequately would doubtlessly require at least a book on its own. Therefore, without even attempting to go too far down that road, I will discuss below only a few potent examples where one might be tempted to attribute an allusion or reference to Nietzsche on Miller's part. This will indubitably only demonstrate the difficulty of the task but hopefully it tells us something about the nature of the influence of Nietzsche on Miller.

According to William Irwin's definition, an allusion is "a reference that is indirect in the sense that it calls for associations that go beyond mere substitution of a referent. An author must intend this indirect reference, and it must be in principle possible that the intended audience could detect it."[34] The indirect nature is one of the attributes that is supposed to distinguish an allusion from reference, which is generally thought to be relatively unhidden. We are not going to be concerned with the differences between the two too much here. What comes up immediately with allusions, however, is the question of how we determine whether an author intended to allude or not. Can an author be unaware of an allusion that he or she is making?

While Irwin allows that "authors are not always conscious of their motivations for alluding or even that they are alluding,"[35] he denies that, in such a case, "the author did not intend the allusion."[36] Instead, he claims that what we have is "a situation in which the author intended an allusion but was nonetheless unaware that he or she was alluding. That is, we have an allusion, unconsciously intended."[37] How this "unconscious intending" can be made visible and accessible, Irwin does not give a straight answer.

In dealing with allusions there is also a danger that we confuse them with accidental associations, which are "intertextual connections readers make independent of authorial intent."[38] According to Irwin, these are not allusions; such associations "simply happen to be."[39] R. F. Thomas calls the same phenomenon "parallel" (as opposed to full-blown reference) and he describes it as "an accidental (and inevitable) linguistic confluence, occasioned by the fact that certain phrases, metaphors, and the like are merely a part of a society's or language's parlance and to that extent defeat any attempt to prove that a given poet's usage is motivated by any other instance of the phenomenon."[40] To our question, how are we to recognize genuine allusions or references, Thomas advices us to use our "judgment" and follow two criteria:

> . . . the model must be one with whom the poet is demonstrably familiar, and there must be a reason of some sort for the reference — that is, it must be susceptible of interpretation, or meaningful.[41]

While this general analysis barely scratches the surface of what is going on in allusion and reference, it will be enough for our purposes here. Let us now try to find passages and fragments whereupon we could genuinely say, taking account what was said above, that Miller indeed alludes to Nietzsche. Let us read, for example, a passage from Miller's *The Colossus of Maroussi*:

> Living openly one becomes a medium, transmitter; living thus, as a river, one experiences life to the full along with the current of life, and dies in order to live again as an ocean. (COM, 210)

At the outset, this fragment may not strike the reader as a particularly promising candidate for being an allusion. We might have a suspicion, however, that the way in which Miller uses the river and ocean theme above may allude to Nietzsche's metaphor that *overman* is the sea. The possible reason for this allusion on Miller's part could be, for example, emphasizing the similarity between his *inhuman* and Nietzsche's *overman*. The basis for this suggestion one could take to lie in the following passage from Nietzsche:

> Verily, a polluted stream is man. One must be a sea to be able to receive a polluted stream without becoming unclean. Behold, I teach you the overman; he is this sea; in him your great contempt can go under.[42]

On the basis these readings, one could be tempted to argue, perhaps, that if for Nietzsche *overman* is represented by a sea, then for Miller *inhuman* is associated with an ocean. They both then could be associated with large waters. While we seem to have satisfied Irwin's criteria of indirectedness and that of the "call for association," we still have to label the above identification as mere accidental association since we don't know anything about Miller's intent to allude to Nietzsche with the fragment above.

Let us try out another possible allusion candidate. We might suspect, as we did above, that Miller may be alluding to the *inhuman* and *overman* similarity through *overman*'s connection to earth. "The overman is," Nietzsche writes, "the meaning of the earth. Let your will say: the overman shall be the meaning of the earth! I beseech you, my brothers, remain faithful to the earth, and not believe those who speak to you of otherworldly hopes!"[43] Nietzsche, on the one hand, speaks here of idealists, most notably Plato, who sought the final truth outside the human realm. On the other hand, he also speaks against modern society as the habitat of the *last man*. Miller seems to exhibit similar attitudes, but he is somewhat more vague on this point than Nietzsche. He stated, as we remember, that he "belongs to earth" as opposed to "humanity" (CAN, 255). He also advocated for "earth time" (HAM, 93) as contrasted to conventional time. That seems to suggest that Miller opposes human *societal* life to more natural *earth* life. He, as an *inhuman*, would be happy to live on the earth but not in human-made society. The earth is then something over and above human societies. Using the word "earth" in this sense and context just randomly on Miller's part seems very unlikely. It looks as if Miller wants to suggest that, like Nietzsche's *overman*, his *inhuman*, too, is the "meaning of the earth." The earth then seems to be an important symbol for both Miller and Nietzsche. Again, since we don't know anything about Miller's intention to allude, there isn't much we can truthfully argue about the possible connection here. Miller's unusual usage of "earth" seems to suggest a stronger connection, however, than a mere accidental association or parallel. Having said that, if we follow Irwin's rules, the best we can do is to say that Miller may have "unconsciously intended" this earth allusion.

Another conceivably Nietzschean motif that keeps reappearing is Miller's ample use of the image of mountains as a symbol of ultimate solitude, where his *inhuman* would find his final peace. Nietzsche's *Thus Spoke Zarathustra* begins with Zarathustra—after having "enjoyed his spirit and his solitude" in the mountains for 10 years—descending to men to spread his wisdom, to teach them *overman*.[44] Since he mainly experiences that people do not understand him (although he manages to find a few disciples), he goes back to the mountains:

> Then Zarathustra returned to the mountains and to the solitude of his cave and withdrew from men, waiting like a sower who has scattered his seed . . ..[45]

Miller seems to view himself and his *inhuman* in quite a similar way. In *Black Spring*, he writes: "Today yet a little while Progress and Invention keep me company as I march toward the mountain top. Tomorrow every world city will fall. Tomorrow every civilized being on earth will die of poison and steel" (BS, 240). Given what we already know about Miller, it seems that he is describing here his well-known contempt for the progressive *traditional present* to which he opposes the "mountain top" where he would withdraw from the atrocities of present-day man. In anticipation, we could even speculate that "the mountain top" stands metaphorically for Miller's *full present*. This suggestion becomes even more likely when we find Miller, in the midst of everyday city life, dream of going to a "high hill":

> Every evening, when I take the garbage down, I think of myself standing on a high hill in resplendent whiteness. It is no sacred heart that inspires me, no Christ I am thinking of. Something better than Christ, something bigger than a heart, something beyond God Almighty I think of — MYSELF. I am a man. That seems to me sufficient. (24)

The Zarathustrian mountain motif is expressed, perhaps, with the strongest Nietzschean undertones on the last pages of *Black Spring*, where Miller describes his leaving the society of *humans* much in the same vein as Nietzsche's Zarathustra left the *last men*:

> Walking toward the mountain top I study the rigid outlines of your buildings which tomorrow will crumple and collapse in smoke. I study your peace programs which will end in a hail of bullets. I study your glittering shop windows crammed with inventions for which tomorrow there will be no use. I study your worn faces hacked with toil, your broken arches, your fallen stomachs. I study you individually and in the swarm — and how you stink, all of you! (242)

Miller ends the book very much in the emotional key of Nietzsche's Zarathustra, once again using the mountain symbol:

> And now I take leave of you and your holy citadel. I go now to sit on the mountain top, to wait another ten thousand years while you struggle up toward the light . . . Tomorrow you may bring about the destruction of your world. Tomorrow you may sing in Paradise above the smoking ruins of your world-cities. But tonight I would like to think of one man, a lone individual, a man without name or country, a man whom I respect because he has absolutely nothing in common with you — MYSELF. Tonight I shall meditate upon that which I am. (242–3)

To end this paragraph with the well-known Zarathustrian paraphrase, "Thus spoke the Inhuman," would have been, stylistically, absolutely perfect mimicking of Nietzsche's Zarathustra on Miller's part.

There seems to be little room for doubt that Miller, consciously or not, alludes to Nietzsche above. While we still do not know anything about Miller's possible intention to allude, and we probably never will, the presented fragments seem too similar to allow mere accidental association or a parallel. Indeed, as these fragments demonstrate, there is more than just intention involved in alluding. In fact, this is where the internalist approach to allusion seems to do have an upper hand. The internalists claim that one text alludes to another when "the internal properties of one text resemble and call to mind the internal properties of an earlier text."[46] The last two Miller fragments do just that; they quite unmistakably "call to mind" the literary style of Nietzsche's Zarathustra. Thus, we could say, Nietzsche's "mountain theme" emerges in Miller as the combination of philosophical resemblance and stylistical allusion.

All of these above examples suggest that even without being able to determine Miller's intention to allude, there are passages in Miller that seem to suggest possible allusions to Nietzsche's works. Interestingly, Miller himself seemed to be quite casual about these matters. There is, for example, a very interesting passage in Miller's *Sexus* where he explicitly mentions Nietzsche:

> The creative life! Ascension. Passing beyond oneself. Rocketing out into the blue, grasping at flying ladders, mounting, soaring, lifting the world up by the scalp, rousing the angels from their ethereal lairs, drowning in stellar depths, clinging to the tails of comets. Nietzsche had written of it ecstatically — and then swooned forward into the mirror to die in root and flower. 'Stairs and contradictory stairs,' he wrote, and then suddenly there was no longer any bottom; the mind like a splintered diamond, was pulverized by the hammer blows of truth. (SEX, 191)

From the outset it seems that what we have here is a direct reference to Nietzsche which is supported by a partial quotation. On a closer examination, however, it appears not to be the case at all. It turns out that the phrase "stairs and contradictory stairs" does not belong to Nietzsche at all, and the rest of the reference to Nietzsche is generic, and not direct.[47] At best, then, we have here a casual reference, which, according to Thomas's typology, is "the use of language which recalls a specific antecedent, but only in a general sense, where the existence of that antecedent is only minimally important to the new context, where, one could say, an atmosphere, but little more, is invoked."[48] That seems to be exactly what is happening with the above fragment. While Miller presents it as a direct reference, it turns out to be only a casual one. A casual reference is still a reference, however, and in this particular case, while it fails to refer to the particular "antecedent" in Nietzsche's works, it nonetheless succeeds in echoing the "atmosphere" of the ecstatical nature of creative life, which Miller precisely wanted to convey.

One who wished to make Miller's case stronger could, of course, venture further and see if he or she could find the passages in Nietzsche that Miller casually referred to but failed to provide solid proof for. Miller's line above "passing beyond oneself," for example, could easily have been influenced by Zarathustra's words "I love him who wants to create over and beyond himself and thus perishes,"[49] where we find almost the identical thought: that is, the creative life means overcoming oneself. In Nietzsche's system, *last man* should overcome himself in order to become an *overman* and, respectively, in Miller's system, *human* should overcome or "pass beyond" himself in order to become *artist/inhuman*. Miller's next sentence, where he expresses the joys of artistic or creative life and compares it to climbing to the sky, bears a similar degree of exaltation to Nietzsche's *Before Sunrise* section in *Thus Spoke Zarathustra* where he says: "O heaven above me, pure and deep! You abyss of light! Seeing you, I tremble with godlike desires. To throw myself into your height, that is my depth. To hide in your purity, that is my innocence."[50] Additionally, Miller's "ascension" in the above passage could also have its roots in the following lines of the same section of *Zarathustra* where he goes on to describe his relationship with heaven: "Together we have learned everything; together we have learned to ascend over ourselves to ourselves and to smile cloudlessly — to smile down cloudlessly from bright eyes and from a vast distance when constraint and contrivance and guilt steam beneath us like rain."[51] The "ascending over ourselves to ourselves" will later reappear in Miller as something the *Artist* (with a capital "a") needs to do.

As we can see, with the help of research, Miller's case can be considerably improved and thus his engagements with Nietzsche also substantiated better. In summary, while studying allusion, reference, accidental associations etc. regarding Miller and Nietzsche opens up a whole new avenue of possible scholarship, it never seems to be possible to rely on these things alone in determining the matter of influence. We saw that, following the intention rule, Miller can never be shown to properly allude even if internally the evidence seems compelling. Likewise, we also saw that even in case of a casual reference, when more evidence is provided, the reference may turn out not to be as casual anymore. Therefore, we can now devote our attention to more properly philosophical investigations of Miller's work.

From art to *China: Inhuman* revolution vol. 2

We have thus far discussed the nature of Miller's *inhuman artist* insofar as he "implicitly sets himself to overthrow existing values" (CAN, 254). Precisely this "overthrowing" or evil *Beelzebub* side of the *inhuman artist* resembles, as we saw, Nietzsche's *Übermensch* the most in declaring univocal war to all that is *human*. While it genuinely describes one dimension of the *inhuman*, it's not all that he does or is. Indeed, in this section, we are going to focus on the "positive program" or *St. Anthony* side of the *inhuman*. This is where Miller's *inhuman artist* is going to "make of the chaos about him an order which is his own . . ." (*ibid*). In a way, it can be viewed as the final stage of Miller's *inhuman revolution*. While in the first stage we saw Miller fighting vehemently against the *traditional present*, in the second stage he starts to build the *full present*.

Since the *inhuman* has been clearly from the beginning meant to be an artist in Miller's system, it is only natural to ask of the role that art plays in the life of the *inhuman*. What is the art of the *inhuman* and what it is supposed to do to him?

In what follows, I argue that, effectively, in the "positive program" of the *inhuman artist*, Miller lays out an ethical conception of art. By invoking *China* as the ultimate realm to which art or artistic activities should lead, Miller assigns an intermediary or transitional role to art. Indeed, it is art whereby a true artist moves from the *traditional present* into *China* or the *full present*. After having "domesticated"[52] the artist, however, art's role in the sense of one's active engagement in producing works of art becomes secondary to life. In this Miller rejects the treatment of art as esthetics, which belongs to the *traditional present* as a part of the *metaphysical ground* of the age.

A call for *inhuman art*

As the reader will have noticed, Miller construes the *inhuman artist* as somebody who should "revive the primitive anarchic instincts of man." The artist's "song" we saw above, was meant to "contaminate." From these brief remarks alone we get a sense that an esthetic experience is not something the *inhuman artist* is overly concerned with. On the contrary, it seems that what the *inhuman artist* does or feels, in Miller's view, bears some important relation to the truth about man's condition.

> I do know . . . why the artist's life is a preparation for the good life. The reason, in a word, is this: the good life is the holy life. (Wholly living, wholly dying.) It is the kind of life in which you do your utmost every day, not for art, not for country, not for family, not for yourself even, but because it's the only thing to do. Life is being, which includes doing and not doing. Art is making. To be a poet of life, though artists seldom realize it, it is the *summum*. (BSOHB, 193)

Since the artist's concern in the passage above appears to be about living a good and satisfying life, and not esthetic pleasure, Miller's conception of art can be seen as a species of ethical thinking. Indeed, he can be interpreted as paving the way toward the ethos of the *inhuman artist* by summarizing the current situation: not only has the modern day lost its vital relationship with arts but also have the artists themselves lost something essential too:

> . . . today we realize that the artist has failed to live up to his trust. He has betrayed the powers that be. And in return he has been stripped from his authority, his privileges. His magic no longer works — not because magic has been disproved — because in him magic is dead . . . What he says is incomprehensible. Perhaps it was always incomprehensible, but in the past this very fact of non-comprehension worked a spell upon the listener. The audience did not ask to understand — men begged to be visited by the demon and the exorcized. (HAM, 69)

Miller is evidently concerned about art and artists in contemporary society. He, it should be remembered, was a rebel among modern writers. While he was definitely pro art, he certainly did not support just any kind of art. As from above, Miller held that some of the art of his day no longer brought release and was in some cases "incomprehensible." Proper art, it seems, should be able to produce "magic" and spell, according to Miller. Similarly to Heidegger, art (or at least much of it), according to Miller, had been reduced to triviality in the modern age. It no longer had the qualities it once had. The *inhuman artist*'s task, so it seems, is then not only to revive the "magical powers" of art and then reintroduce them to the public. Miller also, and equally importantly, calls for a critical inspection within artists' communities themselves: what is the true meaning and value of the art that artists produce today? That by itself seems to reveal the extent of the ethical concern about art's status on Miller's part. Essentially, then, there are two major concerns at stake here: art's relation to man (and public) and a kind of meta-question concerning the nature of artistic practice as such. The questions are generally interwoven, but the former usually takes precedence, at least in terms of urgency and volume in Miller's discussions.

Miller's 1941 essay "Creative Death" importantly adds to the above call for rejuvenating the magical qualities of art. In this text, he also makes direct references to Nietzsche's Dionysian properties of art, which have been described as "ecstatic, feral, iconoclastic, unruly and powerfully connected with our instinctual depths."[53] Along with the Dionysian, Nietzsche also assigns an Apollonian component to art, which he associated with a "dreamlike mental state, where visions of more perfect, soothing, transcendent and beautiful conditions appear."[54] The fusion of the characteristics of these two Greek gods then is what the early Nietzsche saw manifest itself in art.[55] The Dionysian aspect of art and artist, doubtlessly, strongly resembles Miller's *Beelzebub* side of the *inhuman artist* as described before. In his "Creative Death" essay, Miller picks up particularly the Dionysian quality of art as something that needs to be reintroduced in the modern age:

> After the Olympian Goethe the Dionysian race of artists sets in, the men of the 'tragic age' which Nietzsche prophesied and of which he himself was a superb example . . . Once again man must re-enact the mystery of the god, the god whose fertilizing death is to redeem and to purify man from guilt and sin, to free him from the wheel of birth and becoming. (CD, 17)

It is rather evident that Miller thinks that bringing back the Dionysian qualities to the present condition of art of his day seems to be absolutely necessary in order to save it from stagnation and degeneration. Continuing with the citation of one of Nietzsche's most popular slogans, Miller writes:

> It is at this point in the cultural cycle of history that the 'transvaluation of all values' must set in. It is the reversal of the spiritual values, of a whole complex of reigning ideological values . . . The Dionysian art of ecstasies now reasserts its claims . . . Through madness and ecstasy the mystery of the god is enacted and the drunken revellers acquire the will to die —to die creatively. (17)

Here, Miller's agenda seems to be so clearly spelled out. It is reformed, Dionysian-like "mad" art, which still has a chance to inflame the degenerated humans of the *traditional present*, and by becoming "drunk" on this wonderful art, make them want to overcome the "reigning ideological values" and themselves as carriers of them. The new art must make *humans* as *last men* want to "die creatively"; that is, only through this "artistic death" can they hope to resurrect as creators, as *inhumans*. Since neither the seemingly mad qualities of art nor the *Beelzebub* side of the *inhuman artist* exhaust the full potential of the *inhuman artist* for Miller, we must investigate further and see where it leads us.

Setting the belligerent *Beelzebub*/Dionysian dimension of the *inhuman* aside for the moment, what is it that artists—now in the more positive *St. Anthony* sense —have to tell, or do, to people, according to Miller? The *inhuman artist*, presumably by way of his craft, or whatever else he does, "sings about life — how things seem to him, or are" (HAM, 62). He does not seem to force anybody to listen, but rather presents a choice to do so. The artist, according to Miller, does not deliberate, defend, or reason, he simply is. The *inhuman artist* is a man acting upon truth. "Men writing about truth," Miller explains, "are usually diseased; men talking about truth are likewise usually diseased. But men acting upon truth are usually sound and healthy. These men do very little talking or writing—they sing" (118). It is through his way of life, then, as much as it is through his particular works of art, that the *inhuman* introduces another and presumably better life to *humans*. In fact, Miller hardly ever goes into details as to what particular kind of art the *inhuman artist* creates or should create: rather, it is the artistic sense of life itself that Miller is concerned with. It is their "singing" of "truth" in which artists reveal the life of their "very-much-aliveness," Miller says. The artist's "singing" voice of "truth" is supposed to be "heard above the wrack of doom — joyous and prophetic" (70).

Miller's *St. Anthony* side of the *inhuman artist* may seem quite favorable to Nietzsche's Apollonian qualities of "delight, wisdom, and beauty of 'illusion.'"[56] Yet, there are considerations which militate against self-explanatory or immediate likening of Miller's *inhuman artist* with his *Beelzebub* and *St. Anthony* side to Nietzsche's concept of Dionysian ecstatic and Apollonian dream artist in one. A major complication seems to rise from the fact that despite the strong similarities between Miller and Nietzsche, the solution resulting from art for Nietzsche is essentially "the early Greek" solution. To Nietzsche, it has been noted, the Greeks were "the most vigorous, creative, life-affirming people the world has known."[57] Precisely for this reason Nietzsche turned to Greek culture to find an antidote to the "terrors and horrors" of modern man. From Miller's several writings, however, we find out that art and the artist's life are meant to bring forth a condition or state that he labels *China*. How can these culturally and metaphysically entirely different loci—Nietzsche's Greece and Miller's *China*—represent essentially the same view of art? Is it here where Miller and Nietzsche truly part ways? In order to answer these questions, we must first investigate what exactly Miller means to achieve by his *China* concept.

China disclosed

In his *Hamlet letters*, Miller explains that

> An artist like myself, consequently, a late-city-product, so to speak, twin brother to Grosz, Whitman, Van Gogh, Strindberg, the brothers Bosch, all the

> demonologists, finds himself under a supreme obligation, entrusted with a sacred mission. He must escape this death which is engulfing the world in order to protect and preserve his magic role. He flees to imaginary China (hasn't the artist always done this?). (HAM, 70)

China, evidently, is not so much a physical place, as it is a condition of being.[58]

First of all, we might want to ask why Miller chose this term. What is *China* supposed to mean? Leon Lewis has suggested that "China was as good a name as any for a 'place' where a certain spirituality replaced the greed and lust of the West."[59] Robert Ferguson importantly qualifies this by saying that *China* was "a personal shorthand term he [Miller] used to denote the admiration and sympathy he felt for the Taoist philosophy of Lao-Tzu and Chuang Tzu."[60] William Gordon calls *China* a "symbolic realm"[61] and J. D. Brown "a realm of pure being."[62] While they all are right in some respects, I think we have the means to unpack this idiosyncratic concept in even more detail. In the following paragraphs, we will see that the origin and nature of Miller's *China* is, perhaps, best disclosed by a close reading of his *Hamlet letters* and a section of *Black Spring*.

There are several hints and suggestions that may explain the origin and further development of the *China* concept in Miller. The earliest one, perhaps, is a picture depicting a Chinaman walking across Brooklyn Bridge in the rain that, according to Ferguson, Miller had seen in a church hall in the 1890s. "It was an image that seemed shrouded in fascinating and slightly frightening mystery," Ferguson writes.[63] As the Chinese, according him, were "most feared of all immigrants into America," they were "frightening figures" to the "respectable whites and superstitious blacks." As such they apparently appealed to "little Henry Miller" because it would make "his parents shudder."[64] Ferguson also suggests that the aura in the Chinese laundry, where young Miller would go with his father, "filled him with a frightened wonder."[65] Coming closer to Miller's adult life, Ferguson suggests that by 1933 Miller had revisited and penetrated many of his early Chinese mysteries and had, in fact, become "a confirmed sinophile with an indiscriminate fondness for everything oriental."[66] The evidence of Miller's fondness for Lao-Tzu and *Tao Tĭ Ching* is indeed no surprise to a Miller reader.

More concrete evidence, however, of the background of Miller's fascination with *China* in relation to the context we are interested in here—that is, art and the artist's life—we discover in Miller's correspondence with Michael Fraenkel. In the long letter from 19 November 1935, we find Miller quoting extensively on the topic of Chinese life and art without any reference to the source other than the letters *Z* and *Y*. There he says, for example,

> The quality of play in the Chinese character and civilization has impressed alike those who have seen China from afar and by actual contact . . . *Y* remarks how this simple childlike, yet profound attitude towards life results in a liberation of the impulses to play and enjoyment which 'makes Chinese life unbelievably restful and delightful after the solemn cruelties of the West . . .' (HAM, 35).

My research reveals that the passage here quoted is in fact taken from Havelock Ellis's book *The Dance of Life* (1923).[67] *Z* in Miller's letter, it is now evident, stands for Ellis and *Y* for Bertrand Russell whom Ellis, in turn, quotes in this passage. There Ellis also says (and Miller quotes) the following:

> We may understand now how it is that in China, and China alone among the great surviving civilizations, we find that art animates the whole of life, even its morality. This universal presence of art, manifested in the smallest utensil, the humblest stalls, the notices on the shops, the handwriting, the rhythm of movement, always regular and measured, as though to the time of unheard music, announces a civilization which is complete in itself, elaborated in the smallest detail, penetrated by one spirit, which no interruption ever breaks, a harmony which becomes at length a hallucionary and overwhelming obsession. For them the art of life is one, as this world and the other are. Their aim is to make the Kingdom of Heaven here and now.[68]

The sentence beginning "this universal presence . . ." actually belongs to Émile Hovelaque, "an acute yet discriminating observer," according to Ellis. The name, similarly to Ellis's, has been altogether omitted from Miller's letter. Also the sentence "for them the art . . ." Ellis says to belong to "another writer" but he doesn't specify.

What is Miller's purpose in citing those passages? Earlier in the letter Miller touches upon the subject of creativity and fear in modern times. Indeed, precisely these references seem to reveal something about the nature of the problems that the *China* passages are meant to address. Miller writes:

> There are two kinds of loneliness today: the loneliness of the herd which feels that it is being driven over the precipice and the loneliness of the creative individual, now more acute than ever since there is no recoil in the collectivity. The modern neurosis, clearly revealed in the work of the modern artist, expresses itself through fear of life. Fear is a constant in the human equation—there is no dispossessing it. But the old irrational phenomena of fear, linked up with the magic of primitive man, gave way, through building up of Cultures, to a tangible talkable fear of death. The creative process, however, stands beyond, outside both the fear of death and the fear of life. (For the fear of life, which we have today, is but the admission of the breakdown of the cultural form.) The question which concerns us vitally is not the death of art, but the drying up of the creative faculty. (HAM, 30)

As we can see, Miller believes that the rejuvenation of creative powers, which are largely "dried up," is capable of counteracting the fear of life in modern times (which has replaced the equally undesirable fear of death of more religious days). As the letter proceeds, we find out that Miller and Fraenkel had discussed "the problem of purpose and method of art" in person the previous night (they lived in the same building) and that they ended "on the discord of integrity and honesty" (31) regarding the subject matter. Miller's purpose, it seems, is to continue discussing the topic in the letter and explain his view to Fraenkel in more detail. In order to do that, however, Miller wants to make "a grand detour" because, he says, "I have kept among my files certain quotations from other writers which have a tremendous significance for me, more particularly because the expression of these various ideas seems to me so exact — not 'true' or 'false,' I would have you understand, but 'exact'" (31). A little further Miller importantly divulges his true intentions regarding the *China* passages:

> I am coming eventually to the Chinese conception of art and life with which I am in complete sympathy and which, I believe, for the moment marks the quality of difference in our approach to life. (32)

We are able to understand now that Ellis's *China* passages, which Miller quoted earlier, were meant to communicate Miller's growing conviction that, perhaps, precisely in the Chinese concept of art and life rests an antidote to the "crisis of creativity" in modernity. This attitude, which Miller defended in several further letters to Fraenkel, reaches its most powerful surrealistic literary manifestation in the *Walking up and Down in China* section in Miller's *Black Spring*—the book that he was working on at the time of the correspondence. In fact, what we get from the letters to Fraenkel and fragments of some other texts are Miller's discussions of the development of the theory of *China*. The *Black Spring* section, by contrast, seems to be Miller's description of the actual artistic experience of *China*. The two approaches, naturally, importantly complement each other. Before discussing these issues further, it is manifest that in regard to the origin of the idea of *China* as a concept relating to art and living, Miller adopted it from Havelock Ellis and not from somebody else.

Ellis's thesis in the book from which Miller quotes seems to have been directed to the question "is life essentially an art?" Through examining (among other phenomena) Chinese culture, Ellis answers affirmatively: "life may be regarded as art."[69] These ideas evidently stayed with Miller and developed into a transcendental concept which seemed to offer the possibility of finally overcoming his most vexing anxieties: the crisis of man, art, and the modern age, which in the grand scheme of things now appeared to be, if not altogether the same, then, at least, intimately connected. The remedy to these things Miller now saw incisively as rising from his growing sense of art as a means or path to *China*.

Let's finish unpacking the remainder of the important letter. Miller seems to be impressed with the longevity and sustainability of Chinese culture since he quotes from Ellis:

> It's obvious that a natural temperament in which the art impulse is so all-embracing, and the aesthetic sensibility so acute, might well be perilous instability. We could scarcely be surprised if, like that surpassing episode in Egyptian history of which Akhenaton was the leader and Tel-el-Amarna the tomb, it had only endured for a moment. Yet Chinese civilization, which has throughout shown the dominating power of this sensitive temperament, has lasted longer than

> any other. The reason is that the very excesses of their temperament forced the Chinese to fortify themselves against its perils. The Great Wall, built more than 2,000 years ago, and still today the most impressive work of man on earth, is typical of this attitude of the Chinese. They have exercised a stupendous energy in fortifying themselves against the natural enemies of their own temperament . . . Alike in its large outlines and its small details, Chinese life is always the art of balancing an aesthetic temperament and guarding against its excesses . . . Thus, during its extremely long history . . . Chinese civilization has borne witness to the great fact that all human life is art.[70]

The age and sustainability of Chinese culture were no doubt seen both by Ellis and by Miller as a great argument for its supremacy over the "decaying" modern Western culture. While Ellis's understanding of the need for the Great Wall as a protection against "the excess of their own artistic nature," and not, primarily, against various nomadic groups such as the Xiongnu, and later Mongols and Turks, may seem odd and even naïve, it offered to Miller a perfect initial image of a closed and artistically driven realm, totally cut off and impervious to its surroundings. In Ellis's enthralling descriptions of *China*, Miller saw a superb physical realization of the "Kingdom of Heaven here and now": the predecessor and ideal for his transcendental *full present*.

Miller ends the letter with a suggestion that "the French (and not the Germans, as Nietzsche so unjustly said) are the Chinese of Europe" (HAM, 36). Since for Miller personally Paris had offered a new beginning, he believed that, at least for the moment, Paris and France captured something of the spirit of Ellis's *China*. "For when the day comes," Miller continues, "on which this European civilization falls apart . . . it will be the Mediterranean spirit which will survive in the new Culture . . . because there is in the Mediterranean attitude towards life that art germ which has been strangled and well-nigh obliterated by the morose, northern mind" (*ibid*).

Again, it is essentially art or artistic attunement that, according to Miller, will be able to survive the doom of the world.

While Miller, writing that letter, presumably did not yet have the full grasp of the eminence of the *China* concept as it would evolve later, the germ of these important ideas was now irreversibly planted. First of all, he seems to have discovered that there was indeed a place and nation in the world that, contrary to the *traditional present* qua corrupted Western culture, still had their "creative powers." Moreover, these "powers" had enabled the Chinese to enjoy a joyous and healthy life far longer than any other civilization did. It also must have appealed to Miller that their success in preserving their lifestyle derived not from association with neighboring countries, least of all the Western world, but, quite literally, by bricking themselves into their own country. It is precisely this distinction between encircled China and the rest of the world in which *full* and *traditional present* make their first adumbrative appearance. Indeed, in a passage from *The World of Lawrence*, another book that at least in part coincides with the period of the Fraenkel letters, Miller says that "everything Chinese is the extreme opposite of all that we feel, think, do, believe . . . China, I repeat, seems indeed the antithesis of all that we regard the human world to be" (WOL, 138). *China*, then, is the antithesis of world in the same way the *inhuman* is the antithesis of *human*. *China*, to Miller, marked the absolute remoteness and incommensurability of the modern artist in relation to his age: the true artist was as far from *human* and contemporary society as China was from the Western world.[71]

Let's proceed to examine the concept of *China* as Miller described and experienced it in the *Walking Up and Down in China* section of *Black Spring*. "In Paris, out of Paris, leaving Paris or coming back to Paris, it's always Paris and Paris is France and France is China," are the first lines Miller wrote (BS, 185). Miller's aim in this story is to explain, through reverie, his spiritual life journey in terms of repeated deaths and rebirths that he had experienced over the years and which had now come to its climax in Paris: the final rebirth on the threshold of *China*. He elaborates:

> Things happened to me in my search for a way out. Up till now I had been working away in a blind tunnel, burrowing in the bowels of the earth for light and water. I could not believe, being a man of the American continent, that there was a place on earth where a man could be himself. By force of circumstance I became a Chinaman—a Chinaman in my own country! (185)

This captures once again the sense of Miller's feelings toward the former American life of the *traditional present* that "forced" him to look for another "place," both spiritually and physically. "I took," Miller continues,

> . . . to the opium of dream in order to face the hideousness of a life in which I had no part. As quietly and naturally as a twig falling into the Mississippi I dropped out of the stream of American life. Everything that happened to me I remember, but I have no desire to recover the past, neither have I any longings or regrets. I am like a man who awakes from a long sleep to find that he is dreaming. A pre-natal condition — the born man living unborn, the unborn man dying born. (185)

The last sentence, again, indicates the essence of the difference between the *human* of the *traditional present* who, while *de jure* living, is *de facto* "unborn" because of the way he lives, and the *inhuman* of the *full present* who can only be born by his dying in the *traditional present*.

Walking Up and Down in China, then, according to the interpretation taken in this book, is Miller's detailed narration of the birth of the *inhuman* as he is about to enter or be "born" into the realm of *China*. Before that can happen, however, he must let go of the past, time, and his former selves that he identified himself with in the former life of the *traditional present*. "Now I am walking to the grave, marching to my own funeral," Miller writes (186). As "the road to *China*" is a transcendental project, Miller separates his *I* from the body and, it appears, also from that of his other selves. The body he associates with selves and they are viewed as somewhat ephemeral and temporal, whereas *I* is depicted as eternal and inalienable. One's *I* is hidden under the many layers of selves, it seems.

> My body — the places it knew, so many places, and all so strange and unrelated to me . . . Quebec, Chula Vista, Brownsville, Sureness, Monte Carlo, Czernowitz . . .[72] In each and every one of these places something happened to me, something fatal. In each and every one of these places I left a dead body on the sidewalk with arms outstretched. Each and every time I bent over to take a good look at myself, to reassure that the body was not alive and that it was not I but myself that I was leaving behind. And on I went — on and on and on. And I am still going and I am alive, but when the rain starts to fall and I get to wandering aimlessly I hear the clanking of these dead selves peeled off in my journeying and I ask myself — what next? (202)

This is the journey of Miller's life in the course of which an old sense of self has died numerous times. Each time, one more false notion of oneself is "peeled off" and one's *I* reveals itself in a yet truer form. Thus, with each "peeled off" layer, the true and final understanding of oneself comes inevitably closer and closer. "Each city I walked through," Miller writes, "has killed me — so vast the misery, so endless the unremitting toil. From one city to another I walk, leaving behind me a grand procession of dead and clanking selves. But I myself go on and on and on. And all the while I hear the musicians tuning up . . ." (202). Losing the layers of selves is naturally not an easy task. In fact, dealing with the death of each new layer of self is a major crisis at the time. It may also make one wonder, what is it exactly that will eventually remain? Who am I really? The anticipation of facing one's true self is overwhelming. As the revolutionary nature of self-discovery can be foresensed—nothing will be the same after that—the process is both awaited and intimidating.

"What next?" asks Miller anxiously as the "musicians are tuning up" for the funeral of Miller's last false self, for the ceremony of the final death before his rebirth as *Chinaman* qua *inhuman artist*.

In several passages, it seems that Miller draws a parallel to the Great Wall of *China* as a symbolic demarcation line which separates his former life from what's ahead: the *traditional present* from the *full present* and *human* from *inhuman*. Nonsymbolically, the demarcation is that between dream and reality, consciousness and unconsciousness. Walking physically on the streets of Paris, Miller is effectively "walking inside the great Chinese Wall" (205). Sitting in a Paris café over an aperitif Miller is in fact in "communication with the whole earth" and in the "womb of time" (192). It is evident that Paris offered a physical location fitting for Miller's plunge into his own unconsciousness in a way that no place had done before. What he calls "obsessional walks" carried out in the streets of Paris are, symbolically, trips into unconsciousness, each of which carries him ever closer to *China*, as yet another bloody "corpse of himself" is left behind during the "walk."

> Today I am out for another grand obsessional walk. I and myself firmly glued together . . . Beyond the great wall that hems me in the musicians are tuning up. Another day to live before the debacle! Another day! . . . I am walking in blood, my heart on fire. Tomorrow all this will perish, and I with it. Beyond the wall the devils are tuning up. Faster, Faster, my heart is afire! (195–6)

As Miller reaches closer and closer to his "judgment day," the physical reality fades ever further away and *China* comes into prominence.

> I am here in the midst of a great change. I have forgotten my own language and yet I do not speak the new language. I am in China and I am talking Chinese. I am in the dead center of a changing reality for which no language has yet been invented. According to the map I am in Paris; according to the calendar I am living in the third decade of the twentieth century. But I am neither in Paris nor in the twentieth century. I am in China and there are no clocks or calendars here. (191)

We notice how the individual parts of Miller's *inhuman philosophy* now come together. The "timelessness" of one's true being and the requirement of the *full present*, which we saw him defend in Chapter 2, are now firmly incorporated into *China*. The ultimate self is necessarily *atemporal* and *ahistorical*. Toward the end of the story, Miller describes the realization of the *China* experience in its omneity but also in its simplicity and everydayness. After having had a meal with his friend Carl,

> We were talking about *The Merry Widow* and about Max Linder, about the Prater in Vienna — and then suddenly we were in the midst of the Russo-Japanese war and there was that Chinaman whom Claude Farrère mentions in *La Bataille*. Something that was said about the Chinaman must have sunk to the very bottom of him for when he opened his mouth again and started that speech about his mother, her womb, the war coming on and free as a bird I knew that he had gone far back into the past and I was almost afraid to breathe for fear of bringing him to. Free as a bird I heard him say . . .. (209)

It seems that a *China* moment can strike one any time as the result of coming to a resolution with one's past. It is the acceptance of what has been, in the way it has been, and then it ceases to be a problem. Miller was now, as he said elsewhere, "saved from the fear of death, so that he may be able to die" (CD, 17–18). The death he refers to is that of the past. The past vanishes in the moment when he himself dies in the *traditional present* and is reborn in the *full present*. One must go "forward into death! Not backward into the womb," Miller writes (17). Finally, the *China* moment is the peaceful feeling of the "eternal here and now" in which one accepts oneself in his current situation. The feeling may announce itself in the plainest of circumstances.

> There are some radishes in the bowl and Carl is munching them in the dark. "It's so beautiful to be alive, no matter how poor you are," he says. I can just barely see him sticking his hand into the bowl and grabbing another radish. So beautiful to be alive! (BS, 210)

This is where Miller made his peace with his past in the story. Suddenly all his friends from his past are gone. "The whole past is wiped out," he writes. "It's so beautiful to be alive and free as a bird. The gates are open and I can wander where I please" (210). The gates, naturally, were those of *China*.

Inhuman revolution now finished?

Let's now try to summarize Miller's complex view using his entire conceptual arsenal. First of all, Miller distinguished between the *traditional* and *full present*. The former stands not only for the historical, science-oriented modern society but also for common reality as such. *Traditional present* stands for a type of being that needs to be surpassed. "To be," Miller asserts, "is to have mortal shape, mortal conditions, to struggle, evolve" (CD, 4). As an artist type is unable to "adapt himself to [this particular type of] reality", he creates "a reality of his own," that is, the *full present* or *China*: which is "a projection into the spiritual domain of his biologic condition of non-being" (*ibid*). In the *full present*, man, according to Miller, "triumphs over reality, over becoming" (*ibid*). The *full present* started out as a response to the *traditional present* claiming to provide an *ahistorical, atemporal* and also amoral dimension for the artist. *China* is the further qualification, the climax, of that idea. *China* is the "final reality which the artist comes to recognize in his maturity," Miller writes (3). *China* is located "somewhere between the conscious and the unconscious" in which the artist can live out "his unconscious desires, wishes, dreams" (*ibid*). These opposite realms, *traditional present* and *full present* (or *China*) have, according to our reading of Miller, their respective representatives in *human* and *inhuman* where the latter is the antithesis of the former: the *inhuman* becomes a "traitor to the human race." The *inhuman*'s "betrayal" takes a twofold form. With his more destructive *Beelzebub* side, he must reveal and destroy various manifestations of the *traditional present* (history, technology, progress, science but also false kinds of art, etc.). With his more lenient *St. Anthony* side, he pleads for a creative approach to life which ultimately leads to *China*. *China* is only attainable when one has a proper relationship with art. "By living into his art," Miller explains, "he adopts for his world an intermediary realm in which he is all-powerful, a world which he dominates and rules" (7). Art's role is, thus, essentially intermediary.

> Art is only a means to life, to the life more abundant. It is not in itself the life more abundant. It merely points the way . . .. (BSOHB, 349)

Art for Miller does not usually mean works of art but rather what the artist does or feels when he creates a work of art. Art is a creative activity that helps one to get in touch with "non-being" as opposed to the "being" granted by the illusory means and the reality of the *traditional present*. In fact, art should lead toward the death of all the false selves obtained in the *traditional present*. Moreover, art should make one "willing to die" (CD, 12) voluntarily in order to be reborn. By "becoming an end," art and artist "defeat itself" (8). If the artist chooses to live, then, he defeats his own nature, according to Miller. The artist's goal is the ultimate self-discovery and a better life, but as he occupies the realm of *China*, he must "live" only metaphorically or "vicariously":

> Strange as it may seem today to say, the aim of life is to live, and to live means to be aware, joyously, drunkenly, serenely, divinely aware. In this state of god-like awareness one sings; in this realm the world exists as poem. No why or wherefore, no direction, no goal, no striving, no evolving. Like the enigmatic Chinaman one is rapt by the ever-changing spectacle of passing phenomena. This is the sublime, the amoral state of the artist, he who only lives in the moment, the visionary moment of utter, far-seeing lucidity. Such clear, icy sanity that it seems like madness. By the force and power of the artist's vision the static, synthetic whole which is called the world is destroyed. The artist gives back to us a vital, singing universe, alive in all its parts. (2)

One of the best examples of how Miller construed this sort of artist's life qua *Chinaman* we find in his descriptions of his painter friend Hans Reichel. Miller visited him during his Paris years "for instruction in the technique of making watercolors":

> In going to Hans Reichel twice a week I get something far more valuable than mere instruction in the use of a technique. Every time I see Hans Reichel I feel a little more holy. Yes, holy. I think if I were to say to Reichel one day: Reichel, what do you think about the Absolute? — he would look at me in utter amazement. I don't think the word means anything to him. And yet Reichel is living a sort of Absolute life of painting. (HAM, 124)

In Reichel Miller saw what art really can do to a person. Reichel was a personified *Chinaman*, one who "every day . . . paints a fragment of the universe." Reichel's universe was that of the "singing" *full present* and not of the "synthetic" *traditional present.*

> The question of the whole, of the meaning of the universe, never enters his head. But the meaning of the whole is there in every picture he makes, no matter even if it be the size of a pinhead, his painting. (125)

In the presence of Reichel, Miller felt "the eternality of things" which, without a doubt, reminded Miller of Ellis's "eternal here and now." Reichel represented to Miller the artist's ability to transcend the age. "He is living with us in our time under the same conditions," Miller writes, but "he is not in despair" because "this man is really in communication with life . . ." (*ibid*). In Reichel the plight of the modern artist had come to an end. The art had given way to the *inhuman life*, to *China.*

China and Nietzsche

After having fully unpacked Miller's *China* concept, we must, if for a moment, come back to our earlier discussion of Nietzsche and Miller. While we could detect both Dionysian and Apollonian qualities in Miller's previous discussions of the *inhuman artist*, the "Greek way" and "Chinese way" seemed to posit a problem as intuitively too different to essentially describe a similar approach. Are Miller's *China* art and Nietzsche's concept of art, in the last analysis, really that dissimilar?

Both Nietzsche and Miller ascribe an enormous role to art. Indeed, while for Nietzsche art is "the highest human task, the true metaphysical activity,"[73] for Miller, too, it means everything. It is art, according to both of them, with the help of which their age and modern man should be overcome and rejuvenated. There are some crucial differences, however. It is by no means an accident that Miller chose to develop his view of art through the *China* concept, which he borrowed from Ellis, rather than adhering very closely to Nietzsche's ideal artist as captured in the dialectics of Dionysian and Apollonian elements. While both Nietzsche and Miller attacked modern Western man, the solution for Nietzsche still seemed to advance from the cradle of the West—Ancient Greece. For Miller, however, the very basis of the new man and the new art meant something so radically unique that it couldn't have been restored or grafted from the "old shoots." Hence, so it seems, Miller had to find a concept that would express the binary opposition between his notions of old and new, the *traditional* and *full present* more profoundly. In opposing the *inhuman artist* to the human and *China* to the progressive West, Miller projected his phantasy on the centuries-old distinction between the Orient and the Occident. While the new race of *inhuman artists* needn't be Chinese ethnically (the French, we saw, could be new Chinese), in Miller's visions they would have to embrace the essential life-affirming qualities and the glory of art in the way the Chinese do. Another reason why Miller built his philosophy of art around the concept of *China* stems from the fact that, unlike the mythological Greek culture that Nietzsche had so passionately exalted, the Chinese culture was still actually living and breathing. So instead of joining Nietzsche in his attempt to awaken the "dead Greek man," Miller was pointing to the "Chinese way" as an empirically more viable model for the new start. While under the concept of *China* Miller was still able to express very similar criticisms to Nietzsche in regard to the Western human condition, it also provided an intellectual opportunity to offer a principally different source and setup for his ideal of renewed humanity. In his engagements with *China*, then, Miller seemed to be able to overcome the dissensions that he, despite numerous similarities, had with Nietzsche.

China vs. esthetics

The reader will have noticed that Miller's view on art, regardless of its essentially intermediary role, possessed a strong ethical dimension: its goal was to reveal a better and "more abundant" life to man. As such, Miller's view opposes the *estheticized view* of art which concerns itself with esthetic pleasure in artworks. It also can be claimed now that with his transcendental *China* concept Miller can be said to have finalized the "overthrowing" of the *metaphysical ground* of the age since esthetics was the last component of that ground. In what follows, I first introduce the *estheticized view* and lay bare the apparent differences with Miller's position. In addition, as criticisms regarding Miller's view of art seem to be often based on an erratic selection of his texts, I point out the limits resulting from such disordered approaches. I show that several issues raised by critics cease to be problematic once we have acknowledged the features of Miller's *inhuman philosophy* and their inextricable relation to the topic of art.

Now let us start with the relationship between the *estheticized view* and Miller's approach. Esthetics, according to a simple definition, "deals with the arts, and with other situations that involve aesthetic experience and aesthetic value."[74] A successful artwork, according to the estheticized approach to art, is one "which is beautiful" and which possesses "aesthetic appeal."[75] Art, then, is expected to produce "esthetic experiences" and is evaluated solely on that very basis. Although the roots of the esthetic conception of art began in antiquity (most notably with Plato), "only with the advent of modernity, however, did the practice of art become aesthetic," a prominent commentator writes.[76] Esthetics, in the modern sense, has a close relationship with the Enlightenment movement and the view that we have labeled "progressive" throughout the book. The *progressive view*, we remember, radicalized human reason as the ultimate faculty capable of reaching the truth about the world. Science and scientific knowledge, accordingly, were seen as the only proper ways of securing the truth. It was precisely "scientism" or "positivism," the more recent labels for the thinking that derived from the Enlightenment, which "Estheticized" art in the modern world. Plato construed art as mere "representation" [*mimesis*] of the imperfect world of appearances but not that of eternal forms (the ultimate ideas of all reality). The artists were, accordingly, not seen as dealing with the truth. If anything, they were seen as adding to the possible confusions about the truth (and thus excluded from Plato's imaginary ideal republic). The modern age, seeing only reason and scientific knowledge as the ways of disclosing truth, similarly, expelled art from the domain of truth, for the knowledge of art was seen as not susceptible to the rigor expected of scientific inquiry. As art continued to have an impact on people's lives, it suggested, there remained no alternative in the modern age than to assign art "to the realm of feeling."[77]

The above summary of the rise of esthetics is the starting point, for example, for Martin Heidegger's contra-esthetic thinking. Indeed, esthetics in the modern sense for Heidegger belongs to the same age-specific *metaphysical ground* we introduced in Chapter 3 while discussing the question of technology. As Miller's rejection of the *estheticized view* derives from similar, largely age-specific anxieties, a very brief detour through Heidegger's view seems to be of help in making sense of the modernist antiesthetic stance and Miller's relation to it.

Art estheticized

In discussing the value of modern esthetic experience, Heidegger concedes that we value it because it "reposes and relaxes."[78] We enjoy the esthetic state because it is a form of stress relief, a moment of lyric stasis in the midst of busyness, a holiday from the anxious world of willing and working.[79] It is evident to Heidegger, however, that if that is all that modern art is valuable for, "it becomes, for life, of peripheral importance."[80] If art has "nothing about it of action," if it is "harmless and ineffectual," then it fails to be something we need to take "seriously."[81] Importantly, Heidegger adds in his Nietzsche lectures that

> What makes art great is not only and not in the first place the high quality of what is created. Rather, art is great because it is (answers to) an absolute need.[82]

What is that "absolute need" for Heidegger? Contrary to the *estheticized view* of modern art, Heidegger believes that great art, like that in the "magnificent days of Greek art," should be "truth-disclosing": it should disclose to its audience at least the outline, the shape, of the proper way to live. Art, in short, should provide guidance how to live.[83] According to Heidegger, Greek art did indeed grow out of an absolute need, since an understanding of how to live is something we all need. Modern art, being merely stress relief, while it may even be pleasant, answers to no absolute necessity. Moreover, as esthetics, art in the modern condition becomes the province of "the art industry," an industry aimed at providing pleasurable experiences for "connoisseurs." As such, art becomes a "sector of cultural activity." It is also evident to Heidegger that if art exists only as a "sector" on the smorgasbord of "cultural activity," then it exists only for those "sectors" of the population who choose to go in for that particular form of rest and recreation. Since the enjoyment of (at least fine) art requires leisure and education, esthetic art becomes the province of a subcultural social elite. This is why, according to Heidegger, great art "died" in modern times: it descended from greatness to triviality.[84]

We can already detect a few important similarities between Heidegger and Miller. First, art for Miller, too, is not a matter of esthetic experience but very much that of "action" and "truth." The ethical dimension of art is present in both thinkers since art according to both is meant to reveal something important about one's life. It should be evident from Miller's texts that we have already examined, that the attitude toward art as a "part of the art industry" or a "sector of cultural activity" deserves only contempt in his view. Art in that sense belongs to the human realm of the *traditional present*. Art for Miller, however, has yet more meanings. As noted above, Miller is concerned not only with a general modernist attack on the *estheticized view* of art (in terms of which he can be seen, perhaps, as contiguous with the Dadaists and Surrealists), but also with art's sense and purpose among different modernists themselves. It goes without saying that being a modern writer or painter in itself is not enough to satisfy the criteria of being a true artist in Miller's terms. Art for art's own sake, for example, has no meaning to Miller. As becomes apparent from several texts, Miller especially resisted overly intellectual approaches to art, for they had little to do with life as it is lived day by day. He expressed this attitude even toward as prominent modernist writers as Marcel Proust and James Joyce.[85] In *The Universe of Death* section of his Lawrence book, Miller criticizes Proust, for example, for "making of art the final justification but thereby divorcing art from life" (WOL, 91). Miller finds Proust guilty of worshipping art "for its own sake — not for man" (*ibid*). Art in Proust, according to Miller, "is . . .

regarded as means of salvation, as redemption from suffering, as a compensation for the terror of living. Art as substitute for life." (*ibid*) Miller takes Proust to be the "very symbol of the modern artist — the sick giant who locks himself up in a cork-lined cell to take his brains apart" (93). Consequently, Miller deems Proust as suffering from "the disease of the mind" (*ibid*).

James Joyce is equally to blame according to Miller. "Joyce's deformity of vision," Miller writes, ". . . is depressing, crippling, dwarfing: it is a defect of a soul, and not an artistic metaphysical device . . . life to Joyce, as one of his admirers says, is a mere tautology" (95). Miller considered Ulysses "a paean to late-city man" and thought that "most astoundingly varied and subtle means of art are herein exploited to glorify the dead city" (92). Miller concludes that "Joyce reveals the desperate plight of the modern man who, lashing about in his steel and concrete cage, admits finally that there is no way out" (*ibid*).

This should not be misinterpreted, though, as if Miller had exactly the same attitude toward what Proust and Joyce produced that he held toward what any popular artist did at the time. Far from it. Miller, no doubt, considered both Proust and Joyce brilliant masters in depicting the modern condition, but what he found lacking in them was the so-called "positive program" of art. Agreeing with Proust's and Joyce's outcome—"that there is no way out"—would have meant that art changes nothing. It would have meant that art, at best, is capable only of revealing the miserable condition of the modern age but not of offering any solutions for ending it. Acknowledging that would have rendered the whole *inhuman project* meaningless for Miller. Thus, instead of staying stuck in art, Miller believed in its healing potential, its ability to direct us toward a personal *China*: the final liberation through transcendence. Although art's role was viewed as intermediary by Miller, as a role that should "come to its end," the way in which it comes to an end in Proust and Joyce leaves us with nothing to "grow by"; whereas Miller's version of art's end would introduce us to some sort of greater sense of life and understanding of how to nurture it. Edward Mitchell has called this feature of Miller's vision, and that which Proust and Joyce are bereft of, the "seer-quality" since for Miller "the poet and seer are one."[86]

Art and art

The "end-of-art-question" in Miller has not been well understood by most of the critics. While Welch Everman rightly reads in Miller that "art will and must exhaust itself," he wrongly concludes that Miller's own literary pretensions contradict this claim. He asserts:

> Miller's call for an end to literature comes from within literature itself, from within the text of a book . . . that would kill the book by way of the book.[87]

Everman goes on to infer that "if Miller's goal is the end of literature, and if literature itself is to be the means to that end, then his project is impossible, a failure even before it begins."[88] It seems, however, that Everman's deduction is based on the false premise that "literature" or "art" is all the same to Miller. As we have seen, there are important differences between the senses of art that play a crucial role in understanding Miller. First of all, there is literature and art in an esthetic sense. Rejecting both in that sense creates no serious problems for Miller as they belong to an entirely different sphere: the *traditional present*. Second, and more importantly, there is literature in the sense of Proust and Joyce, which has a somewhat higher status, in that it reflects certain Milleresque or *inhuman qualities*, but still isn't exactly that which Miller himself does. In short, it appears that for the sake of clarity it would be useful, if not in fact inevitable, to read Miller in a distinction: between "literature" and "art" on the one hand, and "Literature" and "Art" on the other. The latter, naturally, is what he himself aspired to. Miller's first goal is the end of "art" and "literature": the death of the wrong type of art that has no connection to one's life in the most fundamental levels. But even "Literature" and "Art' must come to end, according to Miller—although this can happen only at another level. It happens on the threshold of the *full present*, on one's path to *China*. It takes place when "Art" has served its purpose in pointing out *China*. It becomes evident now where Everman's main mistake lies. He falsely thinks that Miller attempts to kill "literature" with "literature," whereas he kills "literature" with *inhuman* "Literature" and, once it has served its purpose, he abandons "Literature" too. Miller's *Tropic of Cancer*, then, is not just a "book" but "Book" and should be viewed as fighting two battles at the same time. Being "Literature" it fights "literature" but because of its revealing nature, pointing out the "horizon" (OLSE, 168) for the one who practices it, it then frees the *inhuman artist* from the further need of it. Art frees one to a right kind of living. Art's purpose (and here we indeed mean "Art"), then, disappears for Miller "when the votary achieves his spiritual goal."[89] Miller explicitly reaffirms this in *The Colossus of Maroussi*:

> Art . . . is only a preparation, an initiation into the way of life. The goal is liberation, freedom . . . To continue writing beyond the point of self realization seems futile and arresting. The mastery of any form of expression should lead inevitably to the final expression—mastery of life. (COM, 209)

We can now see clearly that "literature" and "art" should be "killed" according to Miller because they have no potential to do what "Literature" and "Art" can. If they are construed in a purely esthetic sense, they are merely in service of esthetic pleasure and thus divorced from any meaningful relation to life. If they are used in the way in which Proust and Joyce used them, they can have some value, for they can point out some aspects about one's life, but they still fail as "an initiation into the way of life." The death of Proust-Joyce art is nihilistic, whereas the death of Miller's art is creative. The result of the former is death as *exitus letalis*, the result of the latter is another type of life.

Everman's confusion about Miller's notion of art expands further. He thinks that Miller's "project of the artist" is impossible, for "if the artist's job is to put an end to art, then the role of the artist must come to an end as well. On the other hand, if the artist insists on upon remaining an artist — whose job is to destroy art — then art itself must remain, if only to give the artist something to destroy."[90] As there is "art" and "Art," there is also "artist" and "Artist" in Miller. It is plain that Everman finds an "Artist" killing "Art" problematic since "art" and "artist" are not operating on this ontological level and are long past Miller's concern. Everman's reading of Miller is overly one-dimensional, resting on the notion of "killing 'art" (whereby he effectively means the "killing of 'Art'") and taking the death of "Art" literally, whereas it should be read "creatively." The end of "Art," as we saw above, means in Miller transcending the "Artistic" activity. This signifies, however, not so much the death of "Art" or the "Artist" but a change in focus. The "Artistic" activity (writing, painting, playing music etc.) becomes less and less necessary as an "Artist" practices those art forms in the true sense of "Art." The focus of the "Artist," then, transforms from conventionally "Artistic" activities to guiding life. As life itself is now revealed as "Art" in the most primordial sense, the 'Artist' is meant to "die" only conditionally. He dies only in regard to producing works of "Art" but not as a "seer."

> Every one has his own reality in which, if one is not too cautious, timid, or frightened, one swims. This is the only reality there is. If you can get it down on paper, in words, notes, or color, so much the better. The great artists don't even bother to put it down on paper: they live with it silently, they become it. (OLAS, 9)

On the *China* level—and this is what is effectively at stake here—there is no more "destroying" to do as Everman falsely assumes. In the realm of *China*, life becomes "Art" and "Artist" becomes a seer. *China* is the sphere "where great Artists don't even bother" anymore to do "Art" but just live it. This is, I think, the true meaning of the Miller passage Everman quotes but unfortunately misunderstands:

> All art, I firmly believe, will one day disappear. But the artist will remain, and life itself will become not 'an art', but art, i.e, it will definitely and for all time usurp the field. (ROW, 24)

Both "art" and "Art" must indeed "die" according to Miller. "Art" with the capital letter, however, will only "die" in the sense of transcendence or transformation. "Art" becomes life itself and "Artist" now "remains" as a seer.

Eric Lehman seems to make a similar mistake in interpreting Miller. He appears first to acknowledge that "Miller seems to be validating the artist as the man who creates his own reality," but then he goes on to reject that view on the grounds that "throughout the novel [*Tropic of Cancer*], Miller's narrator maligns art and literature as dung."[91] This miscomprehension, as we can now see, is precisely due to not noticing the crucial distinction between the realms of the *traditional* and *full present* and the different roles of *humans* and *inhumans* in Miller's works. The art and literature that Miller condemns or calls "dung" are naturally only "art" and "literature," not "Art" and "Literature." Contrary to Lehman's reading, Miller's "Artist" indeed does create his own reality in *China* or the *full present*. Miller, as we have now seen several times, is very clear about it:

> The artist's dream of the impossible, the miraculous, is simply the resultant of his inability to adapt himself to reality. He creates, therefore, a reality of his own — in the poem — a reality which is suitable to him, a reality in which he can live out his unconscious desires, wishes, dreams. (CD, 4)

Another related confusion of Lehman's needs to be addressed here. On the basis of a few lines in *Tropic of Cancer* ("The cancer of time is eating us away . . . the hero, then, is not Time, but Timelessness"), he rejects the idea that Miller's artist is meant to be seen as being "outside of time."[92] In light of our analysis in Chapter 2, Lehman's misinterpretation clearly derives from not seeing the full scope of Miller's approach to time and history.[93] Miller's artist, as we established, is to be read as being "outside" of the time of the *traditional present*. In creating the ahistorical *full present*, Miller most certainly "creates his own reality." "Timelessness" as a major goal of the *inhuman*, means abandoning the human time and age. Precisely that, however, Lehman fails to see.

Having unpacked Miller's *inhuman philosophy* in its theoretical entirety in this chapter, we'll turn to examining its more practical applications in the next with the view to demonstrating the sensible and continuous importance of Miller's *inhumanism* in his post-Parisian life.

Notes

1 *Oxford English Dictionary Online*, *inhuman*, adj. and n. url: http://www.oed.com.ezproxy.auckland.ac.nz/Entry/96004.

2 An example of a possible ambiguity of this kind can be present in passages like the following from *Sexus*:
As the front door slammed to, Arthur Raymond came to the threshold and said: "You are not letting her go like that, are you? It's a bit inhuman, isn't it?" "Is it?" I replied. I gave him a weak and rather forlorn smile. (SEX, 398).
It is quite possible that Miller does not take "inhuman" here just to mean cruel or barbaric as Arthur Raymond seems to suggest, but something that may have passed this *human meaning* of the *inhuman* in which case the meaning of Miller's act becomes exactly the opposite to the suggested one.

3 Eric D. Lehman, "Henry Miller and Jean Francois Lyotard: The Aesthetics of 'The Inhuman' in Tropic of Cancer," *Nexus: The International Henry Miller Journal*, 5 (2008): 276.

4 I point out shortly that Miller may also have adopted it from Nietzsche.

5 I will discuss this division at length shortly.

6 J. D. Brown, *Henry Miller. Literature and Life* (New York: Ungar Pub. Co, 1986), 46.

7 Leon Lewis, *Henry Miller: The Major Writings* (New York: Schocken, 1986), 23.

8 *St. Anthony* of Padua, born c. 251 in Egypt was a disciple of Paul of Thebes. Anthony began to practice an ascetic life at the age of 20 and after 15 years withdrew for absolute solitude to a mountain by the Nile called Pispir (now Dayr al-Maymun), where he lived from about 286 to 305. During the course of this retreat, he began his legendary combat against the devil, withstanding a series of temptations famous in Christian theology and iconography. See Anthony of Egypt, Saint in *Encyclopædia*

Britannica Online, url: www.original.search.eb.com.ezproxy.auckland.ac.nz/eb/article-9007776.

9 Friedrich Wilhelm Nietzsche, *Thus Spoke Zarathustra: A Book for All and None*, trans. Walter Arnold Kaufmann (New York: Modern Library, 1995), 17.

10 Ibid.

11 Walter Arnold Kaufmann, *Nietzsche: Philosopher, Psychologist, Antichrist* (Princeton, NJ: Princeton University Press, 1974), 309.

12 "How one becomes what one is" is the subheading of Nietzsche's *Ecce Homo*.

13 Kaufmann, *Nietzsche: Philosopher, Psychologist, Antichrist*, 312.

14 Friedrich Wilhelm Nietzsche, *Ecce Homo: How One Becomes What One Is*, trans. R. J. Hollingdale (Harmondsworth: Penguin Books, 1979), 41.

15 Cited in Friedrich Wilhelm Nietzsche, *A Nietzsche Reader*, trans. R. J. Hollingdale (Harmondsworth: Penguin, 1977), 237.

16 Ibid., 241.

17 Nietzsche, *Zarathustra*, 26.

18 Ibid., 12.

19 Ibid.

20 Friedrich Wilhelm Nietzsche, *The Will to Power*, trans. Walter Arnold Kaufmann and R. J. Hollingdale (London: Weidenfeld & Nicolson, 1968a), 369.

21 Nietzsche, *Zarathustra*, 13.

22 Ibid., 64.

23 Ibid., 27.

24 Ibid., 24.

25 Nietzsche, *Ecce Homo*, 16.

26 As an interesting coincidence, a notorious Californian poet, Robinson Jeffers, adopts the *inhumanist* theme in his 1940s' poetry. While Jeffers, too, was evidently influenced by Nietzsche, his *inhumanist* seems only nominally similar to Miller's *inhuman*, predominantly in the critique of the current day *human*. The goal of Jeffers' *inhumanist* is, through "the contemplation of the transhuman magnificence of natural beauty," to achieve an essentially "nonhuman perspective." See Robinson Jeffers, *The Double Axe and Other Poems* (New York: Random House, 1948), 181. There is no information of whether Jeffers knew Miller's works at all.

27 William A. Gordon, *The Mind and Art of Henry Miller* (Baton Rouge: Louisiana State University Press, 1967), 38.

28 Ibid., 47.

29 Lehman, "The Aesthetics of 'The Inhuman' in Tropic of Cancer," 267–77.

30 Ibid., 277.

31 Ibid.

32 Roger Crisp, "Good," in *The Oxford Companion to Philosophy*, ed. Ted Honderich (Oxford: Oxford University Press, 1995), 322.

33 I explain this term shortly.

34 William Irwin, "What Is an Allusion?" *Journal of Aesthetics and Art Criticism* 59, 3 (2001): 293.

35 Ibid., 290.

36 Ibid., 291.

37 Ibid.

38 Ibid., 294.

39 Ibid.

40 Richard F. Thomas, "Virgil's *Georgics* and the Art of Reference," *Harvard Studies in Classical Philology* 90 (1986): 174.
41 Ibid.
42 Nietzsche, *Zarathustra*, 13.
43 Ibid., 13.
44 Ibid., 9.
45 Ibid., 83.
46 Cited in Irwin, "What Is an Allusion?," 289.
47 I am thankful to Prof Julian Young for helping to identify the wrong Nietzsche ascription on Miller's part. "Stairs and contradictory stairs," according to Young, has not been found in any of Nietzsche's major texts.
48 Thomas, "Virgil's *Georgics*," 175.
49 Nietzsche, *Zarathustra*, 67.
50 Ibid., 164.
51 Ibid.
52 I am using this term in the same sense Emerson did in his "Art" (1841) where he required of all artworks "that they domesticate me, not that they dazzle me." See Ralph Waldo Emerson, "Art," in *The Complete Essays and Other Writings* (New York: The Modern Library, 1950).
53 Robert L. Wicks, *European Aesthetics: A Critical Introduction from Kant to Derrida* (forthcoming in Oneworld Publications, 2013)
54 Ibid.
55 Robert Wicks warns us about the limits of how far the Dionysian and Apollonian distinction can be taken, as if it had "a single meaning and value" to Nietzsche. His presentations and valuations of the distinction often appear as "tension-ridden." Ibid.
56 Friedrich Wilhelm Nietzsche, *The Birth of Tragedy and The Genealogy of Morals* (Garden City, NY: Doubleday, 1956), 22.
57 Richard Schacht, "Nietzsche on Art in *The Birth of Tragedy*," in *Nietzsche*, eds. John Richardson and Brian Leiter (Oxford [England]: Oxford University Press, 2001), 188.
58 Leon Lewis reaches a similar conclusion. See Lewis, *Henry Miller*, 129.
59 Ibid.
60 Robert Ferguson, *Henry Miller* (New York: Norton, 1991), 215.
61 Gordon, *The Mind and Art of Henry Miller*, 57.
62 Brown, *Henry Miller*, 33.
63 Ferguson, *Henry Miller: A Life*, 216.
64 Ibid.
65 Ibid.
66 Ibid.
67 Havelock Ellis, *The Dance of Life* (New York: The Modern library, 1929), 21–2. (Miller, in general, seems to have made no secret about his sympathies to Ellis. From Ferguson's biography, for example, we learn that Ellis was among T. S. Eliot, Ezra Pound, Aldous Huxley, and several other modernist writers to receive a complimentary copy of Miller's *Tropic of Cancer* in 1934 (239–40). Lawrence Durrell, in his letter to Miller in 1937, even describes meeting Ellis in person: "Meeting Eliot and Pringle on Thursday. More talk then. Listen, I went down and bearded

Havelock. I should rather say that he bearded me. Magnificent beard. He is covered with hair like a wild boar. Likes your work and promises to write you in detail about the books. Hasn't finished them yet. Disagrees with you about urination!! Lovely old man . . ." DML, 117).

68 Ibid., 26–7.

69 Ibid., 6 and 272.

70 Ibid., 27–9.

71 The *China* theme came up also in the early Durrell-Miller correspondence. In summer 1936, Miller wrote "you know, I'm nuts about China. I always think that that is the place I will eventually wind up in. I feel like a Chinaman very often" (DML, 17). In the letter dated 6 December 1936 Miller is excited to inform Durrell that "I have found an American who thinks he can translate me into Chinese! Am corresponding now with several Chinese men of letters. Want to be translated into Chinese above everything else" (31–2). As Miller, in his letters, revealed much of his ongoing correspondence with Fraenkel and also quoted from the texts he was writing at the time, Durrell was well acquainted with the China topic. In January 1937, in his reply to Miller, he says "I like that bit you quote about writing Chinese. Sounds marvellous. But these people never understand. Fuck the whole trade" (48). At that time, Miller also signed some of his letters to Durrell as the "Prince of China."

72 A list of 80 more places follows.

73 Nietzsche, *The Birth of Tragedy and The Genealogy of Morals*, 17.

74 Christopher Janaway, "Aesthetics, the problems of," in *The Oxford Companion to Philosophy*, ed. Ted Honderich (Oxford: Oxford University Press, 1995), 13.

75 Julian Young, *Heidegger's Philosophy of Art* (Cambridge: Cambridge University Press, 2001), 9.

76 Ibid.

77 Ibid, 14.

78 Martin Heidegger, *An Introduction to Metaphysics*, trans. Gregory Fried and Richard Polt (New Haven: Yale University Press, 1959), 131.

79 Young, *Heidegger's Philosophy of Art*, 11.

80 Ibid.

81 Ibid.

82 Cited in Young, *Heidegger's Philosophy of Art*, 12.

83 Ibid., 9.

84 Ibid., 11–12.

85 Smithline observes correctly that most of the English novelists (with the exception of D. H. Lawrence and, of course, Miller's friend Lawrence Durrell) share this propensity of Miller's as they "remain detached from their art and view their works as a projected imaginary creation." See Arnold Smithline, "Henry Miller and the Transcendental Spirit," *ESQ: A Journal of the American Renaissance* 43 (1966): 51.

86 Edward B. Mitchell, "Artists and Artists: The 'Aesthetics' of Henry Miller," in *Henry Miller: Three Decades of Criticism* (New York: N. Y. U. Press, 1971), 159.

87 W. D. Everman, "The Anti-Aesthetic of Henry Miller," in *Critical Essays on Henry Miller*, ed. Ronald Gottesman (New York: G. K. Hall, 1992), 329.

88 Ibid., 330.

89 Smithline, "Henry Miller and the Transcendental Spirit," 51.

90 Everman, "The Anti-Aesthetic of Henry Miller," 330.
91 Lehman, "The Aesthetics of 'The Inhuman,'" 279–80.
92 Ibid., 281.
93 While the germ of the idea of *ahistoricity* is implicitly present in *Tropic of Cancer*, it is manifested as a thesis a few years later in the Miller-Fraenkel letters. Lehman does not seem to be familiar with the latter source.

5

From *Theoria* To *Praxis*: The Poetry of Life

. . . I shall pass from art to life

—Henry Miller

The 1930s was arguably the most invigorating and fruitful period of Henry Miller's career. The *Tropic* books, *Black Spring*, numerous essays, and the gargantuan correspondence with Fraenkel, Nin, Durrell, and many others (which in some cases reached well into the next three decades) form a kind of "definitive collection" of Miller's work which commentators most often draw upon. It is a commonplace opinion that the post-Paris era, with the emergence of books like *The Colossus of Maroussi* (1940) and *Big Sur and the Oranges of Hieronymus Bosch* (1957), presents us with quite a different Miller. While this may be true in some respects, my aim in this chapter is to make the claim that this common view somewhat misinterprets the continuities in Miller's thought. I argue that, at bottom, Miller remained faithful to the core of his ideas concerning the artist's life he had developed in the 1930s. What is regarded as having changed is, according to my reading, simply a shift of accent from the *Beelzebub* to the *St. Anthony* side of the *inhuman artist.* To an extent, Miller's later period can also be viewed as a search for the transition from *theoria* to *praxis*: from the discussions of the role of art toward "life as art." In what follows, we examine how Miller's *inhuman philosophy* manifested itself not only in some of his post-Paris texts but also in his life. While his later texts are often considered to lack the power of those of the 1930s, they do provide, I contend, valuable additions and important qualifications to the ideas we have been examining in this book. The question of the possibility of the artist's life in modern society never lost its appeal and pertinence for Miller. We will see that while Miller in several of his later texts kept alive his discursive interest in defending the artist's life against society, it was in fact the *praxis* of *China*—constantly looking for the possibilities of freeing himself to life as art—that was the ultimate driving force and *raison d'être* in the later period of Miller's life and work.

Greece: Transition to *St. Anthony* and the *Artist*

It seems that by early 1939 Miller had reached a point where he needed another great change, and once again, both spiritual and geographical. Since several of his friends had left Paris in the fear of the approaching war, Miller too, was contemplating going back to America. Encouraged by Durrell's invitation, however, he decided to go to Greece instead. As much as he may have dreaded the war, a biographer remarks, "he also feared the prospect of being locked in his own country."[1] It was precisely in Greece where Miller's visionary tendencies started to blossom in full swing and he, it could be argued, came to see the possibility of the "poetry of life" *here and now* which he had vigorously dreamt of in Paris. Having already been called the "Sage of Villa Seurat" in his Paris days by a critic, Miller came to play the role of the "wisdom-giver" more and more. While in his *Tropic*-books and *Black Spring* Miller, perhaps, had mainly only wanted tell his story, now he "wished to convince people of the benefits of knowledge acquired through his suffering,"[2] Jay Martin observes. Erica Jong has similarly suggested that it was indeed in Greece where Miller found his true calling as an "author/sage" with the mission to "liberate his readers."[3]

On account of the beginning of World War II, Greece marked the end of Miller's 10-year exile in Europe. Yet, it wasn't only the war that signaled the end of an era for Miller. Greece designated a more personal closure for him: "When I arrived to Greece I knew that I was finished with Europe," Miller wrote to Perlés a few years later (MM, 454). In Greece, the rebellious tones of *Tropic of Cancer* started to give way to tranquil feelings of peace. *Beelzebub* in Miller was gradually turning into *St. Anthony*; the roar of an uncompromising radical artist was turning into the whispering of a sage. If Miller's *artist/inhuman* arsenal in *Cancer* consisted mainly of "sword and fire", then, in *The Colossus of Maroussi*, the book about Miller's Greek experiences, he has little besides his heart and kindness as his armaments. The *St. Anthony* side of his *inhumanity* totally triumphed in Greece over its belligerent counterpart. Brown, for example, observes that while *Tropic of Cancer* and Paris had given birth to the artist, in Greece, Miller's sense of himself as artist "discovers a greater self" and that these are the "metaphysical forces" and "nature and spirit"[4] which Miller is concerned with in his Greek book. Indeed, based on the distinctions made earlier, we can now go even further and say that in Greece the "artist" in Miller had started to turn into the "Artist." Lewis has suggested that *The Colossus of Maroussi* was "Miller's first attempt to show how an artist can live successfully as a part of a society which supports him and draws strength from his work."[5] This can be seen as an important exploration of the *China* concept on Miller's part. He yearned to find practical evidence to support his Parisian-born and now increasingly evolving *theoria* that in the end art reveals to one a more authentic way of life. In this, Greece seems to have served in the role of midwife: it assisted the birth of this realization.

From peace to *China*, from art to life

Despite the war that was coming closer every day, Miller, paradoxically, found himself at this particular point having arrived at a feeling of utmost tranquillity. "Over thirty years," said Miller in describing his current situation, "I had wandered, as if in a labyrinth. I had tasted every joy, every despair, but I had never known the meaning of peace. En route I had vanquished all my enemies one by one, but the greatest enemy of all I had not even recognized — myself" (COM, 83). We notice here how Miller can be said to repeat the need to overcome or "kill" his former false notions of self that we saw him manifest in *Black Spring.* When the Durrells left for Athens, Miller enjoyed some quality time by himself. "A wonderful period of solitude set in. . . . It was the first time in my life that I was truly alone. It was an experience which I enjoyed deeply," Miller wrote (43). Characteristically, when civilians had to be evacuated from Corfu because the war was coming closer, Miller said that he had been "more concerned about the interruption of my blissful vacation than about the dangers of impending war" (26). The war still had a strong, personally symbolic meaning for Miller's thinking. It was an event that—given his attitudes about mankind disclosed thus far—came as no great surprise to Miller. War is something that *humans* do after all. But, for the same reason, the war was of little importance to him because he was *inhumanly* striving against the sphere where such things take place: the *traditional present.* In the war, Miller perhaps even saw a certain healing dimension of *humankind*:

> This is one of the lowest moments in the history of the human race. There is no sign of hope on the horizon. The whole world is involved in slaughter and bloodshed. I repeat — I am not sad. Let the world have its bath of blood — I will cling to Poros. . . . I can see the whole human race straining through the neck of the bottle here, searching for egress into the world of light and beauty. May they come, may they disembark, may they stay and rest awhile in peace. And on a glad day let them push on, let them cross the narrow strait, on, on, a few more miles — to Epidaurus, the very seat of tranquillity, the world centre of the healing heart. (57–8)

The war was yet more evidence of the failure of the course of humanity driven by rational-scientific ideologies in the *traditional present.* Miller saw the war as the ultimate failure of human reason: the calculative and technically driven mind inherited from modernity. It was high time, then, to turn to one's heart, Miller seemed to suggest. Already in *Cancer*, Miller had privileged the honesty, and thus the power, of one's heart in comparison to that of one's mind. The truth, then, was to be discovered in one's heart and not in one's mind. "If any man ever," Miller goes on to describe the ultimate power of one's heart, "dared to translate all that is in his heart, to put down what is really his experience, what is truly his truth . . . the world would go to smash" (CAN, 250). In *Capricorn*, too, the book he had finished before his Greece trip, Miller expressed a similar attitude: "If you're trying to improve your mind, stop it! There's no improving the mind. Look at your heart and gizzard — the brain is in the heart" (CAP, 269). Continuing with Miller's Greek experiences, it is very much in terms of the kindness of one's heart that we see Miller expressing himself. After visiting Eleusis, he wrote:

> Here the light penetrates directly to the soul, opens the doors and windows of the heart, makes one naked, exposed, isolated in a metaphysical bliss which makes everything clear without being known. (COM, 48)

The reader sees that Miller is contrasting the "wisdom of the heart" with "knowing." The truth reveals itself via experience rather than thinking. Miller also sees Epidaurus, the most celebrated healing center of the Classical world, a place where sick people went in the hope of being cured, as a symbol both for his own new beginning and hopefully that of others:

> The road to Epidaurus is like the road to creation. One stops searching. One grows silent, stilled by the hush of mysterious beginnings. If one could speak one would become melodious. There is nothing to be seized or treasured or cornered off here: there is only a breaking down of the walls which lock the spirit in . . . It is the morning of the first day of the great peace, the peace of the heart, which comes with surrender. (80–81)

The possibility of the overwhelming sense of peace, which Miller now experienced, doubtlessly added more experiential content to his Paris-born idea of *China*. Indeed, he explicitly compares Greece to China, which is "a world of illusion," and the Greeks to Chinamen who are "everywhere" (52). He uses his very own *China* cosmology also to describe a situation whereby he would "talk Chinese" to the local village mayor, which, apparently, is the universal language to Miller (21). If thus far the ideas of the *full present* and *China* had been more or less a passionate vision, Miller's Greek experiences seemed to provide an empirical testimony of the actual realization of these ideas. Indeed, this sense of peace is in fact so compelling that Miller sees this now as the end of searching: there is no need to go any further or do anything anymore. The "road to Epidaurus," in a way, seems to have then finalized Miller's long journey from the *traditional present* of New York via "Art" in Paris, to *China* in Greece. Just as sick people went to Epidaurus to be cured, Miller, by going to Epidaurus (both symbolically and experientially), found his proof of *China* as absolute peace. This all-encompassing peace-experience, at least at the time, seemed to be the highest positive manifestation of Miller's *inhuman philosophy*:

> To be free, as I then knew myself to be, is to realize that all conquest is vain, even the conquest of self, which is the last act of egotism. To be joyous is to carry the ego to its last summit and to deliver it triumphantly . . . The wise man has no need to journey forth; it is the fool who seeks the pot of gold at the rainbow's end. (84)

One could interpret that, with the phrase "to carry the ego to its last summit," Miller pinpoints the idea that the "ego," in the case of the "artist," usually militates against its surrender. An "artist" in doing "art" merely continues to feed his "ego." He who experiences this immense peace, however, realizes that "art" and even "Art" were never meant to be ultimate goals but only guiding aids toward self-realization and peace. Once one becomes aware of this, there is no "need to journey forth" and one is ready to "deliver his ego triumphantly." In this, one also senses the influence of Miller's readings of Krishnamurti who likewise advocates for the deliverance of an artist's ego in favor of one's "own living experience" (BIML, 155). According to Krishnamurti, artists wrongly assume that "it is their ego which is great or sublime," whereas in the moment of true inspiration, it is precisely their ego that is absent (154–5). Clearly taken by these ideas, Miller took a step back from his Parisian "ego" while in Greece. In fact, and if Jay Martin is right, the whole Greece journey for Miller was partly directed by the hope to find "something other than ego."[6]

Miller's formerly proud sense of self as an author and artist certainly took a backseat in Greece, and he didn't feel the need to write anything but letters during his stay. In fact, Miller even declared that after Greece there might not be any need to write at all anymore:

> There are friends who tell me that I will never stop writing, that I can't. But I did stop, for a good interval while in Greece, and I know that I can in future, any time I wish, and for good. I feel under no compulsion to do any particular thing. I feel, on the contrary, a growing liberation, supplemented more and more by a desire to serve the world in the highest possible way. What that way is I have not yet determined, but it seems clear to me that I shall pass from art to life, to exemplify whatever I have mastered through art by my living. (COM, 208)

Art, it is evident now, for Miller is indeed only a means to a yet greater life, and not the goal in itself. "Art . . . is only a preparation, an initiation into the way of life," he writes (209). Miller in New York and Paris had believed that "art was superior to life" and he had used his writing to understand and "live his life through art."[7] Having manifested, and in a way exhausted, this conviction so powerfully in his Paris books, he seemed to have come to miss the non-artistic life. The fundamental goal for Miller during his Greece stay is "liberation, freedom" and "mastery of life" (*ibid*). The "mastery" over life to Miller, however, is not mediated by literature and writing anymore but precisely by refraining from it, by not yielding to the lure and temptations of his artistic ego.

In the end of *The Colossus of Maroussi*, Miller felt that he was spiritually prepared, although not overjoyed, to go back to America: the idea he had obstinately resisted in the beginning of the trip. "The prospect," Miller wrote, "no longer filled me with dread. Greece had done something for me which New York, nay, even America itself, could never destroy. Greece had made me whole again." (213)

America: Search for the *Inhuman* in the land of hopes and dreams

Half compelled and half wished, on 27 December 1939, Miller boarded the *Exochorda*, an American cargo boat, for the long journey back to America. While he knew only too well that the return would not be easy, he seemed to be in good spirits and even reasonably optimistic about seeing his home country again. Miller reflected later that on leaving Greece he was "confident that for the first time in my life I would look upon

New York and what lay beyond it without a trace of loathing or disgust" (ACN, 2). These hopes, sadly, were soon to appear premature. When the boat was approaching Boston, Miller was immediately disappointed because the American coast looked "bleak and uninviting":

> . . . It was *home,* with all the ugly, evil, sinister connotations which the word contains for a restless soul. There was a frigid, moral aspect to it which chilled me to the bone. (*ibid*)

Shortly after his return, Miller wanted his dream to materialize of writing a book about America, a project he had already planned in Paris. He felt the need "to effect a reconciliation with my native land" (*ibid*). Since at the time Miller had no intention of staying to America for very long, he only "wanted to have a last look at my country and leave it with a good taste in my mouth . . . I wanted to embrace it, to feel that the old wounds were really healed, and set out for the unknown with a blessing on my lips" (*ibid*). Miller was also, without a doubt, directed by the secret hope of rediscovering his artistic drive in America. He needed to see for himself whether there were signs of ever attaining the possibility of *China* in America as he had in France and Greece. Miller wanted to see whether he, as a representative of the new type of *inhuman artist*, would be as unwelcome in America as he felt he had been in the 1920s. The meeting with his long-admired writers, Sherwood Anderson and John Dos Passos, shortly after his arrival, set a promising tone for Miller's plan. As both writers spoke "wonderfully of American small towns and the still-evident continuity of American life,"[8] Miller sensed that there indeed could be hope for his *inhuman artist* type in his native land.

Miller ended up making a year-long road trip throughout America and his account of these experiences was realized in *The Air-Conditioned Nightmare* (1945). The trip according to Miller proved to be "fruitless."

> I had to travel about ten thousand miles before receiving the inspiration to write a single line. Everything worth saying about the American way of life I could put in thirty pages. (10)

In December 1941, he wrote to Durrell: "You know, I am back from the tour. Covered about 25000 miles. A year wasted, I'd say" (DML, 172). Before *The Nightmare* was even finished, Miller came to hate the book he was writing. He felt that it was his weakest writing since pre-*Cancer* days. He also thought that the book might get him into trouble with authorities: war years usually are not the best time for attacking one's country's achievements and values.[9] Miller was not the only one disappointed: the manuscript of *The Air-Conditioned Nightmare* was turned down by its initial publisher, Doubleday, Doran & Co., and Miller had to pay back the advance, which had enabled him to organize the trip in the first place. By the time it was finally published in full in 1945, most of its episodes had already appeared in various magazines. The book, according to Brown, "was only of slight interest, lacking focus and stylistic force."[10] *The Nightmare* was widely considered to be inferior to Miller's previous works because of its lack of personal engagement. To quote Lewis, "Miller seemed like a European visitor, often looking with disdain at the various vulgarities of popular culture and other facets of America."[11]

Whatever its literary merits, or the lack thereof, *The Air-Conditioned Nightmare* provides important evidence of Miller's ongoing concern with the possibility of living the life of an alternative artist in America. He had hoped to relive, at least according to Brown, a kind of "Whitmanesque journey"[12]: to find that there was indeed something valuable and meaningful in America for the true "Artist" kind. Indeed, Martin also suggests that Miller "would have liked to be a second Whitman," somebody who had, in the end, become a beloved writer "through his positive vision of America and of the new American man."[13] Unfortunately, nothing of the sort materialized for Miller. Instead, what he discovered on the trip only confirmed his earlier negative dispositions. The real America, not quite living up to the dreams, both his own and those of his literary icons, soon destroyed the stability and peace of mind he had achieved in Greece. After visiting New Hope, the famous art colony in Pennsylvania, Miller felt, ironically, that there indeed was "no hope for the artist":

> The only artists who were not leading a dog's life were the commercial artists; they had beautiful homes, beautiful brushes, beautiful models. The others were living like ex-convicts. This impression was confirmed and deepened as I travelled along. America is no place for an artist: to be an artist is to be a moral leper, an economic misfit, a social liability. A corn-fed hog enjoys a better life than a creative writer, painter or musician. (ACN, 2)

We can see that the reason for Miller's discontent is the dominant practice of art in the sense of "art" and not "Art" as distinguished in Chapter 4. The contrast of "commercial" and "creative" echoes this crucial difference. His mid-1930s' distinction between *human* and *inhuman* had once again proved its relevance: dull but popular *human* art still reigned in America:

> I had the misfortune to be nourished by the dreams and visions of great Americans — poets and seers. Some other breed of man has won out . . . It is not a world I want to live in. (15)

Miller clearly still felt very much *inhuman*, among "some other breed" or *humans* whose "art museums are crammed with lifeless junk" (25). America was evidently bereft of Miller's Rimbaud-like artist ideal—"the dreamer, the inspired madman" that he thought the country desperately needed (TOA, viii). The root cause of the "wrong kind" of life in America was still the same as it had been in the 1920s—the *progressive view* of life:

> Everything that was of beauty, significance or promise has been destroyed and buried in the avalanche of false progress. In the thousand years of almost incessant war Europe has not lost what we have lost in a hundred years of 'peace and progress.' (26)

Miller's verdict in *The Air-Conditioned Nightmare* is, thus, unsurprising and unambiguous: there was very little "Art" in America and attaining *China* in this country seemed as unreachable as ever under the dominant mentality. While perhaps mediocre artistically, *The Nightmare* still expressed Miller's genuine account of his debate with himself about his native land.[14] In order to even think about moving on with his life in "the land of hopes and dreams," he needed to test America once more. Unfortunately, America failed the test the second time over.

Inhuman in need of human help

Miller continued to exhibit his worries about the artist's life in America in a rather peculiar but unmistakably Milleresque way: by asking the public to support him. Although already past 50, he was still very much an object of charity. As Erica Jong has humorously put it, Miller's financial life reads like a "surrealist farce."[15] While it was himself who was constantly in need of support, he often pled his case as a representative of a whole breed or type of artists who were being continually neglected by the public. By asking for money (or even clothes, food, or painting supplies), Miller had, thus, found another way to draw attention to his *inhuman artist.* After having condemned bourgeoisie and popular artists with such vigor in his Paris books, this may seem a very odd thing: basically, to ask money from his fiercest enemy. On the other hand, it only goes to show Miller's perseverance for staying true to his artistic lifestyle and, perhaps, to his still unfailing *St. Anthony* or wisdom-giver side: to educate the public in matters of art, using his own life and struggles as an example. Moreover, since Miller generally saw no pride in having money and he loathed the American view that "poverty is moral turpitude,"[16] he, conversely, seemed to feel no shame in asking for money either.

In his essay "Artist and Public" published in *Remember to Remember* (1947), alternatively titled, vol. 2 of *The Air-Conditioned Nightmare*, Miller proposes a public financial scheme for the support of artists. In line with his distinction between genuine "Artists" and mere "artists," he had no concern with "those who receive a fair share of what they produce in their lifetime" nor with "the mediocre ones who pander to the public taste — the public will provide for them handsomely" (AP, 408–9). His scheme would be, he thought, for the benefit of those artists "who are denied, rejected, killed off" and who "receive nothing but jeers and insults for their pains" (408). Naturally, Miller spoke of his own kind, that is, *inhuman artists.*

Miller's plan was that artists themselves would band together in accumulating funds. Artists should, according to Miller's suggestion, "present the case to the public in detail and then appeal to the communities, to start the fund" (410). The idea was to raise enough money to support artists for all their active and productive life: approximately 50 years. Miller had even calculated the cost of maintaining one artist for such a period: 125,000 dollars. Naturally, there arose the question of how to select those worthy for such a maintenance program. While Miller was well aware of the problem, he did not seem too worried about it:

> . . . Give it in the name of art, which includes good and bad works, successful and unsuccessful artists. The first thing is to give. (409)

Miller saw great benefits arising from such an artist-keeping scheme. As artists would manage the affairs themselves, the "art dealer" would be eliminated and . . . "exhibits would be arranged by the artists, and in their own galleries" (411). Furthermore, in Miller's grand vision, "art would be brought to the public — it would belong to the public in a live way, and not to private collectors, museums, morgues and crematories" (*ibid*). If only, Miller envisages, "just three artists — a poet, a painter, a musician — could be assured a lifelong protection, it would be something" (413).

It is evident, however, that Miller's greater aim was not merely to collect funds from an artistically minded public but in effect to connect the public more firmly with the world of art and then, hopefully, also to "Art."

> Art has to be re-introduced, not via gallery and museum, but via the individual home. There has to be reborn a desire to do things with the hands, to work from within out, to make the home itself a work of art . . .. (414)

In his appeal to one's "creative instinct," which he believed to be "the dominant one" and to exist to some degree in every one, Miller clearly echoed his *China* vision. He wanted to "awaken desire" so as to advance one's own unique life beyond the one offered by society. This ethos would reveal itself as soon as more people actually started to practice the arts. It is clear to Miller that in the end, if the arts in any given society are hindered, it is a loss for the public, and not merely for the artist.

Once again, then, Miller stresses the opinion that art is a weapon against modern society. Art would make one see that the comforts of modern society are deceptive and inauthentic. Miller remained convinced that society has to "foster the artist in every human being, see to it that everything one handles, sees or hears is imbued with art. Art must penetrate through and through, from the humblest to the most exalted domain" (415). Miller's message is plain: the longer the public restrains the evolution of art the longer they will be fooled by the dictates of the *traditional present.* Through large-scale financial support systems, many more artists would be able to "create" and thus live life according to their own principles in the *full present.* Once more and more communities are involved in supporting the artists, they themselves would become more aware of the truth it reveals and hopefully also awaken their own artistic desires. Hence, every artistically driven person, according to Miller, who has been liberated to practice art, is truth's gain and falsity's loss. Unfortunately, this "manifesto of art" of Miller's started no "revaluation of all values" and not even a public discussion.

What did start a discussion, albeit an infamous one, however, was when Miller found a yet more personal way to communicate the worries of the creative artist: his notorious open letters. In those letters, published mainly in literary magazines, Miller described his situation and asked for financial support from his readers. In his "On Open Letter to All and Sundry" (1944), he explains that it is clear that everyone, and perhaps especially the artist, would like to make a living by doing what he enjoys. The problem arises particularly with non-commercial artists, such as himself:

> If he remains faithful to his art he compromises in life, by begging and borrowing, by marrying rich, or by doing some stultifying work which will bring him a pittance. (OLAS, 6)

In this letter, Miller offers his watercolors for whatever price people are willing to pay for them to keep him "afloat." Although, Miller admits, the paintings may not be worth much at the time, the situation might be different: "if upon my death I should have any fame as a writer these water colors which I have been turning out for my own amusement and the amusement of my friends will have real value" (6).[17] Thus, in a way, Miller offered the paintings in advance of his presumptive fame. Miller made it abundantly clear that he was not painting those works for the money: "Should this scheme, which I am now broaching, prove a failure I will still go on making water colors. I will paint my own grave and lie in it . . ."(10). At the end of the letter, he added a *post scriptum*, which reads:

> Any one wishing to encourage the water color mania would do well to send me paper, brushes and tubes, of which I am always in need. I would also be grateful for old clothes, shirts, socks, etc. I am 5ft. 8 in. tall, weigh 150 pounds, 15, 5 neck, 38 chest, 32 waist, hat and shoes both size 7 to 7, 5. Love corduroys. (10)

While some found his specification about corduroys pretentious, Miller apparently received "several hundred responses" ranging from soldiers to housewives who all offered support of some description (old clothes, newly baked bread etc.). According to biographer, Mary Dearborn, "donations poured in."[18] Miller's "begging," however, was also greeted with less enthusiastic feelings by the editors of *Time* magazine who reported the story but whose "tone of reporting was one of condescension" according to Ben Porter, the editor of the collection of Miller's open letters (11). That incident initiated several additional responses from Miller who felt the need to explain his motives and views on artists' situations in general. Effectively, he turned these responses into yet another paean for the *inhuman artist* and also into a campaign against the American way of life.

As Miller's *Tropic* books were still banned in America, he set out to juxtapose Europe and America, painting the former as liberal and welcoming, and the latter as restrained and hostile toward artists. "Only in Paris," Miller writes, "was I able to find a publisher courageous enough to print my work . . . For ten years I wrote without a line of my work appearing in print — in America"(17). Miller realized that the obvious question, which many people would raise, is why wouldn't he take a job, and wanted to settle this matter once and for all:

> Why don't I do as other men, other writers? Because I am different, for one thing. And because I know that if I work eight hours a day at something which I am

> totally disinterested in I shall have no desire to write the kind of books I am now engaged, and have been engaged, in writing. I intend to do nothing but to write and paint as I please. (20)

Writing scripts for the movies, copy for advertising agents, gags for the radio, and stories for paying magazines, Miller regarded as nothing more than "high class prostitution" (*ibid*). Miller saw "absolutely no reason why in a supposedly prosperous country such as America the artist should starve or else prostitute himself" (21). Miller repeated once again that the life of a people resides in its artists, its men of visions, its creators (*ibid*). By supporting an artist such as himself people would be, in effect, helping themselves, Miller thought. Once again, we see Miller giving voice to his belligerent *Beelzebub* side of the *inhuman*:

> The creative ones are no respecters of race, country or creed. They destroy whatever is evil and ugly in order to make room for creation. The people who are helping me are not doing so to help me personally, or to preserve the status quo, know that. They are helping me because I help them to liberate themselves. They are struggling to throw off the chains which bind them. They are not throwing me a bone or a crust, they are throwing me encouragement. They are encouraging me to give the courage. (34)

Miller, thus, brilliantly connected the help that he was receiving to the ethos of the "Art" of the *inhuman*. People wouldn't be just giving money to a struggling artist but would, in effect, be promoting an alternative and more fulfilling view of life. Via Miller, then, people would help themselves.

The woods of Arcady are alive: Big Sur

In 1944, Miller settled down in Big Sur, California. It was the place he probably came closest in realizing the *China* dream in his post-Europe era. The change from France to Big Sur, Jay Martin notices, "seemed almost tantamount to saying: from art to life, civilization to primitivity, self to selflessness."[19] In a similar vein, Brown has suggested that for Miller "Big Sur was Eden in the New World, a place as primitive, spectacular, untrammelled, and visionary as the Old World Eden he had discovered in Greece."[20] Dearborn adds that Miller's choice "represented his rejection of traditional American society" and that his decision to live there was, perhaps, "the closest he would come to making a political statement."[21]

Miller's reasons for choosing to settle in Big Sur might seem practical enough: he desperately needed a home but could not afford one so he took up an offer of a cabin to live there for free during the war years. But it also seems evident that in envisaging what the life would be like in Big Sur, *China* and "the idea of a paradise for artists was in the forefront of his thoughts."[22] Since Partington Ridge, the area in which Miller first settled, became more and more popular among artistic types, we find Miller before long revisiting his well-worn interest in the artist and society. Miller, it seems, wanted to interpret the fact that artists were growing in number in the area and led their relatively solitary lives outside of big cities as a sign of his prophesies of the artist's life as *summum bonum* coming to realization. In them, Miller saw the germs of the "new breed" or "race" he so fervently fantasized about in his earlier days and had until then been unable to track down elsewhere in America. "Utterly disillusioned," Miller writes,

> this new breed of experimenter is resolutely turning his back on all that he once held true and viable, and is making a valiant effort to start anew. Starting anew, for this type, means leading a vagrant's life, tackling anything, clinging to nothing, reducing one's needs and one's desires, and eventually — out of a wisdom born of desperation — leading the life of an artist. Not, however, the type of artist we are familiar with. An artist, rather, whose sole interest is in creating, an artist who is indifferent to reward, fame and success. (BSOHB, 17)

Miller's dichotomy between "artist" and "Artist" is well laid out here again. Noncommercial "Artists" seem to discern the true value of creation and thus abandon the society that does not share their vision. Also, with these fellow artist types coming to live in Big Sur, Miller saw this as a sign that more people were becoming aware that American society was coming closer to an end, and this would, again, prove the rightness of his stentorian premonitions concerning the collapse of the Western world, premonitions expressed throughout his works:

> The presence of these 'renegades,' small in number though they may be, is but another indication that the machine is breaking down. When the smash-up comes, as now is inevitable, they are more likely to survive the catastrophe than the rest of us. At least, they will know how to get along without cars, without refrigerators, without vacuum cleaners, electric razors and all other 'indispensables' . . . probably even without money. (18)

Miller was pleased to see that people were now concerning themselves with themselves, their being. They were turning from outside to inside, from their former *human* living to an *inhuman* one, as it were:

> The most important thing I have witnessed, since coming here, is the transformation people wrought in their own being. Nowhere have I seen individuals work so earnestly and assiduously on themselves. Nor so successfully. Yet nothing is taught or preached here, at least overtly . . . In a paradise you don't preach or teach. You practice the perfect life — or you relapse. (26)

Clearly, Miller's attitudes on education and religion are reflected in his proud claim that "nothing is taught or preached here"; that a person's transformation is "wrought in their own being" can been seen as a confirmation for Miller that once people abandon *human* education systems, and religion, there is a good chance that they'll turn toward their true and innermost selves. Here, we also notice Miller's insistence on the *praxis* of "Art" over *theoria.*

Despite now living in Big Sur with his third wife and two children, Miller praised the virtues of solitude much in the fashion of a Nietzschean "free spirit." For the second time after Corfu, Miller could truly experience and appreciate aloneness in Big Sur:

> To be alone, if only for a few minutes, and to realize it with all one's being, is a blessing we seldom think to implore . . . Only when we are truly alone does the fullness and richness of life reveal itself to us. In simplifying our lives, everything acquires a significance hitherto unknown. When we are one with ourselves the most insignificant blade of grass assumes its proper place in the universe. (34)

While it's clear that Miller's life at Big Sur wasn't always as idyllic as the above passages may indicate (he had major quarrels with his now third wife Janina Lepska, for example, which led to their divorce in 1954), he seems to have learned to be content, at least at times, with what he had. "Serve life and you will be sustained. That is a truth which reveals itself at every turn of the road" (396), he wrote toward the end of the book. He remained true to his credo, expressed so many times through his oeuvre, of keeping up one's creativity: "To live more intensely, to participate more fully, to keep all channels of communication open — that seems to be my bent . . ." (398).

It seems that Miller was almost ready to abandon his artistic activities, which, if we recall, were only "a means to a better life." The final goal is, Miller reminds us once more: "to make life itself an art" (400). Becoming more and more popular, however, Miller was interrupted constantly by visits from assorted admirers. That, naturally, affected his working habits and the vision of "making life an art." In a letter from 1957 to Durrell, Miller describes the downsides of his *inhuman* life.

> It gets more and more difficult to do any continuous work here. Living on the land, two children, endless visitors, endless chores, no recreation except ping-pong and a half hour's reading a day — no more! — no contact with vital people, no interest in the cultural, or less and less, desirous only of learning how to live easy and relaxed and in the world but not of it, the urge to write recedes. (DML, 321)

We notice that, although Miller was complaining of not being able to work, he also sought to transcend his work for "easy and relaxed living" beyond that of everyday goings-on, including writing. In a letter written 2 years later, Miller seems to grow even more indifferent toward the need to write:

> Writing seems so foolish, so unnecessary now . . . I seem to feel that all I have done is to create a booby hatch. Now I can throw the letters away without replying. It's easy. The next step is to throw myself away. That's harder. One thing seems certain — that I've built on sand. Nothing I've done has any value or meaning for

> me any longer . . . Years of struggle, labor, patience, perseverance have yielded nothing solid. (366)

Miller confirms his Greece-born idea that writing after self-discovery is meaningless. While it goes without saying that the writing "I" needs to be surpassed and the "artist" thrown away, even the "Artist" life may appear problem-laden: particularly if one has cherished his 'artist' ego for too long. Miller realized that once one has given up one's artistic ambitions, the "new" life needs to have other things in it in order for one to enjoy it as "Art":

> . . . wanting desperately to become a writer, I became a writer. In the process I sinned. I became so involved with the Holy Ghost that I betrayed my wife, my child, my friends, my country. I fell in love with the medium. I thought — if one makes a stroke on the blackboard that is the thing in itself, the reality. (376)

The evidently negative thoughts about the role of his own conception of art shouldn't be hastily interpreted as essentially undermining Miller's belief in the *inhuman philosophy.* These pessimistic feelings seem sporadic and more or less invoked by his marital problems at the time. The Big Sur years, overall, were one of the happiest in Miller's life.

C'est tout!: Pacific Palisades

In 1964, the year when the US Supreme Court finally ruled that *Tropic of Cancer* was not an obscene book, Miller moved to Pacific Palisades, Los Angeles. The reasons for moving were more to do with Miller wanting to be closer to his children, who now went to school in Los Angeles, rather than being a direct response to the outcome of the long legal proceedings. It should be remembered also that Miller was now in his seventies and Big Sur's rustic lifestyle and endless chores simply became too much to handle for the aging man. Being at the height of his fame and with some financial security he was able to afford a house in a suburb where he would be frequented by Hollywood actors and famous musicians. It seems, however, that the "pennies from heaven" didn't ruin him, for he still owned "but one suit" and used his bicycle to get around (CHM, 66). Indeed, despite living now among bourgeoisie *humans* par excellence, he seemed to remain *inhuman* to the core. His interviews from that era until his death in 1980 indicate that his views on the *metaphysical ground* of the age, which he had begun criticizing some 40 years earlier, had not changed in the least. In the interview published in *Cavalier*, for example, Miller sounds as Spengleresque as ever:

> Here we've based our thoughts about the civilization on the idea that man gets more refined, more ethical, moral and so on, and we have arrived at the very opposite of that. We are worse than any age that has ever lived, worse than the stone man; more barbarous, more cruel, more ruthless, more heartless, conscienceless. This is the end of all our ethical upbuilding. (75)

American life qua the *traditional present* was still Miller's number one concern.

> For seventy-two years I have been waiting to see some breakdown of the artificial barriers surrounding our educational system, our national borders, our homes, our inner being — a shattering of the wretched molds in which we've lived — but it never happens. We have the dynamite but we don't set it off. (97)

The *Beelzebub* side of the *inhuman artist*, too, was still a part of Miller; for he wanted to see "everything swept away to clear the ground for something new . . . to get beyond civilization to what has been called the prehistoric state and see the new man who will live without all the restrictive, inhibiting barriers that hedge us in" (97). The status of literature, and of art in general, also seems to have remained essentially unchanged for Miller: "Ninety per cent of all writing — in fact, 90 per cent of all the arts — is junk. It could be wiped out entirely with no loss to civilization" (138). When asked about his view of contemporary America in 1969, Miller answered: "I think that in literature, in politics, in almost every phase of its existence, this country is going through a process of deterioration and disintegration. I see very little left of what inspired the founding fathers" (*ibid*). Although the *traditional present* evidently still reigned at this time, Miller never really lost his faith in both "Art" and the "Artists'" power to change things one day: ". . . my belief is that if you trust the artist, you'd have a crazy world, maybe, but a delightful one. An insane one, maybe. But it'd be far better than this one that we have now. Over the years, we've tried every possible kind of government. Except this poetic one" (179).

The words of wisdom: To whom and what for?

While it is certain that Miller never found America to be ready for the rise of the *inhuman artist*, he still dreamt of a "poetic government" and seemed to believe in the power of art. Yet, by the time he reached his early eighties, Miller seemed to bother less and less about writing. "I don't want to write a single word that isn't necessary. Now I primarily just want to live . . . Being, to me, has become more important than doing" (172–3). Does the latter remark suggest that Miller really was "passing from art to life" and entered into his *China* as he had proclaimed he would ever since the Paris-era? The question does not have a straightforward answer. It looks as though Miller still put confidence in Art's power as a philosophical thesis but vehemently resisted suggestions that he himself had, through his writing, "found a way to get through life":

> This is an error, to say that I've found the way — I'm getting credit for that all the time. No. I am still searching. I'm not writing, I'm not expressing it anymore. I don't need to assuage my soul by writing. I am not the man who knows the answers, and has arrived at that place where he's serene, on the path and skating, you know what I mean? No. It'll always turmoil in me, and chaos, and bewilderment. But in a different order from that, you have another man, on another level. (172)

A critical way to read this late testimony would be to concede that Miller indeed admitted to have failed in achieving his life-long philosophical goal: a full release from the *traditional present.* A somewhat more sympathetic reading, however, is equally plausible. We remember that Miller declared in his Greece period that he was a "sage who was also a seeker."[23] In light of the above passage, this "searching" seems to be still an important integral part of Miller's psyche. For he does not say that he has given up his *belief* in *China* completely but suggests that he simply has not arrived there yet. Additionally, the seeming contradiction between "serenity" and "turmoil," we should always keep in mind, is effectively built into Miller's very notion of the Artist as *both St. Anthony* and *Beelzebub.* As a consequence, and quite in line with what Dearborn suggests, acceptance for Miller always also meant rebellion and he, at the same time, would "continue to rail against the world" but also "claim to be at peace with it."[24] Having a kind of artistically schizophrenic nature, there is no conflict here for Miller. Rather, it is a question of which side of the *inhuman artist* dominates at any given time. It cannot be ignored also that whatever his occasional self-doubts, Miller never went back to living a *human* life. Even if in his later years he never exactly reached *China*, he most certainly was not another Tom, Dick, or Harry of the *traditional present.* The philosophical demarcation lines of his yesteryears survived his personal defeats.

It should also be remembered that Miller never promised to provide a doctrine for the masses. The *inhuman philosophy*, in the last analysis, is a deeply individual concept. It's not a thesis for a group to live by. The world cannot be changed by a "special group" but by the way people live "individually" according to Miller (171). The individuality requirement is precisely why Miller always resisted art as an agenda for movements. Art is a profoundly personal thing. It, thus, cannot provide universal answers to mankind but, at best, can only change an individual. Hence, *inhumanism* cannot be taught in the fashion of political rhetoric but only "lived out" personally. This is why Miller resists the possibility that he has a "message" which can be taken as a slogan for mass movements. The hippy movement seems to be a case in point: "they claimed me as one of them, but I had no use for the hippies. I looked on them as a bunch of bums. You should do something, work or be creative, not just idle your life away" (227). Indeed, the cornerstone of Miller's thinking, "creativity," seems to have been confused with the essentially political goals of the "flower children" in their marching rallies.

We should, it seems, construe Miller's philosophy predominantly not as providing "the answer" but more as a method providing many uniquely personal answers. One starts with a critical inspection of the *traditional present* and then, through his personal craft or art, he discovers, hopefully, a personal satisfaction in the *full present.* When many people have found their personal *China*, or at least striving for it, then mankind as a whole, perhaps, ends up living better too. Of course, there are no guarantees that this *inhuman* "method" always brings the expected results in every particular case, for people are different. The *full present* and *China* are concepts with validity for everyone, but that by no means guarantees success for those who adopt them in life.

Miller himself declared that the importance of his work lies in his "vision of life and of the world" (82) and that his own life symbolizes the fact that he "had the guts to stick it out . . ." (212). That may well be something worthwhile to take away from our *inhuman* journey with Miller. With the stubbornness of an ass, he fought against this age by trying to find a way out through art. And even if he did not get out of it completely, his *inhuman* struggle at least suggested a personal model for how to "be in it, but not of it" (171).

Notes

1 Jay Martin, *Always Merry and Bright: The Life of Henry Miller* (Santa Barbara: Capra Press, 1978), 339.
2 Ibid., 335.
3 Erica Jong, *The Devil at Large* (London: Vintage, 1994), 147.
4 J. D. Brown, *Henry Miller: Literature and Life* (New York: Ungar Pub. Co, 1986), 55.
5 Leon Lewis, *Henry Miller: The Major Writings* (New York: Schocken, 1986), 134.
6 Martin, *Always Merry and Bright*, 356.
7 Ibid., 357.
8 Ibid., 367.
9 Ibid., 381.
10 Brown, *Henry Miller: Literature and Life*, 69.
11 Lewis, *Henry Miller: The Major Writings,* 149.
12 Brown, *Henry Miller: Literature and Life*, 66.
13 Martin, *Always Merry and Bright*, 376.
14 Ibid., 383.
15 Jong, *The Devil at Large*, 171.
16 Ibid., 160.
17 Miller's original paintings today have an asking price of $8000–40,000 USD. It is another question, however, how many of them actually get sold.
18 Mary V. Dearborn, *The Happiest Man Alive: A Biography of Henry Miller* (New York: Simon & Schuster, 1991), 226.
19 Martin, *Always Merry and Bright*, 405.
20 Brown, *Henry Miller: Literature* and Life, 87.
21 Dearborn, *The Happiest Man Alive,* 229.
22 Martin, *Always Merry and Bright*, 404.
23 Ibid., 206.
24 Dearborn, *The Happiest Man Alive*, 229.

Conclusion

In the beginning of this book, we set ourselves the task of examining whether meaningful philosophical readings of Henry Miller could still be offered. We have now seen that this is indeed possible. Through the discovery and elaboration of Miller's notions of *traditional* and *full present*, in conjunction with the idea of the *inhuman artist* and *China*, we are able to contend that Miller's philosophical dispositions were, at core, directed against the most dominant metaphysical features of the modern age. Having called attention to Miller's oeuvre as a decidedly *modernist* literary quarrel against Western metaphysics, aimed at transcendental release, we now have a new philosophical paradigm for explaining his much-debated legacy. The value of the conceptual framework suggested in this book lies predominantly in the fact that it is comprehensive: it enables one now to explain coherently a vast number of Miller's ideas and show that they belong to one substantial philosophical standpoint. We have also now learned that what has often been treated as mere philippic on seemingly unrelated topics, such as *history, time, progress, technology, work*, and the *esthetic* notion of art, is in fact an assault upon a series of concepts all metaphysically connected in the *traditional present* as its ground. Appreciating this, it is evident that Miller was not merely offering a random social or literary commentary in his works but was genuinely driven by certain philosophical concerns. Likewise, the elaboration of Miller's *full present* allows us now to make sense of his concepts of "art" and "Art" and their relation to *China*, which until now has caused a fair amount of confusion among critics and commentators. By disclosing these two oppositional realms—*traditional* and *full present*—as the very source of the conflict between Miller's *inhuman artist* and the modern world, we have formulated an all-embracing view, which we may now positively call Henry Miller's *inhuman philosophy*.

While indeed offering a comprehensive picture, Miller's *inhuman philosophy* is by no means finished or final. On the contrary, it is very much open to additions, qualifications, and juxtapositions stemming first from the greater realm of *Milleriana* and also from other paths of philosophy and literary theory. A greater number of close readings and comparisons of parts of Miller's *inhuman philosophy* with the ideas of other modernist writers is still needed, too. Setting myself the task of formulating the main philosophical structure of Miller's writings, this type of comparative research, while indeed present in parts, could not have been carried out in great depth throughout this book. For that I take full responsibility. Also, new philosophical insights are likely to emerge from the investigations on the impact of Chinese and Indian philosophical thinkers on Miller's works: the area of the Miller discourse that to this day remains largely unexplored in the strong scholarly sense.

Bibliography

Aleksic, Branko. "The Unpublished Correspondence of Henry Miller & André Breton, the 'Steady Rock', 1947–50." *Nexus: The International Henry Miller Journal* 5 (2008): 150–72.

Arendt, Hannah. *The Human Condition*. Chicago: University of Chicago Press, 1958.

Baldick, Chris. *The Modern Movement*. Oxford English Literary History v. 10, 1910–40. Oxford: Oxford University Press, 2004.

Bartlett, Jeffrey. "The Late Modernist." In *Critical Essays on Henry Miller*. Edited by Ronald Gottesman. New York: G. K. Hall, 1992.

Bell, Michael. "The Metaphysics of Modernism." In *The Cambridge Companion to Modernism*. Edited by Michael H. Levenson. Cambridge: Cambridge University Press, 2011.

Benjamin, Walter. "Central Park," trans. Lloyd Spencer, *New German Critique* 34 (Winter 1985): 50.

— *Illuminations*. Edited by Hannah Arendt. New York: Schocken Books, 1986.

Blinder, Caroline. *A Self-Made Surrealist: Ideology and Aesthetics in the Work of Henry Miller*. Columbia, SC: Camden House, 2000.

Bloshteyn, Maria R. *The Making of a Counter-Culture Icon: Henry Miller's Dostoevsky*. Toronto: University of Toronto Press, 2007.

Borgmann, Albert. *Technology and the Character of Contemporary Life: A Philosophical Inquiry*. Chicago: University of Chicago Press, 1984.

Bradbury, Malcolm. "The Name and Nature of Modernism." In *Modernism: 1890-1930*. Edited by James Walter McFarlane and Malcolm Bradbury. Harmondsworth, NY: Penguin Books, 1976.

Breton, André. "First Surrealist Manifesto." In *Surrealism*. Edited by Patrick Waldberg. New York: McGraw-Hill, 1971.

Brown, James Dale. *Henry Miller* (Literature and Life). New York: Ungar Pub. Co, 1986.

Bullock, Alan. "The Double Image." In *Modernism: 1890-1930*. Edited by James Walter McFarlane and Malcolm Bradbury. London: Penguin, 1976.

Bury, John Bagnell. *The Idea of Progress: An Inquiry into its Origin and Growth*. New York: Cosimo Classics, 2008.

Calinescu, Matei. *Five Faces of Modernity: Modernism, Avant-Garde, Decadence, Kitch, Postmodernism*. Durham: Duke University Press, 1987.

Calonne, David Stephen. "Euphoria in Paris: Henry Miller Meets D. H. Lawrence." *Library Chronicle of the University of Texas* 34 (1986): 88–98.

Childs, Peter. *Modernism*. 2nd ed. The New Critical Idiom. London: Routledge, 2008.

Comte, Auguste. *The Positive Philosophy of Auguste Comte*. Vol. 2. Translated by Harriet Martineau. New York: Cambridge University Press, 2009.

Crisp, Roger. "Good." In *The Oxford Companion to Philosophy*. Edited by Ted Honderich. Oxford: Oxford University Press, 1995.

Danius, Sara. "Technology." In *A Companion to Modernist Literature and Culture*. Edited by David Bradshaw and Kevin J. H. Dettmar. Malden, MA: Blackwell Pub., 2006.

Dearborn, Mary V. *The Happiest Man Alive: A Biography of Henry Miller.* New York: Simon & Schuster, 1991.

Decker, James M. *Henry Miller and Narrative Form: Constructing the Self, Rejecting Modernity.* Context and Genre in English Literature. New York: Routledge, 2005.

Deiman, Werner J. "History, Pattern, and Continuity in Virginia Woolf." *Contemporary Literature* 15 (1974): 49–66.

Derr, Jonathan. "The Poet's Place in Modernity: Heidegger, Eliot and Pound." PhD dissertation. Chicago: Loyola University, 2002.

Ekberg, Kent. "Studio 28: The Influence of the Surrealist Cinema on the Early Fiction of Anaïs Nin and Henry Miller." *Deus Loci: The Lawrence Durrell Quarterly* 4, 3 (1981): 3–4.

Eliot, Thomas Stearns. "The Idea of a Christian Society." In *Selected Prose of T. S. Eliot.* Edited by Frank Kermode. London: Faber, 1975a.

— "Tradition and the Individual Talent". In *Selected Prose of T. S. Eliot.* Edited by Frank Kermode. London: Faber, 1975b.

Ellis, Havelock. *The Dance of Life.* New York: The Modern library, 1929.

Emerson, Ralph Waldo. "Art." In *The Complete Essays and Other Writings.* New York: The Modern Library, 1950.

Everman, Welch P. "The Anti-Aesthetic of Henry Miller." In *Critical Essays on Henry Miller.* Edited by Ronald Gottesman. Critical Essays on American Literature. New York: G. K. Hall, 1992.

Ferguson, Robert. *Henry Miller: A Life.* New York: Norton, 1991.

Fjågesund, Peter. *The Apocalyptic World of D. H. Lawrence.* London: Norwegian University Press, 1991.

Flaxman, Amy M. *New Anatomies: Tracing Emotions in Henry Miller's Writings.* MLA-IB. Belfast, ME: Porter, 2000.

Fóti, Véronique Marion. *Heidegger and the Poets: Poiesis/Sophia/Techne.* Philosophy and Literary Theory. New Jersey: Humanities Press International, 1992.

Fowler, Roger. *A Dictionary of Modern Critical Terms.* London: Routledge & Kegan Paul, 1987.

Fraenkel, Michael. *The Genesis of the Tropic of Cancer.* London: Village Press, 1973.

Gifford, James. "Surrealism's Anglo-American Afterlife: The Herbert Read and Henry Miller Network." *Nexus: The International Henry Miller Journal* 5 (2008): 36–64.

Gini, Alfred R., and T. Sullivan. "Work: The Process and the Person." *Journal of Business Ethics* 6, 8 (1987): 649–55.

Gordon, William A. *The Mind and Art of Henry Miller.* Baton Rouge: Louisiana State University Press, 1967.

Gross, Harvey Seymour. *The Contrived Corridor: History and Fatality in Modern Literature.* Ann Arbor: University of Michigan Press, 1971.

Guyer, Paul. "Immanuel Kant." In *Routledge Encyclopedia of Philosophy.* Edited by E. Craig (1998, 2004) url: http://www.rep.routledge.com/article/DB047.

Hamsun, Knut. *Hunger.* Translated by George Egerton. London: Duckworth and co., 1921.

Hegel, Georg Wilhelm Friedrich. *Lectures on The Philosophy of World History.* Translated by H. B. Nisbet. Cambridge: Cambridge University Press, 1998.

Heidegger, Martin. *An Introduction to Metaphysics.* Translated by Gregory Fried and Richard Polt. New Haven: Yale University Press, 1959.

— *What Is Called Thinking?* Translated by J. Glenn Gray. New York: Harper & Row, 1968.

— "The Age of The World Picture." In *The Question Concerning Technology, and Other Essays.* Translated by William Lovitt. New York: Harper & Row, 1977a.
— "The Question Concerning Technology." In *The Question Concerning Technology, and Other Essays.* Translated by William Lovitt. New York: Harper & Row, 1977b.
— "The Turning." In *The Question Concerning Technology, and Other Essays.* Translated by William Lovitt. New York: Harper & Row, 1977c.
— *Being and Time.* Translated by John Macquarrie and Edward Robinson. New York: HarperPerennial/Modern Thought, 2008.
Hopkins, David. *Dada and Surrealism: A Very Short Introduction.* Oxford: Oxford University Press, 2004.
Horkheimer, Max. *Eclipse of Reason.* New York: Continuum, 1985.
Hotho-Jackson, Sabine. "Virginia Woolf On History: Between Tradition And Modernity." *Forum for Modern Language Studies* XXVII, 4 (1991): 293–313.
Hoy, David Couzens. *The Time of Our Lives: A Critical History of Temporality.* Cambridge, MA: MIT Press, 2009.
Ibargüen, Raoul Richard. "Narrative Detours: Henry Miller and the Rise of New Critical Modernism." PhD dissertation. Yale University, 1989.
Inwood, Michael. "Ontology and Fundamental Ontology." In *A Heidegger Dictionary.* Oxford, UK: Blackwell Publishing Ltd., 1999.
Irwin, William. "What Is an Allusion?" *Journal of Aesthetics and Art Criticism* 59, 3 (2001): 287–97.
Jackson, Paul R. "Henry Miller, Emerson and the Divided Self." *American Literature* 43, 2 (1971): 231–41.
Jahshan, Paul. *Henry Miller and the Surrealist Discourse of Excess: A Post- Structuralist Reading.* New York: P. Lang, 2001.
Janaway, Christopher. "Aesthetics, the problems of." In *The Oxford Companion to Philosophy.* Edited by Ted Honderich. Oxford: Oxford University Press, 1995.
Jeffers, Robinson. *The Double Axe and Other Poems.* New York: Random House, 1948.
Jong, Erica. *The Devil at Large: Erica Jong on Henry Miller.* London: Chatto & Windus, 1993.
Jung, Carl Gustav. *Modern Man in Search of a Soul.* London: Routledge & Kegan Paul, 1961.
Kaufmann, Walter Arnold. *Nietzsche: Philosopher, Psychologist, Antichrist.* 4th ed. Princeton, NJ: Princeton University Press, 1974.
Kennedy, Gerald J. "The Secret Paris of Henry Miller." In *Imagining Paris: Exile, Writing, and American Identity.* New Haven : Yale University Press, 1993.
Kermode, Frank. "John Betjeman and Henry Miller." In *Puzzles and Epiphanies: Essays and Reviews, 1958-1961.* New York: Chilmark Press, 1962.
— *The Sense of an Ending; Studies in the Theory of Fiction.* New York: Oxford University Press, 1967.
— *Lawrence.* London: Fontana, 1973.
— "D. H. Lawrence and the Apocalyptic Types." In *Modern Essays.* London: Fontana, 1990.
Kern, Stephen. *The Culture of Time and Space 1880-1918.* Cambridge, MA: Harvard University Press, 1983.
Ladenson, Elizabeth. "Henry Miller: A Gob of Spit in the Face of Art." In *Dirt for Art's Sake.* Ithaka & London: Cornell University Press, 2007.

Lawlor, Leonard and Valentine Moulard. "Henri Bergson." In *Stanford Encyclopedia of Philosophy*, Edited by Edward N. Zalta (2010) url: http://platostanford.edu/entries/bergson/.

Lawrence, David Herbert. "Why the Novel Matters?" In *Selected Literary Criticism.* Edited by Anthony Beal. London: Heinemann, 1955.

— *Apocalypse*. Edited by Richard Aldington. London: Heinemann, 1972.

— "The Novel." In *Complete Works of D. H. Lawrence*. Kindle Edition, Delphi Classics, 2011.

Lehman, Eric D. "Henry Miller and Jean Francois Lyotard: The Aesthetics of 'The Inhuman' in *Tropic of Cancer*" *Nexus: The International Henry Miller Journal* 5 (2008): 272–85.

Lewis, Leon. *Henry Miller: The Major Writings*. New York: Schocken, 1986.

Lewis, Wyndham. *Time and Western Man*. Boston: Beacon Press, 1957.

Marcuse, Herbert. *One Dimensional Man; Studies in the Ideology of Advanced Industrial Society*. Boston: Beacon Press, 1964.

— "Some Social Implications of Modern Technology." In *The Essential Frankfurt School Reader*. Edited by Andrew Arato and Eike Gebhardt. New York: Urizen Books, 1978.

Marinetti, Filippo. "The Founding and Manifesto of Futurism." In *Futurism: An Anthology*. Edited by Lawrence Rainey. New Haven: Yale University Press, 2009.

Martin, Jay. *Always Merry and Bright: The Life of Henry Miller: An Unauthorized Biography*. Santa Barbara, California: Capra Press, 1978.

McCarthy, Harold T. "Henry Miller's Democratic Vistas." *American Quarterly* 23, 2 (1971): 221–35.

Masuga, Katy H*enry Miller and How He Got That Way*. Edinburgh: University of Edinburgh Press, 2011.

— *The Secret Violence of Henry Miller*. New York: Camden House, 2011.

Mitchell, Edward B. "Artists and Artists: The 'Aesthetics' of Henry Miller." In *Henry Miller: Three Decades of Criticism*. New York: N. Y. U. Press, 1971.

Mokyr, Joel. *The Second Industrial Revolution, 1870-1914*. url: faculty.wcas. northwestern.edu/~jmokyr/castronovo.pdf.

Mumford, Lewis. *Technics and Civilization*. London: Routledge & Kegan Paul, 1934.

Nelson, Jane A. *Form and Image in the Fiction of Henry Miller*. Detroit: Wayne State University Press, 1970.

Nesbit, Thomas. "Death, Rebirth, and the Self in Tropic of Cancer." *Nexus: The International Henry Miller Journal* 1 (2004): 149–62.

— *Henry Miller and Religion*. New York: Routledge, 2007.

Nietzsche, Friedrich Wilhelm. *The Birth of Tragedy and The Genealogy of Morals*. 1st ed. Garden City, NY: Doubleday, 1956.

— *The Will to Power*. Translated by Walter Arnold Kaufmann and R. J. Hollingdale. London: Weidenfeld & Nicolson, 1968a.

— *Twilight of the Idols; and, The Anti-Christ*. Translated by R. J. Hollingdale. Harmondsworth: Penguin, 1968b.

— *A Nietzsche Reader*. Translated by R. J. Hollingdale. Harmondsworth: Penguin, 1977.

— *Ecce Homo: How One Becomes What One Is*. Translated by R. J. Hollingdale, Harmondsworth: Penguin Books, 1979.

— *Thus Spoke Zarathustra: A Book for All and None*. Translated by Walter Arnold Kaufmann. New York: Modern Library, 1995.

— "On the Uses and Disadvantages of History for Life." In *Untimely Meditations*. Translated by R. J. Hollingdale. Cambridge: Cambridge University Press, 1997.

Nisbet, Robert. *History of The Idea of Progress*. Transaction Publishers, 2008.
Online, Encyclopaedia Britannica. Anthony of Egypt, Saint. (2001) url: www. original. search.eb.com.ezproxy.auckland.ac.nz/eb/article-9007776.
Online, Oxford English Dictionary. inhuman, adj. and n. (1989) url: http://www. oed.com. ezproxy.auckland.ac.nz/Entry/96004.
Orwell, George. "Inside the Whale." In *Henry Miller and the Critics*. Edited by George Wickes. Carbondale: Southern Illinois University Press, 1963.
Parkin, John. *Henry Miller, The Modern Rabelais*. Lewiston, NY: E. Mellen Press, 1980.
Peterson, Leland D. "Ezra Pound: The Use and Abuse of History." In *American Quarterly* 17, 1 (1965): 33–47.
Raaberg, Gwendolyn. "Surrealism in the Works of Henry Miller and Anaïs Nin." In *Actes du VIIe congres de l'Association Internationale de Litterature Comparee/Proceedings of the 7th Congress of the International Comparative Literature Association, I: Litteratures americaines: Dependance, independance, interdependance/Literatures of America: Dependence, Independence, Interdependence*. Edited by Milan V. Dimić and Juan Ferraté. Stuttgart: Bieber, 1979.
Schacht, Richard. "Nietzsche on Art in *The Birth of Tragedy*." In *Nietzsche*. Edited by John Richardson and Brian Leiter. Oxford Readings in Philosophy. Oxford [England]: Oxford University Press, 2001.
Short, Robert. "Dada and Surrealism." In *Modernism: 1890-1930*. Edited by James Walter McFarlane and M. S. Bradbury. Harmondsworth: Penguin, 1976.
Smith, Michael. "Recourse of Empire: Landscapes of Progress in Technological America." In *Does Technology Drive History? The Dilemma of Technological Determinism*. Edited by Merritt Smith and Leo Marx, 37–52. Cambridge, MA: The MIT Press, 1994.
Smithline, Arnold. "Henry Miller and the Transcendental Spirit." *Emerson Society Quarterly: A Journal of the American Renaissance* 43, 1 (1966): 50–6.
Solomon, William. "Laughter and Depression: Henry Miller and the Emergence of the Technocarnivalesque." In *Literature, Amusement, and Technology in the Great Depression*. Cambridge Studies in American Literature and Culture. New York: Cambridge University Press, 2002.
Sorokin, Pitirim Aleksandrovich. *Modern Historical and Social Philosophies*. New York: Dover Publications, 1963.
Spengler, Oswald. *The Decline of the West*. Translated by Charles Francis Atkinson. New York: Knopf, 1926.
— *Man and Technics: A Contribution to a Philosophy of Life*. London: G. Allen & Unwin, 1933.
Starck, Stephen L. "Hacking Away with an Ax: Henry Miller and Modernity." PhD dissertation. Norman, Ok: University of Oklahoma, 1999.
Stinson, Emmet. "Literary and Cultural Contexts: Major Figures, Institutions, Topics, Events." In *The Modernism Handbook*. Edited by Philip Tew and Alex Murray. London: Continuum, 2009.
Stirner, Max. *The Ego and His Own: the Case of the Individual Against Authority*. Translated by James J. Martin. New York: Dover Publications, 2005.
Tew, Philip and Alex Murray. *The Modernism Handbook*. London: Continuum, 2009.
Thomas, Richard F. "Virgil's Georgics and the Art of Reference." *Harvard Studies in Classical Philology* 90 (1986): 171–98.
Trotter, David. "The Modernist Novel." In *The Cambridge Companion to Modernism*. Edited by Michael H. Levenson. Cambridge: Cambridge University Press, 1999.

— "Modernism and Empire: reading The Waste Land." In *Critical Quarterly* 28, 1 (2008): 143–53.

Tzara, Tristan. "Dada Manifesto, 1918." In *The Dada Painters and Poets: An Anthology.* Edited by Robert Motherwell. Cambridge, MA: Belknap Press of Harvard University Press, 1989.

— "Manifesto of Mr. Antipyrine." In *The Dada Painters and Poets: An Anthology.* Edited by Robert Motherwell. Cambridge, MA: Harvard University Press, 1989b.

Whitman, Walt. *The Portable Walt Whitman.* Edited by Malcolm Cowley Mark Van Doren and Gay Wilson Allen. New York: Viking, 1985.

Whitworth, Michael H. *Modernism.* Blackwell Guides to Criticism. Malden, MA: Blackwell Pub, 2007.

Wickes, George. *Americans in Paris.* New York: Doubleday, 1969.

Wicks, Robert L. *European Aesthetics: A Critical Introduction from Kant to Derrida.* Manuscript. Forthcoming in OneWorld Publications, 2013.

Williams, Raymond. *Television: Technology and Cultural Form.* Routledge Classics. London: Routledge, 2003.

Wilson, Edmund. "Twilight of the Expatriates." In *Critical Essays on Henry Miller.* Edited by Ronald Gottesman. New York: G. K. Hall, 1992.

Wilson, Leigh. "Historical Context of Modernist Literature." In *The Modernism Handbook.* Edited by Philip Tew and Alex Murray. London: Continuum, 2009.

Wright, G. H. von. "The Myth of Progress." In *The Tree of Knowledge and Other Essays.* Leiden: E. J. Brill, 1993.

Yeats, W. B. "The Lake Isle of Innisfree." In *The Collected Poems of W. B. Yeats.* London: Macmillan, 1958a.

— "The Second Coming." In *The Collected Poems of W. B. Yeats.* London: Macmillan, 1958b.

— "The Song of the Happy Shepherd." In *The Collected Poems of W. B. Yeats.* London: Macmillan, 1958c.

Young, Julian. *Heidegger's Philosophy of Art.* Cambridge: Cambridge University Press, 2001.

Zimmerman, Michael E. *Heidegger's Confrontation with Modernity: Technology, Politics, and Art.* The Indiana Series in the Philosophy of Technology. Bloomington: Indiana University Press, 1990.

Index